Finding Our Way?
TOWARD
MATURITY
IN
U.S.-LATIN
AMERICAN
RELATIONS

Finding Our Way?
TOWARD
MATURITY
IN
U.S.-LATIN
AMERICAN
RELATIONS

HOWARD J. WIARDA

AMERICAN ENTERPRISE INSTITUTE FOR PUBLIC POLICY RESEARCH
Washington, D.C.

Howard J. Wiarda is a resident scholar at the American Enterprise Institute and director of its Center for Hemispheric Studies. He is a professor of political science at the University of Massachusetts, Amherst, where he served as the director of the Center for Latin American Studies. He is the author of *The Communist Challenge in the Caribbean and Central America* and editor of *Rift and Revolution: The Central American Imbroglio.*

Distributed by arrangement with
UPA, Inc.
4720 Boston Way
Lanham, Md. 20706
3 Henrietta Street
London WC2E 8LU England

Library of Congress Cataloging-in-Publication Data

Wiarda, Howard J., 1939–
 Finding our way?

 Includes bibliographies and index.
 1. Latin America—Foreign relations—United
States. 2. United States—Foreign relations—Latin
America. 3. United States—Foreign relations—1981–
I. Title.
F1418.W649 1987   327.73O8   87-14485
ISBN 0-8447-3631-7
ISBN 0-8447-3632-5 (pbk.)
AEI Studies 460

Printed in the United States of America

Contents

PART TWO
CRITICISM, ISSUES, AND AGENDAS

Preface

This book is intended as a complement to other work in progress or already published through the Center for Hemispheric Studies at AEI—on human rights and U.S. human rights policy,[1] Central America,[2] the current crisis in Latin America,[3] the Communist challenge,[4] the Kissinger Commission,[5] the role of the state in Latin American development,[6] Latin America's alternative futures,[7] the relations between Spain and Latin America,[8] Southern Europe,[9] and U.S. policy toward Latin America.[10]

The outlook presented here contrasts in certain ways with the more pessimistic viewpoints expressed in our earlier Central America study and with the skepticism of the author's earlier study of U.S. foreign policy in Latin America. The title of that foreign policy study, *In Search of Policy,* implied that the United States was still groping for and had not yet found an appropriate foreign policy for Latin America. At the time the book was written in 1982–1983, that observation was essentially correct. The title of this volume, *Finding Our Way?,* suggests that during the period 1983–1986, when the essays for this book were written, the United States had achieved a firmer hand on policy in Latin America and had developed a coherent and rational strategy for carrying it out. That is not intended to imply, however, that such a firmer and more enlightened policy can or will be continued. The question mark in the title implies continued uncertainty about the future; it is also a device that academics use to preserve their scholarly credentials.

The fact is, our relations with some parts of and some sectors in Latin America remain strained; and we have by no means solved all the problems. To the extent we think we have "solved" the problems in El Salvador and elsewhere, and therefore can now return to a policy of "benign neglect," this book issues some strong warnings: the problems have not been solved, and if we choose again to ignore Latin America, we will surely invite further explosions later. Hence, where difficulties and problem areas remain in U.S.-Latin American relations, this book does not hesitate to point them out in quite forceful terms. But I do believe overall American foreign policy toward Latin America is more sophisticated and more discriminating than in the past, that we are now more certain where we are going and what our goals are, and that our grasp of the handles of foreign policy is now surer. There has been a learning process under way in the administration with regard to Latin America in the past several years, as there was with earlier administrations.

It takes at least two years for any new administration, particularly those organized by Washington outsiders, to begin to understand what we can do and, of at least equal importance, what we cannot do in Latin America, which policies and approaches are feasible and realistic, and how we can carry out these policies effectively. One of our problems in implementing an effective foreign policy over the past quarter century is that not one of our presidents has served two full terms (In the twenty-four years between 1960 and 1984, we have had six presidents, an average of one every four years, or the equivalent of one term each.) Our administrations have been so short-lived that when one after some time finally learns how to operate abroad, in Latin America or elsewhere, its tenure ends—and hence the learning process must begin anew.

Under President Reagan it appeared for a time that not only would we have some continuity in policy but also that the policy itself would become more subtle and sophisticated. One of the chapters included here even suggests that at long last we may be on the point of establishing a mature relationship with the Latin American countries, which will finally put our relations on a sounder basis. Hence, although this volume contains criticisms where its seems appropriate and does not shy away from major problem areas, it also includes an entire section on these new and positive steps. Whether these more hopeful steps can be sustained through the last two years of the administration, or whether they will be forgotten and submerged in the wake of the so-called Iran-contra scandal, cannot be determined at this moment (February 1987).

An author sometimes hesitates to pull together a collection of his own earlier papers, articles, and essays. Such volumes always suffer from both a certain disjointedness and some repetition; and the effort seems a bit immodest. In this case I have been persuaded by friends, readers, and colleagues that such a collection is useful and worthwhile because (1) the papers collected here either were published in diverse and often obscure places or were not previously published at all; (2) the issues are of such importance that a serious discussion of them merits wider dissemination; and (3) the themes are timely and should be considered at this stage of U.S. policy development. The chapters have been lightly edited to update them and to remove some repetition, but essentially appear as they were originally written.

These papers were all written at the American Enterprise Institute for Public Policy Research in Washington, D.C., where I have served as resident scholar and director of the Center for Hemispheric Studies. AEI is one of the country's premier "think tanks," a wonderful place to do research, to write, to debate with colleagues of diverse viewpoints, and to observe (as well as participate in) the Washington policy process. We like to say, only half facetiously, that in its diversity, intellectual stimulation, and policy-oriented research, AEI is just like a university except that it has neither students nor bureaucracy nor committee meetings—and what could be better than that!

I am especially grateful to Pamela Robertson and Louise Skillings, our outstanding secretaries; to Janine Perfit, who has served as indispensable research assistant; to my former colleague Mark Falcoff, who stimulates my thinking although we disagree on certain particulars; and to the entire AEI "family" that makes my work possible: the conference staff, the administration, the kitchen staff, the office management and logistics staff, the library staff, and others. Without these people AEI could not function in its present form; that staff support, cheerfully and usually anonymously offered, is what enables the scholars and fellows at AEI to do their jobs.

I am also indebted to the "core" group of several score Latin Americanists in Washington, from the government, journalism, other think tanks, Congress, and so forth, who go to all those endless receptions and forums, not only where the day's gossip is exchanged but where a good deal of policy is discussed, winnowed, and shaped. Without these friends and colleagues on the Washington circuit, my understanding of how policy is made and implemented would be far less than it is now.

But my greatest debt is owed to Dr. Iêda Siqueira Wiarda, who for some reason continues cheerfully and unflinchingly to read and criticize all that her husband sets before her, while also superbly managing a family and household, to say nothing of her own professional career. It is to this *"supermadre"* (after the title of our friend Elsa Chaney's book)[11] that this volume is dedicated.

Howard J. Wiarda

Notes

1. Howard J. Wiarda, ed., *Human Rights and U.S. Human Rights Policy* (Washington, D.C.: American Enterprise Institute, 1983).

2. *Rift and Revolution: The Central American Imbroglio* (Washington, D.C.: American Enterprise Institute, 1984); "The Crisis in Central America," special

PREFACE

issue of the *AEI Foreign Policy and Defense Review,* vol. 4, no. 2 (1982), Howard J. Wiarda, guest editor.

3. Howard J. Wiarda, ed., *The Crisis in Latin America: Strategic, Economic, and Political Dimensions* (Washington, D.C.: American Enterprise Institute, 1984).

4. Mark Falcoff and Howard J. Wiarda, with Ernest Evans and Jiri and Virginia Valenta, *The Communist Challenge in Latin America* (Washington, D.C.: American Enterprise Institute, forthcoming).

5. "U.S. Policy in Central America: Consultant Papers for the Kissinger Commission," special issue of the *AEI Foreign Policy and Defense Review,* vol. 5, no. 1 (1984), Howard J. Wiarda, guest editor.

6. Howard J. Wiarda, *The State and Economic Development in Latin America* (Washington, D.C.: American Enterprise Institute, in preparation).

7. "The Alternative Futures of Latin America," special issue of the *AEI Foreign Policy and Defense Review,* vol. 5, no. 3 (1985), Howard J. Wiarda, guest editor.

8. Howard J. Wiarda, ed., *The Iberian-Latin American Connection* (Boulder, Colo.: Westview Press, 1986).

9. "Socio-political Change in Southern Europe—and Its Foreign Policy Implications," *AEI Foreign Policy and Defense Review* (1986).

10. Mark Falcoff, *Small Countries, Large Issues: Studies in U.S.–Latin American Asymmetries* (Washington, D.C.: American Enterprise Institute, 1984); and Howard J. Wiarda, *In Search of Policy: The United States and Latin America* (Washington, D.C.: American Enterprise Institute, 1984).

11. Elsa Chaney, *Supermadre: Women in Politics in Latin America* (Austin, Tex.: University of Texas Press, 1979).

xvi

1
Introduction:
Toward a More Sophisticated
U.S. Policy in Latin America?

The Latin America policy of President Ronald Reagan got off to a terribly rocky start. First, there was the situation "on the ground." The Nicaraguan revolutionaries who had seized power in 1979 were becoming increasingly Marxist-Leninist, were intent on spreading the revolution elsewhere in Central America, and had moved toward an alliance with Cuba and the Soviet Union—so much so that the outgoing Carter administration, which had initially been sympathetic to the Sandinistas, had become thoroughly disillusioned. In Grenada, the New Jewel Movement had seized power in 1979 and was in the process of being converted from a romantic and almost comic-opera revolution into an outpost for further Cuban and Leninist expansionism.[1] And in El Salvador the war was not going well: both the government and the army were teetering on the brink of collapse, and there was the ominous prospect of a fourth "Cuba" in the Caribbean Basin area.

In Washington the administration's Latin America policy had a similarly uncertain beginning. José Napoleon Duarte, then as now the head of government in El Salvador, was told by members of the National Security Council that the new administration was not favorably disposed toward agrarian reform and that he should not expect much help in pursuing that route. Reagan's first nominee for the post of assistant secretary of state for human rights and humanitarian affairs said that he intended to abolish the position and the program for which he was being considered. Some of the position papers prepared by the incoming Reagan administration foreign policy advisers contained strident statements which, although understandable and rational in the context of a U.S. domestic political campaign, had the added unfortunate and unintended effect of seeming to give almost carte blanche to some of the most destructive and repressive elements in Latin American society. And then Secretary of State

1

Alexander Haig made exaggerated comments indicating that El Salvador's civil war was purely an East-West struggle, that the Cold War would be decided there, and that "going to the source" of the Central American troubles implied action against Cuba, a step that would likely have resulted in a major confrontation with the Soviet Union and that would probably have devastated the prospects for a successful Reagan presidency.

The legacy of these early missteps haunts the Reagan presidency and its foreign policy today. Critics and the Democratic opposition are still using some of the overblown rhetoric of 1980 to damn the administration and to hamstring, as much as possible, its foreign policy agenda. Others believe that although the administration has changed its rhetoric about democracy, human rights, and agrarian reform, its real agenda is still the original hard-nosed military-strategic one. On both sides, the 1980 election campaign is continually being refought.

But in fact there have been major changes in administration policy since 1981—and they are many. Further, even if the critics are right—that behind the democracy and human rights agenda is still the military-strategic one—the reality of domestic politics in the United States is that once an administration states publicly its support for democracy and human rights, it is forced to carry out effective policies in those areas. Moreover, the administration has learned that it is good politics, domestically and abroad, to stand firmly for democracy and human rights. Perhaps it would be preferable if all politicians "really believed" in all the policies they carried out and certainly that would be more acceptable to purists. But the facts of politics are that even stating one's preference for (and there is no doubt President Reagan really does have a strong commitment to democracy and human rights) a certain option obliges one to follow through on that policy. In addition, pressures from the media, the Congress, public opinion, and our allies oblige any American administration in this day and age to incorporate the defense of democracy and human rights as major components of our foreign policy.

Actually, the Reagan administration's Latin America policy has evolved significantly since January 1981 and become far more nuanced and mature. These changes have often been obscured because the domestic debate is still strongly shaped by the rhetorical flourishes, hyperbole, and verbal overkill that prevailed during the election campaigns of 1980 and 1984; the continued partisan and therefore exaggerated nature of the debate has also served to cloud the accomplishments. But in fact the changes over the past several years have been many and profound, leading to a more complex and sophisticated policy than prevailed in the early weeks of the administration. Those changes, as well as the continued false starts and problem areas in Latin America policy, are what this book is about.

The Reagan Phenomenon[2]—and the Critics

The 1960s were a pivotal decade in American politics. They began with the election of John F. Kennedy and closed with Vietnam and Kent State. In the course of that decade the political consensus on social and economic programs at home and on America's role abroad was broken. Then came Watergate, Jimmy Carter, and Ronald Reagan, adding new and controversial issues and further elements of polarization to our political system. The older elites in both political parties were forced to yield to newcomers, while the economy moved uncertainly toward a new era of international markets and high technology. The New Deal and the New Deal coalition that had dominated our discourse and our politics for thirty years began to come apart. In many ways, the 1960s wrote the final chapter to one era—that begun by Franklin Roosevelt—and the first chapter of another, whose story is still unfolding. It is in this context of fundamental change and increased polarization that any discussion of current American foreign policy must be placed.[3]

Under Jimmy Carter U.S. foreign policy swung considerably to the left. The McGovern wing of the Democratic party monopolized almost all the foreign-policy-making positions in the new administration—particularly at the assistant secretary level in the State Department—at the expense of the more conservative or Henry Jackson wing organized in the Coalition for a Democratic Majority. These newcomers to foreign policy, at State and on the National Security Council, were younger and more radical, shaped strongly by Vietnam, and determined not to repeat that experience elsewhere in the third world. They also had a new foreign policy agenda sometimes at odds with the historic mainstream of U.S. policy. They emphasized human rights and a strong U.S. human rights policy as distinct from the historic concern for security interests, the North-South dialogue (as distinct from the East-West one) and U.S. obligations to the third world, and the peaceful resolution of all disputes. Now, these are not altogether bad goals; the problem was they became virtually the only goals. Other considerations (economic, strategic) were not taken adequately into account, and implementation was often spotty, incompetent, and not even-handed.

But there was a learning process that went on in the Carter administration—as there would be under President Reagan. By midterm, the Carter administration had become more realistic and pragmatic and less romantic. The president himself had his eyes opened about the Soviets (inconceivably, *while* he was president), some of the "looser cannons" were removed from the administration or shunted aside, and policy became more tempered. In Latin America the administration became disillusioned with the Sandinista regime in Nicaragua (after first being supportive); and it was Jimmy Carter who, in his last major act in office in January 1981, authorized U.S. military assistance to the government of beleaguered El Salvador.

The Reagan administration was, in a sense, a reaction to the Carter administration—and both of these more ideological presidencies were products of the breakup of the older 1960s consensus. Reagan's political advisers were determined to reverse the main thrusts of the Carter administration: to deemphasize human rights, to hang tough on North-South negotiations, to reemphasize the East-West dimensions of policy. Those convictions gave rise to some of the strident and sometimes unfortunate statements of the administration's early weeks. But eventually, a variety of things happened to temper these statements as well as actual policy and to push it—as had occurred under Carter—back toward the center. These moderating forces included the resurgence of the foreign policy professionals in the State Department and elsewhere; the role of the press and public opinion in defining acceptable policy; the opposition to administration initiatives in the Congress, which forced various compromises; the need to ameliorate "world public opinion," which led the administration to reevaluate its views and to pursue a more nuanced strategy; and the considerable learning process that went on within the administration itself.[4] Thus emerged a more complex and sophisticated policy.

The details of this process of policy development and its various components are discussed in the chapters that follow. Here, only a brief listing of some of the key elements in the process is given:

• We must distinguish between the administration's harsh rhetoric—largely for domestic political purposes—and its more restrained actions. We have *not* sent U.S. ground forces to El Salvador, we have *not* invaded Cuba or Nicaragua, we have *not* sought a confrontation with the Soviet Union in the Caribbean, and we have *not* created a new Vietnam in Central America. Instead, U.S. policy has been quite measured and restrained—despite the president's sometimes exaggerated hyperbole. Americans are not used to and are sometimes uncomfortable with a government whose words and deeds are not always in exact congruence (we tend to call it "hypocrisy"); Western Europeans are more used to these contradictions, and their political and intellectual leadership strongly favored Reagan over Mondale in the 1984 campaign.[5] But the point is that actual U.S. policy has been considerably more tempered than the early rhetoric would indicate; in fact, the gap between the rhetoric, for a home audience, and the implementation of policy (quite moderate) is fairly wide. We should not be surprised by this, let alone appalled; often it is simply good politics—if it can be brought off successfully.

• We need to keep in mind the shifting coalitions within the administration. Clearly the State Department professionals under Secretary George Shultz emerged by early 1985 as dominant. That is not by any means an unmitigated blessing, as one of our chapters makes clear, but it does reflect the gradual diminishing of ideological arguments within the administration and the growing influence of pragmatists and career professionals.

• Good policy can seldom be separated from reelection and partisan considerations. Policy is not based on a simple "rational actor model" but emerges from a myriad of factors, including political, organizational, and bureaucratic elements. Hence we must distinguish between what the administration (or its critics in Congress) say or do for the purpose of cementing or increasing electoral advantage and actual policy, which has generally been much more prudent.

• There is now in Washington a powerful tendency toward paralysis in U.S. foreign policy (see chapter 11), toward stalemate, and immobilism. This has to do with a more independent and assertive Congress, the new and more activist role of the media, the proliferation of interest groups, as well as other factors. By charisma and sheer force of personality, to say nothing of two overwhelming electoral mandates, President Reagan has succeeded in overcoming the now natural tendency of the American foreign-policy-making system toward paralysis and in focusing unprecedented attention on Latin America. The results of this new attention, in terms of U.S. aid to and interest in the area, are not altogether bad. The more balanced policy that gradually emerged from this process shows the American foreign-policy-making system *working*—and not altogether inadequately.

• The administration has actually listened to and has occasionally been stung by the criticism of the media, the Congress, and the academic community. Such criticism does not always sit well, naturally enough, but it has helped to change policy—whether in regard to supporting agrarian reform, pursuing the "death squad" killers in El Salvador, backing away from the Chilean regime, or favoring

5

democracy and human rights. These criticisms have also served to moderate policy.

• Rather like Jimmy Carter, the administration has undergone a learning process in the Latin America policy area. President Reagan's comment to the press that there are really different countries "down there," though it sounded ludicrous to academics and particularly to Latin Americanists, was a reflection of the learning process he has gone through; so also were the findings of the Kissinger Commission on Central America. The public forums and publications of such moderate and influential think tanks as AEI have also had considerable influence. The administration now has a more realistic grasp of what it can and cannot do in Latin America and of what the area is all about.

• Policy has also begun to reflect some of the new realities in Latin America and in U.S.–Latin American relations. The administration's sense of what the United States can accomplish in Latin America, of the limits on our capacity to effect change in the area, about which levers to manipulate to accomplish these purposes, and of the changing nature of the inter-American relationship has grown significantly stronger.

• Policy has become more sophisticated. The emphasis on democracy and human rights, on economic and social assistance as well as military aid (as incorporated in the Caribbean Basin Initiative and the Kissinger Commission Report), on balancing strategic with other concerns, on the North-South dimensions as well as the East-West ones, on developing long-term policy goals rather than simply reacting to the crisis of the moment all represent significant steps in developing a better and more multifaceted Latin America policy. To professional Latin Americanists, of course, these seem like very modest steps indeed; but given the historic inattention to Latin America practiced by most previous U.S. administrations, they must be viewed as significant. They are a part of the learning and maturing process.

• A new consensus on Latin America policy in Washington has finally begun to emerge. The Kissinger Commission Report embodied this bipartisan consensus, which involves economic *and* military aid; social and political *and* strategic concerns; democracy, human rights, *as well as* security interests.[6] Now, if the Congress can stop playing politics with the issue (unlikely) and if we can proceed with the agenda the Commission set forth, which, while not perfect, is the best possible in the present context and on which virtually all of political Washington is agreed, then an even more coherent and sustained policy for Latin America may evolve.

Three further points require brief commentary. The first is the paradox that anti-Americanism in quite a number of Latin American countries seems to be increasing—especially among the younger generation—just at the time that U.S. policy there is becoming more mature and sophisticated. The reasons for this probably have to do with the U.S. stance on Nicaragua, the debt issue, some popular perceptions (or misperceptions) of President Reagan, and doubtless other factors; but there is no doubt that in the last two years a considerable change has occurred in Latin American attitudes toward the United States. The anti-Americanism often ranges across the political spectrum; it sometimes encompasses the center and right as well as the left. Such a shift augurs ill for future U.S.–Latin American relations and is particularly unfortunate if it comes at a time when U.S. policy in the area is actually becoming more constructive. The subject merits more detailed discussion.

The second point is that the window of opportunity to pursue a more sophisticated policy in Latin America may be brief and likely to close soon, in terms of the domestic U.S. context. Nineteen eighty-five was not an election year and was therefore a good time to proceed with U.S. Latin America policy. But 1986 *was* an election year, and in the meantime the sweepstakes for 1988 had already begun. Once these election campaigns begin—and they now begin so far in advance that there is virtually no between-elections respite—foreign policy will probably again be overwhelmed by domestic political considerations (witness the 1986 conflict over aid to the contras). In the process, a more rational foreign policy toward Latin America may again be sacrificed. Hence the question of whether our policy toward Latin America will in fact continue to mature or whether it will be subordinated to other considerations must remain unanswered.

The third point relates to the problems of complacency within the American government over Latin America. As compared with a few years ago, Central America is now out of the headlines and therefore no longer a major preoccupation for the administration. The sense is strong among some influential policy makers in the White House, in the National Security Council, and in the Congress that the Latin America issue has been "solved." They believe that if it is solved, we need no longer pay serious or top-level attention to Latin America, and our aid and other programs can be allowed to wither.

That is a very dangerous and short-sighted stance to take. This book makes clear that Latin America's problems have not by any means been solved. El Salvador policy, for example, although positive and hopeful, nevertheless still hangs by very weak threads. If, under the pressure and headlines of crises elsewhere in the world, we revert to our traditional stance of largely ignoring and neglecting Latin America, we will again invite the crises there that we have devoted so much energy to averting. Latin America may again slide into the abyss.[7] We need therefore to sustain the balanced policy we have achieved with so much difficulty, to follow through on the Kissinger Commission recommendations, and to keep our attention focused on Latin America. If we do not, if we return to a posture of benign neglect and indifference, the wrenching problems and hard choices for American policy in the region will come back to haunt us. Benign neglect is no longer, if it ever was, an adequate basis for U.S. Latin America policy; instead it is a formula for disaster. Benign neglect during much of the 1970s is, after all, what produced the crises in Nicaragua and El Salvador to begin with. It is incumbent on our policy makers to listen to this warning—and to heed it.

This volume essentially covers the period from the early 1980s (or earlier, in the case of the more historical chapters) through 1986. It does not deal with the implications of the Iran-contra scandal that began in late 1986 or the events that have unfolded since then. In quite a number of passages the book sounds a hopeful and optimistic note—certainly more hopeful and optimistic than was the case in my earlier book *In Search of Policy,* and probably more hopeful and optimistic than it would sound had it been written in 1987. At this stage no one can say for certain what the outcome of the Iran-contra scandal will be but we do know that as a result of those events and the revelations that have come to light the presidency has been severely damaged, the administration has suffered some severe blows, and foreign policy making is in considerable disarray. Hence while we remain optimistic that U.S. policy toward Latin America can still be placed on the more sophisticated and mature basis called for in this book, we are at the same time fearful that the themes developed in chapter 11, of fragmentation, disarray, and paralysis in foreign policy-making, may become the dominant ones.

The Book: A Preview

This book deals with U.S. policy in Latin America in the broad sense. That is, it deals with the problem of increasing our policy-relevant understanding of Latin America, as well as with specific trends and policy issues.

The three chapters in part one emphasize understanding. They concentrate on the major approaches, concepts, and ways of looking at and comprehending Latin America. Chapter 2, on the political systems of Latin America, discusses the nature and history of Latin

American development, sets forth a typology of Latin American regimes, and assesses the main models and approaches used to analyze contemporary events in the area. Chapter 3 discusses the phenomenon of economic and political statism in Latin America—why the state plays such a strong role both in the economies of the area and in the polities. Chapter 4 examines the systems of political representation in Latin America, from the historic corporatist forms to the newer liberal-democratic as well as "neo-corporatist" types.

Part two offers criticism and addresses some major issues affecting U.S.–Latin American relations. Chapter 5 focuses on the new democracy agenda and the quest for democracy in U.S. policy toward Latin America, and offers both a critique and more positive suggestions concerning that strategy. Chapter 6 deals with the problem of ethnocentrism in U.S. foreign policy and with our persistent inability to deal with Latin America on its own terms or to fashion development policies appropriate for the area. Chapter 7 deals with spiraling population growth, internal unrest, and U.S. security interests in Latin America. Chapter 8 discusses U.S. containment policy in Latin America and the need, in the face of new realities in both the United States and Latin America, to revise and update our stategic policy. Chapter 9 examines John F. Kennedy's touted Alliance for Progress—whether the alliance "lost its way," whether it was based on the wrong assumptions to begin with, and whether those same assumptions are still with us in such programs as the Caribbean Basin Initiative and the recommendations of the Kissinger Commission.

Part three focuses on the *processes* of making foreign policy. It deals with the actual politics and machinations that help determine policies, as distinct from the policies themselves. A chapter on the National Bipartisan (Kissinger) Commission on Central America, based on my work as a lead consultant for the commission, explores the political dynamics of presidential commissions and examines the processes by which this commission reached consensus. Chapter 11, The Paralysis of Policy, deals with our divisive, fragmented, stalemated foreign policy-making process, which makes it virtually impossible for any administration to formulate a rational and coherent foreign policy. The chapter also discusses whether we may now be overcoming our immobilism.

Part four emphasizes the newer and more positive policy thrusts in Latin America. Chapter 12 on the future of Latin America suggests that Latin America, contrary to many current assessments, actually has a future and that it may not be all that bleak. Chapter 13 on U.S. policy toward South America suggests that, although all the headlines have been focused on our troubles with Central America, our rela-

9

tions with most of the South American countries are quite good and that these relations are becoming sounder and more mature. Chapter 14 analyzes the prospects for U.S. Latin America policy during President Reagan's second term and suggests that we can expect more of the same: some verbal overkill but a policy that is actually quite tempered and prudent. The final chapter, prepared for the Kissinger Commission, assays the options and possibilities for democratic political development in Latin America and what the United States can reasonably do to promote it.

Notes

1. An especially good study is Herbert J. Ellison and Jiri Valenta, eds., *Grenada and Soviet/Cuban Policy: Internal Crisis and U.S./OECS Intervention* (Boulder, Colo.: Westview Press, 1986).

2. After the title of Jeane Kirkpatrick's book, *The Reagan Phenomenon* (Washington, D.C.: American Enterprise Institute, 1983).

3. Based on the symposium "The 1960s and the Future of American Politics," University of Massachusetts/Amherst, April 25–27, 1985, with presentations by, among others, Everett Ladd, Robert Kuttner, Cornel West, William Kristol, Theodore Lowi, Hendrick Hertzberg, George Gilder, and Michael Robinson.

4. For some early indications of these dynamics see Howard J. Wiarda, *In Search of Policy: The United States and Latin America* (Washington, D.C.: American Enterprise Institute, 1984).

5. See the op-ed article by Michael Harrison, *The New York Times*, October 23, 1984, p. 33.

6. *Report of the National Bipartisan Commission on Central America* (Washington, D.C.: U.S. Government Printing Office, 1984). See also the special issue of the *AEI Foreign Policy and Defense Review*, "U.S. Policy in Central America: Consultant Papers for the Kissinger Commission," vol. V, no. 1 (1984), Howard J. Wiarda, guest editor, and with papers by Mark Falcoff, Carl Gershman, Margaret Daly Hayes, Robert E. Hunter, William H. Luers, Alan Stoga, and Howard J. Wiarda.

7. See Howard J. Wiarda, *Latin America at the Crossroad: Debt, Development and the Future* (Boulder, Colo.: Westview Press, 1987).

PART ONE
Approaches and Background

2
The Political Systems of Latin America: Developmental Models and a Taxonomy of Regimes

Themes and Variations in Latin American Politics

The nations of Latin America share a common language (Spanish or, in the Brazilian case, Portuguese), a common religion (Catholicism), a common history dating back to the discovery of the Americas in 1492, and many common political, economic, cultural, and sociological features. Yet they are also very different from one another—and increasingly so. Paraguay is different from Argentina, Venezuela different from Colombia, Costa Rica different from the other Central American countries, and so on. This theme of diversity amidst unity is the first fact we must understand in coming to grips with the political systems of Latin America.

We must also understand the *systematic* nature of Latin American politics. Because North Americans usually think of the area as chaotic and devoid of all system, it is often difficult for us to realize that, in fact, Latin American politics are quite regular and systematic. Even the instability of the area has a rationale and logic, constituting a normal, recurring, almost everyday fact of political life. It is not that Latin American politics is unsystematic; rather, our difficulty in understanding its system of politics is that it is so different from ours.

Another point to remember, related to the previous one, is that Latin America is increasingly following its own developmental routes. In its quest to modernize, Latin America does not conform closely—

Prepared for a volume edited by Jack W. Hopkins, *Latin America: Perspectives on a Region* (New York: Holmes and Meier, 1987).

except in the broadest of terms—to the developmental models with which we are familiar. There are industrialization, class changes, and growing pluralism in Latin America; but the precise nature of these changes, the institutional arrangements for dealing with them, and the developmental outcomes do not fit the expectations we have formed on the basis of our experiences in the already industrialized nations. Hence although some common characteristics of development in the West apply to Latin America, we need also to be aware of the nuances and distinct patterns of Latin American development. We shall return to these themes later in the discussion.

The Historical Pattern of Latin American Development

Colonial Spain and Portugal bequeathed to their American colonies a form of government that was authoritarian and hierarchical. Because the indigenous Indian institutions were often similarly authoritarian and hierarchical, the indigenous and the imposed colonial institutions complemented and reinforced each other. Both the pre-Columbian Indian civilization and the Iberian colonizers had systems of rule organized on an organic or highly unified and centralized basis, based on the wedding of civil and religious authority, and structured on a segmented or corporate system of social groups: military, oligarchy, religion, or priesthood.

What was remarkable was not that the colonial systems established by Spain and Portugal should be founded on an authoritarian, hierarchical, organic, and corporatist basis; that was the dominant European pattern in the early sixteenth century. What was truly remarkable was the longevity of these institutional arrangements in the Iberian colonies. They survived not only three centuries of colonial rule but also the transition to independence early in the nineteenth century. There is abundant evidence, furthermore, that these same oligarchic and authoritarian traditions are alive today throughout Latin America, although now undergoing transition.

Five distinct periods may be identified in the overall historical process of the Latin American nations since independence. The first, from the 1820s to the 1850s, was marked by general instability and some social and economic retrogression. The rule of Portugal and Spain (except in Cuba and Puerto Rico) had ended, leaving a political and institutional vacuum in the colonies. The constitutions adopted by the new states of Latin America were liberal and democratic, but their underlying social and political institutions remained authoritarian and aristocratic. The landed oligarchies often alternated in power with the newly created armies and "men on horseback" that had emerged out of the independence wars, producing anarchy and chaos. The economies of the area also suffered from the political disruption and the detachment from Spain.

The second period, the 1850s to the 1890s, saw greater order emerge from the prevailing chaos. Some of the vexing political issues of the first thirty years (church-state issues, federalism, boundary controversies) were resolved. The first generation of *caudillos* passed from the scene. New political parties were organized. Foreign capital (chiefly British at the time—later it would be American) began to come in, and the pace of economic life quickened. The population increased and there was greater organization of governments, bureaucracies, and armies. Although there were still frequent coups and alternations in power, the political system settled down somewhat and became more regular. New interest associations and organizations helped fill the institutional vacuum that had existed. The countries of the area began their march toward modernization.

Economic and political takeoff occurred in the third period, which ran from the 1890s to 1929. By the 1890s the landed elites had reconsolidated their hold on power, often using new and more centralized armies to cement their position. In several of the Central American and Caribbean countries, U.S. Marine occupations established stability and contributed to institutional development while also provoking some nationalistic resentments. Foreign capital helped develop roads and port facilities so that the primary products of the area—sugar, coffee, bananas, tin, copper, rubber—could be shipped to Europe and the United States. Large estates were consolidated and more and more peasants were, correspondingly, relegated to a marginal position. It was a period of stability and prosperity in Latin America, although prosperity was reserved for very few. This stable and oligarchic system came tumbling down along with the world market crash of 1929.

The period from the 1930s until the 1960s was a period of reordering in Latin America. A new middle class had grown sufficiently in size and influence to challenge the traditional elites. Trade unions were organized. A variety of new political parties came into existence. Industrialization was stimulated and social change began to accelerate. New social services were created and the government bureaucracy grew. The economies of Latin America experienced newfound growth and modernization. Under both military and civilian auspices, an older oligarchic system began to give way to a newer urban and middle class-dominated system, but without a radical and revolutionary restructuring of society.

A fifth period began in the 1960s, and neither its precise contours nor its final outcome is yet certain. In general, this has been a period of increased societal fragmentation, of revolutionary challenges to the status quo, and of deepening divisions over social and political issues. In several of the larger countries—Argentina, Brazil, Chile—an authoritarian regime, responding to increased revolutionary challenges, replaced civilian governments. The Latin American systems had proved more or less capable of adapting to the earlier middle-class challenges, but they began to unravel when faced with rising mass challenges. The growing economic crisis in Latin America in the 1970s and 1980s has also made it more difficult to maintain the older accommodative system. Political sclerosis set in in several regimes— Guatemala's, Nicaragua's, El Salvador's—which, instead of bending to change, became more brutal, corrupt, and repressive. Fragmentation and polarization became endemic. Democracy eventually reemerged in several countries, but the severe economic and social crisis of the area kept its future in doubt.

This brief survey illustrates that the Latin American political systems have not historically been as rigid and unchanging as is often thought. Instead, they have been quite flexible and accommodative— at least to a point. That "point" seemed to come in the 1960s when a new period of instability set in; the societies and polities of Latin America frequently seemed incapable of dealing with accelerated change; and a situation of crisis and polarization arose in many countries. That is the context in which Latin America now finds itself.

A Classification of Latin American Political Systems

Although the Latin American political systems have undergone vast change in the past 175 years, there are many variations in the patterns. Some nations have lagged behind, others have forged ahead. Some had large indigenous Indian populations, others had small; some had rich natural resources, others meager. The starting points of development are thus different for the several nations of the area, as are their several routes and end points. There is no one inevitable or unilinear route to development for the Latin American nations; instead the routes crisscross, take numerous detours and wrong turns, and have multiple starting points as well as a great variety of destinations.[1]

Recognizing that any scheme of classification involves some degree of simplification, we may nevertheless divide the Latin American political systems into five categories.[2] An attempt is made to use categories that reflect Latin America's own history and traditions, not artificial categories imposed from the outside. The five categories are:

(1) traditional authoritarian regimes; (2) closed corporatist regimes; (3) open corporatist regimes; (4) genuinely democratic regimes; and (5) revolutionary, or what one scholar has called Trotsko-Populist, regimes.[3]

Traditional Authoritarian Regimes. This type of regime used to be dominant throughout Latin America and corresponds to many of our old stereotypes about the area. It was particularly prevalent in the nineteenth century; now there are only vestiges remaining—Alfredo Stroessner's regime in Paraguay may well be the last.

The traditional authoritarian regime is characteristic of a "sleepier" and more traditional society, of which there are few left in Latin America. Traditional authoritarian regimes tend to come to power in countries where wealth and power are concentrated in a small landed elite, where the majority of the population is poor and apathetic, where the middle class is small, and where there are few competing or pluralist groups. These conditions no longer apply in most of Latin America, where major economic, societal, and political changes have been under way during much of the twentieth century.

To interject a personal anecdote, in my university courses on Latin American politics organized in a two-semester sequence, one focused on South America and the other on Central America and the Caribbean, I used to begin each semester, respectively, with a discussion of Stroessner's Paraguay and Somoza's Nicaragua. That was done to provide the students with an idea of what Latin America *used* to look like in its pre-modern past. The course would then proceed to discuss the various alternative routes to development in the more modern or modernizing countries of the area. Well, the Somoza family is no longer in power, Duvalier has fled, and even in Stroessner's Paraguay a great deal of social and economic change has taken place in recent decades which will, sooner or later, relegate this anachronistic political regime to the sidelines. Traditional authoritarianism is largely a category of the past in Latin America.

Closed and Open Corporatist Regimes. These two categories are considered together for several reasons. First, the lines between them are not always clear cut, which is unfortunate for purposes of neat categorization but does reflect the reality of Latin American politics. Second, several of the Latin American nations have oscillated between these two types in recent decades and therefore may fall under one category at one moment and under the other at another. Third, treating these categories in conjunction, almost as mirror images of the same phenomena, enables us to say some general things about Latin

American politics, the nature of the change processes there, and how these are often different from the U.S. experience.

At one level, the differences between closed and open corporatist regimes may be viewed as corresponding to the differences between dictatorship and democracy. That formulation, however, paints the difference between the two in stark either-or terms; it derives more from Anglo-American criteria than from Latin American ones; and it ignores the fact that many Latin American regimes consist of complex mixes, halfway between dictatorships and democracy, that overlap or alternate rapidly between the two forms of government. The closed and open corporatist categorizations provide a more satisfactory means for understanding these dynamics than does the dictatorship-democracy dichotomy; they also correspond more closely to Latin American realities.

The choice (and often alternation) between open and closed corporatist systems in Latin America originated in the 1930s when the traditional oligarchic and authoritarian regimes of the region began to break down and Latin American politics became more differentiated and complex. The question facing the elites and middle-class sectors at the time was: How can we preserve the system of authority, hierarchy, and order of the past while also responding to, even accommodating, the newer forces of change? Although many Latin American countries experimented with several formulas in the 1930s and into the postwar period, most of them eventually settled on an updated form of corporatism, in both its open and its closed varieties.

Corporatism is the tendency to view the political community as the sum total of the functional interests in the society, with each of these interests deemed to have a defined position and a legitimate right to participate in the political society.[4] Under a corporatist system, however, participation is determined largely by sector rather than by U.S.-style egalitarian elections based on one-man, one-vote. The typical corporations or corporate interests in such a system are the landowners, the armed forces, the church, businessmen and industrialists, professionals, and, most recently, organized labor. In practice most Latin American states have combined such a corporatist system of functional representation with one form or another of electoral representation.

The corporatist system still leaves much of the population in Latin America—chiefly unorganized peasant and indigenous elements—unrepresented. That of course was the purpose of the elite and middle class who designed the system and who have never been entirely convinced that all men deserve an equal say in the selection of their leaders. Corporatism also limits participation within the government to those whom the state recognizes as having a legitimate right to bargain in the political process. Those not so recognized are generally excluded from participation. The vertical, hierarchical, and usually personalist principles on which the separate corporations—and indeed the entire national system—are organized mean that the real decision makers are few in number. The system is nondemocratic, at least as North Americans understand that term, and was fashioned in part to keep the masses in check and to prevent them, in the new era of mass society, from overwhelming the system from below.

Although these Latin American systems were nondemocratic and often antidemocratic in nature, they were not necessarily inflexible. Indeed, it was largely to deal with the spiraling pressures of the interwar period—from the rising commercial class, from the middle class, and from the emerging trade unions—that these corporatist and semicorporatist schemes were first concocted. Rather than standing fast against all change, the Latin American nations tried to adjust to it—but without allowing change to get out of hand.

Since the 1930s, therefore, the Latin American systems have been dominated no longer by just one elite class. Rather the tendency has been to incorporate more and more "corporations" into the system. These included first the rising commercial class, then the middle sectors, finally organized labor. An effort was made to accommodate the new forces while leaving intact much of the traditional hierarchic order. As Mark Falcoff has written, much of Latin American political life consists of the effort to stamp a "Western," "modern," and "democratic" gloss (U.S.-style elections, political parties, and the like) on an indigenous and corporatist system that operates according to a logic of its own.[5]

Closed corporatist regimes. In the closed corporatist systems the number of groups that rule and that are allowed to participate is kept small and "closed," with power concentrated in the hands of the landed and business elites, the armed forces, and perhaps some middle-class professionals and technicians; peasants, workers, students, and the lower middle class are generally excluded or controlled from above. In the open corporatist systems these latter groups or sectors are included in one form or another but generally still under state or elite auspices and regulation.

The closed corporatist regimes included the dictatorships of Rafael Trujillo in the Dominican Republic, of Anastasio Somoza in Nicaragua, of Jorge Ubico in Guatemala, of Fulgencio Batista in Cuba (especially during his second administration in the 1950s), of Getulio Vargas in Brazil (1930–1945), of Carlos Ibañez in Chile, and of Juan

19

Perón in Argentina (1946–1955; later Perón came back and won a democratic election, as did Brazil's Vargas).

There were, to be sure, major differences among these regimes. Trujillo's is considered the bloodiest and most repressive; the others represented various forms of somewhat milder authoritarianism. The systems of the smaller Caribbean and Central American countries were less well articulated and organized than those of Argentina and Brazil. In these latter, the corporatist systems were sufficiently well articulated that they conjured up memories of Italian-style fascism.

Open corporatist regimes. The open corporatist systems were at least equally diverse. Precise categorization is made even more difficult, however, because of the frequent overlap of open corporatist systems with more democratic forms. Included within this category would be the Mexican political system: one-party dominated but with elections every six years; corporately organized within the one party but providing some degree of choice (rather like a U.S. primary election in a one-party state); authoritarian in many of its features but not entirely undemocratic.

Colombia is another example. Colombia may be described as an elite-directed democracy. Unlike Mexico with its one-party system, Colombia has two parties that have long alternated in power according to either an informal gentlemen's agreement or a formal pact. The principle of alternation and coparticipation also operates in the bureaucracy where appointments are divided up on a quasi-corporatist basis. Venezuela is another example of a system that is democratic at some levels and in some areas and corporatist in others; it has been referred to as a system of "tutelary pluralism."[6]

Similarly, Costa Rica and Chile have (or had, in the Chilean case) well-articulated political party systems and regular elections. They had evolved to incorporate the rising middle class and, to some degree, the lower classes into what we might call the "participatory nation"—those who actively participate in the national social, economic, and political life. But much of the political life in these countries is still dominated by the elites; and the structure of labor relations, social security, peasant participation, and business activity is still often governed by corporatist or semi-corporatist features.

The differences between the open corporatist regimes and the closed corporatist regimes are not always as clear as we would prefer for the purposes of a precise categorization of regimes in Latin America. Closed corporatist regimes have often evolved into more open types (and even into democracy), while open corporatist regimes have frequently reverted to the more closed types, and there are various

mixed forms. Such frequent changes make a neat classification difficult, but that is an important point: the lines in Latin America between
democracy and dictatorship are often fuzzy and vague; there is no one
unilinear evolutionary path; indeed the composite governments (incorporating both authoritarian and democratic features) that the Latin
Americans have a knack for improvising are what make their political
systems so interesting and give them their dynamism.

The problem of classification is further complicated by the fact
that a number of the Latin American countries have alternated between these two types while others have in fact actually evolved in
fairly definitive directions toward true democracy.

Let us look first at the alternating countries. Since the 1930s
Argentina has gone back and forth several times between military and
civilian rule, between more open and closed forms of corporatism—
none of which have been able to resolve that country's massive problems. In Brazil after Vargas, a more open form of corporatism prevailed from 1945 until 1964, when the military came back to power
and reinstituted a closed and authoritarian form of corporatism, but
the Brazilian *abertura* (opening) brought the country back in a more
democratic direction. Peru, Ecuador, Bolivia, and Panama have similarly alternated between military and civilian governments, between
closed and open corporatist regimes. In both Chile and Uruguay,
countries with long and strong democratic traditions, albeit with
powerful vestiges of authoritarianism and corporatism, strongly repressive corporatist regimes returned to power in the early 1970s. In
many of these closed corporatist regimes there is now renewed movement toward democracy and a more open system; some have
achieved democracy.

Now let us examine the evolving regimes, of which there are two
types. The first includes those, especially in Central America, that
seemed for a time to be evolving from closed to open forms of
corporatism. The second includes those that are moving away from all
forms of corporatism toward genuine democracy; in some countries
this evolution has proceeded far enough that a new "democratic"
category is required. Both these trends have important implications
not only for the countries affected but also for U.S. policy.

El Salvador from 1948 until 1972 provides the best example of the
transition from a closed to a more open corporatist form and back
again, with disastrous consequences. In that country a more-or-less
nationalist and progressive military regime came to power in 1948.
Modeling itself in part after the Mexican-style corporatist, nondemocratic regime, the El Salvadoran government over this twenty-
four-year period carried out a number of reform projects, allowed

21

some trade unions to organize, generally respected human rights, aligned itself with the U.S. Alliance for Progress, and ruled in an open and not entirely undemocratic way. The current crisis in El Salvador can be traced to 1972 when a brutal and repressive, "closed," military regime replaced the open one, thus providing a fertile breeding ground for radical and revolutionary movements to flourish in the late 1970s and for polarization to set in.

Much the same thing—although not quite so well defined— occurred in the other two crisis countries of the area, Guatemala and Nicaragua. In Guatemala the two more-or-less centrist regimes (one military and one civilian) of the 1960s gave way in the 1970s to a viciously brutal regime that closed off all possibilities for change and sought to turn the clock back. In Nicaragua, the mild authoritarianism of Anastasio Somoza and his son Luis gave way in the 1970s to the brutal and unacceptably corrupt rule of Anastasio Jr., which closed off the possibilities for a more open form of corporatism and precipitated the radical shift toward Marxism when Somoza was overthrown in 1979 by the Sandinistas.

In all these cases, had a more open system of corporatism been allowed to emerge and prevail, we would not now be encountering such problems in that area. An open corporatist system had maintained stability while also adjusting to change. In contrast, a closed corporatist system in a charged political atmosphere did not provide stability but precipitated its own downfall by creating conditions in which guerrilla movements would flourish. It is not coincidental that those countries that reverted from an open to a closed corporatist regime in the 1970s are experiencing the greatest conflict and upheaval and present the greatest difficulty for U.S. policy.

Democratic Regimes. Although the precise line between closed and more open corporatist systems is often fuzzy, so too is the line between open corporatism of the type practiced in, let us say, Mexico or El Salvador in the 1960s and full-fledged democracy. Nevertheless, some of the Latin American countries have undertaken or are undertaking this transition also, and it merits consideration as a separate category.

In countries such as Costa Rica and Venezuela there has been a definite transition to democracy. These countries have not just imported the institutional paraphernalia of democracy—elections, electoral commissions, and political parties—but have implanted a genuinely democratic civic consciousness. Public opinion research in these countries indicates that a fundamental shift from a mentality of corporatism (elitism, hierarchy, the sectoral organization of society) to a civic political culture of democracy is taking place. Indeed, it may be that in these countries democracy rather than corporatism is now the dominant strain. If the trend is sustained it will mark a sea change in public opinion as well as the arrival of true democracy in Latin America.

The change is, of course, more marked in some countries than in others. It seems to be strongest in Costa Rica and Venezuela but growing in the Dominican Republic, Honduras, Ecuador, Panama, Colombia, Peru, perhaps El Salvador and Guatemala, and elsewhere. The democratic political culture that was once strong in Chile and Uruguay was reversed in the 1970s and now may again be going back toward democracy. In 1983, accompanied by a widespread public outpouring in favor of democracy, Argentina installed a new democratically elected government. Democracy was reinstituted in Brazil in 1985. Mexico may also reform its aging corporatist regime in more democratic ways.

So far, in many of these transitional regimes, the democratic sentiment is often inchoate and may still be reversed, but there does seem to be growing sentiment for the values of a civic, participatory, and democratic political culture.

Revolutionary Regimes. To this point, Latin America now has only two revolutionary regimes, Cuba and Nicaragua. Grenada appeared to have joined this group, but in 1983 that was reversed by U.S. military intervention. Guyana and Suriname have moved in some parallel trajectories, but the transition in these two countries remains uncertain and incomplete. Bolivia had its revolution in 1952 and may be again headed in a radical direction; and early in the century Mexico also had a profound social revolution that for a time seemed quite radical.

The causes for the coming to power of these radical-revolutionary, or Trotsko-Populist, regimes are clear. In both Cuba and Nicaragua revolution had its roots in the transition backward from an open to a closed corporatist regime. We have no record of an open corporatist regime in Latin America ever giving way to radical revolution; rather it is the closed kind that provides the breeding ground for revolutionary upheaval. The regimes of both Batista in Cuba and Somoza in Nicaragua sought to revert to a more closed and repressive form after an initial opening and when their peoples had come to expect something better.

Several lessons may be learned from these experiences. First, one cannot turn the clock back in Latin America unless one is willing to use brutal repression to accomplish it, which may in the long run

23

provide the conditions in which revolutionary sentiment can flourish. Second, an open corporatist system, even though not fully democratic, is much to be preferred to a closed one, from the point of view of the peoples affected and of the implications for U.S. foreign policy. The third lesson is that the mixed closed-and-open systems—such as those in El Salvador, Guatemala, and Honduras—bear especially close watching. Should the pendulum in any of these three countries swing definitively toward a closed and brutal form of government, then radicalism will almost certainly spread and a revolutionary upheaval inimical to U.S. interests is likely. On the other hand, if openness can be maintained and expanded, both the interests of the peoples of these countries and of U.S. policy will likely be enhanced.

There are three main difficulties with the revolutionary regimes of Cuba and Nicaragua. First, they have opted for an alliance or for close ties with the Soviet Union, substituting one form of external dependence for another. Second, political liberty and freedom have been sacrificed in the face of what otherwise seems to be a rising tide of sentiment in favor of democracy throughout Latin America. Third, the economies of these two countries are unsuccessful. The Cuban and Nicaraguan economies are both disasters. Nicaragua has steadily run downhill since 1979 and now has food lines, rationing, and a lowered standard of living. In Cuba the economy some twenty-five years after the revolution has about reached the level it was in the late 1950s; the Cubans are now worse off in per capita terms than many of their capitalistic or semicapitalistic neighbors whom they once were ranked ahead of, and alone among the socialist countries of the world Cuba has shown relatively little progress since 1960. The two regimes have probably improved education, housing, and health care; otherwise, however, they have merely redistributed and democratized their poverty. Eventually, these regimes must produce concrete accomplishments in the way of material goods and services, not just rhetoric, if they are to succeed, if their peoples are to remain contented, and if the revolutionary option they offer is to be attractive elsewhere in Latin America.

Explanatory Models

The history and mechanisms of the political systems of Latin America are fairly clear to those who study the area, but the models we use to interpret the region's development are less clear. Let us review the major interpretations to sort out what is useful and not so useful in each.

Marxism. The Marxian intellectual framework may sometimes be useful, at its most general level, in helping us understand the broad course of Latin American development since the nineteenth century. But many scholars find it less useful as a guide to the more specific events, movements, and regimes of today. There has been in Latin America since the last century a long-term process in which feudalism has come to be supplanted by more capitalistic structures; and, in some countries a further transition from capitalistic to more social-democratic and socialist forms has taken place.

Moreover, the force in these transformations has been economic development. Economic development helped undermine the old land-owning class, stimulated the rise of a new business-entrepreneurial elite, paved the way for the growth of the middle class, and eventually gave rise to trade unionism. These changes in the class structure, in turn, worked a profound transformation in the political structures as well, particularly from the 1920s and 1930s on when the pace of change accelerated.

The Marxian paradigm thus provides a large map, a set of general contours, for the understanding of the broad sweep of Latin American history from the past to the present. That framework is less useful, however, (1) the closer one moves to the present, and (2) the more specific one seeks to become. For example, although virtually all Latin American clerics and military officers are now from the middle class, the Marxian class categories do not tell us much about why one officer corps or group of clerics moves to the left and the other goes to the right, or about the divisions *within* their respective ranks. Nor do these categories get us very far in helping us understand some aspects of Latin American bureaucratic behavior, political party machinations, the role of the state, circulations in power by various groups, and so forth. The Marxian explanation is useful to a degree in all these areas, but it tends to ignore both the strong force of cultural continuity in Latin America and the genuine independence of political variables. The fact is that these cannot simply be subordinated to economic or class determinants. Hence the Marxian explanation carries us only a limited distance, leaving a great deal of Latin American political phenomena unexplained and unaccounted for.

The Developmentalist Model. The developmentalist model derived from the literature on social, economic, and political development of the 1960s and strongly undergirded such U.S. assistance programs as the Alliance for Progress (see chapter 9). The developmentalist approach offered a non-Communist route to development and was presented as an alternative to Marxism. The approach was based on the developmental experiences of the United States and Western Europe and assumed that these processes were unilinear, inevitable, universal, and repeatable. The developing nations of Latin America were thus viewed as somewhat backward versions of the United States, but fated inevitably to follow our footsteps if only enough economic assistance and technological know-how could be applied.

Hence the United States, through the Alliance for Progress, supported economic growth in Latin America with the hope that it would lead to development and a higher standard of living. Economic growth, it was also presumed, would lead to a stable middle class, a more moderate and nonpolitical trade unionism, professionalism on the part of the military and less inclination to meddle in civilian politics, and, ultimately, a stable, democratic, socially just political system that would closely resemble our own.

These assumptions were not borne out in the Latin American setting. Considerable economic growth occurred in Latin America during the 1960s under the Alliance, to be sure, but the social and political concomitants that were supposed to follow from this growth did not follow. The middle class did not become a bulwark of stability, the trade unions remained highly politicized and often revolutionary, greater professionalism led frequently to more military intervention rather than less, and stability and democracy were not ensured.

The problems with the developmentalist approach were several. Most important was that the grand universal categories put forth in the literature had but limited relevance to Latin America. Latin America is not "non-Western" but it does represent a special (Iberian) fragment of the West to which the experiences of the Northern nations of Europe and America have long had only partial relevance. Second and the reverse side of this coin was the fact that the developmentalist approach was based on an appalling lack of knowledge about Latin America—about the middle class, the military, trade unions, and the like. Indeed what was said about the Marxian approach could also be said about the developmentalist approach: both were based on a grand global theory or model that had only limited utility when applied to Latin America.

The Andersonian "Power Contenders" Model. To help remedy those deficiencies in both the Marxian and the developmentalist theories, Charles W. Anderson of the University of Wisconsin, one of the nation's leading Latin Americanists, formulated a new theory of Latin American politics based on the actual experiences of Latin America, not on models imported from the outside and only partially applicable there.[7] For a considerable period in the 1960s and 1970s this approach served as the dominant one in the field.

Anderson argued that in Latin America the political system consists of a variety of rival power contenders—church, army, oligarchy—roughly comparable to the "corporate" groups of this analysis. These groups vie for influence and political power in accord with specific rules—rules that are quite different from those prevailing in the United States but not entirely unviable or unworkable in Latin America. Anderson suggested that elections in Latin America are tentative rather than definitive and constitute only one among several routes to power, that coups are a normal part of the political process, and that politics often involves the circulation of several elites into and out of power. In these regards, Anderson's model corresponds closely to the discussion here of alternations between closed and open corporatist regimes.

The *system* of Latin American politics Anderson described was not rigid but in fact quite flexible. New groups could be accepted into the system if two conditions were met: (1) they had to demonstrate that their strength could threaten the system, and (2) they had to agree to moderate their demands so as to allow the older power contenders to continue to have influence.

The Andersonian model was particularly useful where the Marxian and developmentalist frameworks left off. It increased our understanding of the dynamics of *political* change in Latin America and the overlap of its traditional and modern aspects. But the Andersonian model was excessively optimistic, a product of the hopeful years of the early 1960s. It pictured the Latin American political systems as almost infinitely flexible and accommodative, but did not adequately explain the return to more authoritarian practices in the mid- to late 1960s. It demonstrated that the Latin American middle sectors could be assimilated in the time-honored way the area had long dealt with change, but it was not able to account for the breakdown of the system under rising mass pressures in the 1960s and 1970s. Nor did it adequately account for international or external forces.

The Corporatist Model. The corporatist model, as outlined earlier in this chapter, was a complement to and extension of the Andersonian model. It derived from dissatisfaction with the incompleteness of the Marxian categories and with the inadequacies of the developmentalist approach that undergirded the U.S. foreign assistance program and from a need to update and modify Anderson's theory. It also sought to understand Latin America on its own (often Catholic, authoritarian, organic, hierarchical, corporatist) terms rather than according to an ethnocentric U.S. set of political preferences.[8]

The corporatist model was meant not as an all-encompassing and complete explanation of Latin American politics but as a partial explanation designed to shed light on phenomena not adequately explained by other models. It sought to explain the almost inherently corporate and sectoral organization of Latin American social and political life, as contrasted with the interest group pluralism of the United States. It was useful also in enabling us to understand better the structure of Latin American labor-employer relations, the guiding and paternalistic role of the state, the nature of group interaction, the quasimercantilist nature of the economy (see chapter 3), the special position of the church and the army, the system of social security, and the functions of the bureaucracy.

The corporatist model caused a considerable stir because of the presumed identification of corporatism with fascism. Fascism, however, is only one particularly venal form of corporatism; in Latin America corporatism generally took more benign, Catholic, and nontotalitarian forms. Others believed the corporatist approach to be excessively pessimistic about the likelihood of democracy's ever taking firm root in Latin America. Corporatism could and did, however, have democratic or open forms as well as authoritarian ones—as we have seen. The corporatist model, especially when considered in conjunction with other approaches, added greatly to our understanding of Latin American politics.

The Bureaucratic-Authoritarian Model. The bureaucratic-authoritarian and the corporatist models arose at about the same time and for several of the same reasons. Both sought to explain why Latin American development failed to correspond to the developmental models of the already industrialized nations and why, particularly, the most advanced of the Latin American nations—Argentina, Brazil, and Chile—reverted in the 1960s and early 1970s to authoritarian rule, albeit modernized bureaucratic-authoritarian rule, as distinct from the traditional one-man dictatorships of the past.

The growth of bureaucratic authoritarianism, its advocates argued, was caused by the failure of Latin America's development strategy of import substitution—that is, of a strategy to produce locally what had previously been imported. The effort resulted in rising unemployment, economic stagnation, growing balance-of-payments problems, and rising mass unrest. To stem the unrest from below, the military (the bureaucratic authoritarians) were obliged to step into power to prevent revolutionary upheaval and to forge a new and more conservative development strategy.

This approach had its usefulness but it was also problematic. In the writings of some of its best known proponents, the analysis of the bureaucratic-authoritarian approach took on a quasi-Marxist form that seemed overly rigid and deterministic. Second, questions arose whether this approach had accurately assessed the import-substitution strategy. Third, it failed to fit all the countries equally well. And fourth, the new political openings and movement toward democracy of the later 1970s meant the inevitability of bureaucratic-authoritarianism needed to be seriously reconsidered.

Dependency Theory. The dependency model, largely formulated by Latin Americans themselves, argued that the fundamental problem of the area's underdevelopment derived from its dependency on the outside world, that is, on the United States. It suggested that development in the United States had come at the cost of leaving Latin America underdeveloped. Instead of pursuing development in tandem, this approach suggested, the two Americas were fundamentally antagonistic.

Dependency theory has its crude as well as its sophisticated formulations, as do all the models dicussed here. But let us face facts: Latin America *is* excessively dependent on the outside world, the United States sometimes *does* become too involved in its internal politics, major U.S. multinational corporations have sometimes engaged in some nefarious practices in Latin America, and the international banks *do* in part dictate the rhythms of Latin American development.

Excessive enthusiasm for dependency theory should also be tempered, however. Dependency is by no means the only cause of Latin American underdevelopment; and too often the dependency model has been used by Latin Americans to blame all their problems on the United States instead of looking to their own societies for the causes. Some writers have used the dependency approach as a shorthand for Marxist-Leninist arguments about U.S. imperialism and as a justification for guerrilla war. Like the corporatist model, dependency analysis offers a worthwhile approach, particularly if its importance is not exaggerated. But again, one needs to be careful not to elevate a useful but still partial explanation into a single and all-encompassing one.

The Struggle-for-Democracy Approach. An updated version of the developmentalist model, the struggle-for-democracy approach holds that the U.S. model still has considerable relevance for other nations

and that the United States can and should assist democratic development in Latin America. Its backers view Latin America as locked in a
constant struggle between democracy and dictatorship. They believe
that U.S. institutions can be exported to Latin America and that U.S.
capital, technology, and know-how can accomplish these goals (see
the further discussion in chapter 5).

Others are skeptical. They doubt that U.S. institutions can be
transplanted to nations where the culture and history are different
from our own. They doubt that the United States has the will, the
capacity, or the resources over the long term to effect these ends or
that the Latin American nations want necessarily to replicate the U.S.
model. The political problem in Latin America is often devising formulas that combine and reconcile the diverse features in its political
history, not choosing between dictatorship and democracy.

Still, there is a democratic opening in Latin America that merits
attention and support. We have portrayed it here, however, not always as a struggle for democracy but often as a trend from closed to
more open forms of corporatism in some countries and from open
corporatism to a genuine civic culture in others. That is a more
accurate description and enables us to avoid some of the exaggerated
expectations—and the frustrated hopes—that the dictatorship-versus-
democracy dichotomy gives rise to.

Conclusions and Implications

Latin America has a system of politics uniquely its own. Some parts of
this system are borrowed from abroad (from the U.S. constitutional
tradition, from the French system of legal codification), but the most
salient features are indigenous. These have developed, even "modernized," over time into complex patterns, processes, and institutional arrangements. Corporatism, or the sectoral organization of
society, as well as representative government, have been incorporated
into the Latin American systems as dominant forms of social and
political structure.

This chapter uses five categories to classify Latin American political systems: (1) traditional authoritarian regimes, (2) closed corporatist regimes, (3) open corporatist regimes, (4) genuinely democratic
or "civic" regimes, and (5) radical-revolutionary regimes. The traditional authoritarian regime is becoming an anachronism, with only
one left in Latin America. Genuinely radical and revolutionary regimes are also relatively rare in the hemisphere.

The real political struggle, therefore, has been between closed
and open corporatist regimes and the combinations and oscillations

between them as well as the newer trends toward democracy. We may prefer full-fledged democratic regimes in Latin America, but for some countries that is not now an entirely realistic possibility. The "mixed" or "half-way house" of an open corporatist regime represents an intermediate stage, and is certainly to be preferred over the closed corporatist regimes and over full-fledged authoritarianism. Open corporatist regimes have the advantage both of being closer to the historical traditions of Latin America and of representing an opening toward democracy. Particularly in the strife-torn nations of Central America, and maybe in some of those in South America as well, an open corporatist regime may be the best that we can realistically hope for in the present circumstances.

We also surveyed the various models that scholars and policy analysts have used to interpret Latin America. Both the Marxian and developmentalist approaches offer some useful broad categories and insights, but they become less helpful when applied in very specific circumstances. For understanding Latin America on its own terms and in its own context, many scholars find a combination of the Andersonian, corporatist, bureaucratic-authoritarian, and dependency theories of development most useful—especially if they are free of ideological baggage and employed pragmatically and eclectically. The struggle-for-democracy approach also has utility in the appropriate circumstances.

We await a synthesis of these various approaches. Most openminded students of the area see no reason why we cannot selectively combine the best insights of each into a useful and panoramic whole.

We now have considered literature on each of these approaches; what is required is both further testing and refinement of these theories *and* a building of bridges between them. We require such a grand synthesis as a way of broadening and enriching our understanding of Latin America and the interpretations we use to comprehend the area.

Notes

1. Philippe C. Schmitter, "Paths to Political Development in Latin America," in Douglas Chalmers, ed., *Changing Latin America* (New York: Columbia University Press, 1972).

2. These formulations derive from the author's own writings, *Politics and Social Change in Latin America*, 2nd rev. ed. (Amherst: University of Massachusetts Press, 1982), and *Corporatism and National Development in Latin America* (Boulder, Colo.: Westview Press, 1981); and from Mark Falcoff, "The Politics of Latin America," in R. Daniel McMichael and John D. Paulus, eds., *Western Hemisphere Stability—The Latin American Connection* (Pittsburgh, Pa.: World Affairs Council of Pittsburgh, 19th World Affairs Forum, 1982).

3

Economic and Political Statism in Latin America

My remarks address the general nature of the political economy of Latin America and also the place of foreign investment and perhaps domestic investment there. The presentation is not entirely pessimistic, though pessimism about Latin America is much at large these days; it does serve to highlight from a new perspective the difficulties of relying on direct private investment in resolving Latin America's problems.

A Model of State Capitalism in Latin America

I would like to discuss a model of the Latin American political-economic systems. The model obviously applies more to some countries than others. My presentation is necessarily general and is intended as a heuristic device, not necessarily as a reflection of reality in any particular country. My use of the term "model" implies neither approval nor disapproval but rather how things are in this part of the world, and perhaps expresses some facts that we must face realistically.

The theme I want to develop is the following: that the political economy of Latin America conforms very poorly to any of the models with which we, from our background, training, intellectual life, and academic perspectives, have much familiarity. We are dealing with a system, I suggest, that at its heart is mercantilist, with various neo-feudal aspects, and perhaps can be defined as state-capitalist. In its basic features this system does not conform closely either to the North American or Northwest European model of capitalism or, in most of

This chapter is adapted from Michael Novak and Michael P. Jackson, eds., *Latin America: Dependency or Interdependence?* (Washington, D.C.: American Enterprise Institute, 1985). This chapter is based on the transcript of an oral presentation made at the conference out of which the book grew; it is therefore more conversational than academic.

the countries of the area, to a Marxian model of socialism. Rather it represents a distinctive intermediary between these two. Indeed that is how I want to define the state capitalism that prevails in Latin America: a system of national production and organization intermediate between that of liberal market capitalism, where private interests dominate and where there is laissez faire in both the economic and the political realms, and a full-blown command system, where the state dominates in both economic and political affairs.[1]

The implication that might be drawn from these introductory remarks is that when we discuss or criticize capitalism in Latin America, we should be quite clear what precisely we have in mind. The form of capitalism that exists in Latin America, if it can be called that at all, is so much at variance with the familiar models of our own historical experience that it does not fit our usual categories. Furthermore, in studying or operating in these sytems, academics and business people who go to Latin America often make major mistakes of assessment and interpretation; they do not know how to function effectively in that context because the form of capitalism there is quite unlike our own U.S. version.

Characteristics of the Region's Political Economy

Let me set forth a framework, a kind of systemization of characteristics, of what this mercantilist or state-capitalist system of political economy is all about.

First, if one looks at the percentage of GNP that is generated through the public sector, one finds that all the countries of Latin America have very large public sectors, with some very interesting differences. The state sector is so large, and its activities so extensive, that one comes to think the system is unlike U.S. capitalism. But in most countries it is not socialist either. Rather, one must think of a continuum between capitalism and socialism. If one, so to speak, spaces out the various countries of the world on that continuum, one finds the United States at one end as the most laissez-faire economy. The figures that I have seen recently indicate that roughly 30 to 35 percent of our GNP is generated through the public sector. If one uses the measure of the percentage of capital generated through state-owned enterprises, then the figure for the United States is even lower—4.4 percent—making the United States far and away the least statist of the world's major economies.

At the other end of the continuum one finds the Soviet Union, with roughly 95 or 96 percent of GNP generated through the public sector. Other countries are strung out at various points between these two positions. Poland generates rougly 85 percent of its GNP through the public sector, allowing considerable small-scale farming and commercial enterprises in private hands.

Where does Latin America fit in this continuum between laissez faire and complete statism? It fits in an intermediary position, by and large, with virtually all the countries of the region spaced between the complete statist and the laissez-faire types. The form of state capitalism in Latin America is so distinct from, so different from, the North American conception of laissez-faire or liberal capitalism that it is a quite different type of political economy with which we must grapple, not simply a slightly different version or pale imitation of the U.S. model of capitalism.

In the various countries of Latin America, one finds a wide range of percentages of state-generated GNP. It extends from about 35 to 40 percent (roughly equivalent to our own) in some of the lesser-developed countries, Honduras or Guatemala, for example, to 50 or 55 percent in the Dominican Republic and to roughly 60 percent in Nicaragua. It further extends to about 65 or 70 percent in Mexico (with the nationalization of the banks and the various private concerns under the banks' domain) to about the same figure in Brazil, and to roughly 92 percent in Bolivia, according to the latest figures that I have seen. One could say that there is almost nothing left to nationalize in Bolivia.

The percentage of GNP generated through the public sector in Bolivia is higher than that of Poland or most of the Eastern European countries, yet we think of Bolivia as a capitalist country and the countries of Eastern Europe as socialist countries. As we examine these statistics about the percentage of GNP generated through the public sector, it becomes clear that we are dealing with a different form of capitalism in Latin America from that in the United States. It is a type that I have chosen to define as a system of state capitalism or, if one thinks historically, perhaps an updated twentieth-century version of mercantilism. It is definitely not the system of laissez-faire capitalism one finds in the United States.

A second, related feature of these systems is the size of their bureaucracies, and here the figures more or less reflect the percentage of GNP in the public sector. That is, we are dealing with countries in which, by and large, 50, 60, or 65 percent of the gainfully employed work force in fact work for the state in one form or another. The state hence becomes one of the key hubs around which the national system revolves: employment, patronage, spoils, social status, career enhancement.[2]

Many have written about the heavy hand of bureaucracy in these countries, and if one looks at the percentage of the work force employed by the state, one again gets a certain sense that we are dealing with a system of economy, or maybe of political economy, that is quite different from our own. In the United States, where the number of persons who work for the state has been steadily rising since the 1930s, the percentage is still far below that of the Latin American bureaucracies. In Latin America the figures indicate that overwhelmingly the state is the largest employer, particularly of educated middle-class persons, almost all of whom look first to the state for employment and only second to private possibilities.

The figures also indicate that the state is, in the absence of many effective social security or social assistance programs, de facto a large social security agency. Sinecures, patronage, and nepotism are used to keep on the public payroll virtually the entire educated middle class and much of the organized working class as well, in this way providing the social services and levels of income support largely nonexistent through the social security system itself.

This phenomenon of large-scale public employment in Latin America also raises questions about the usefulness of certain prescriptions that economists often offer. One prescription has it that these state-owned enterprises ought to be returned to private hands because they are more profitable that way. Another suggests that the way to solve the economic crisis in the region, particularly the debt crisis, is to impose such strict austerity programs that they force massive layoffs of personnel working in the state system. Such prescriptions may seem economically rational, but the political costs would be immense, especially in the absence of any viable social safety net. No government in the area can afford to fire or lay off workers who are its own bases of patronage support and loyalty.

The third feature of these state-capitalist systems in Latin America involves close government control and regulation even of the fairly modest private sector that remains. In virtually all of the Latin American countries, even in those that call themselves capitalist, a vast range of government controls and regulations is in place that makes our own web of regulations in the United States seem very modest by comparison. These controls reach not only into what we would think of since the 1930s as more or less normal regulatory areas, but also include government control and regulation, in some countries and some economic sectors, of such basic areas of the economy as prices, wages, and production.

One finds throughout Latin America a mixed situation: the market sets prices and wages and determines production in some areas, while the state sets prices and wages and determines production in others. The state in Latin America thus not only owns a great deal and generates a very high share of the GNP, but has regulatory powers considerably more vast than those of the United States as well.

A fourth feature of these statist systems in Latin America is government suspicion of and regulation of investment, both foreign and domestic. I think this attitude is now changing. There was a great wave of romantic sentiment in Latin America and indeed some action toward the nationalizing of foreign firms in the late 1960s and early 1970s. There is still a strong thrust toward regulation of these firms, and the ancient suspicions of capitalism, especially emanating from foreign sources, remain. But we are now seeing in countries like Jamaica, for example, considerable national lamenting that Reynolds Aluminum is pulling out. In the Dominican Republic the firm that was long a kind of national phobia for Dominican politicians, the Gulf + Western Corporation, has also sold its holdings, a move now being lamented by left-wing and Marxist politicians as well as others. With the large multinationals pulling out, the jobs and capital they provided are being sorely missed.

The countries of Latin America are turning around to the extent that they would now welcome investment of virtually any sort, with some degree of control and regulation on their part, precisely at a time when American companies themselves are leaving the region as quickly as possible. I have some figures from the Chase Manhattan Bank that suggest that nowhere in all of Central America and the Caribbean is there an American company with more than 10 percent of its holdings there. Those who are old enough to remember some of the machinations of the giant Gulf + Western Corporation in the 1960s or maybe the United Fruit Company in the 1950s—those traditional bugaboos of Latin American politics—may be surprised by these figures. But we have to deal with a new reality: the multinational firms, rather than clarmoring to enter either Central America and the Caribbean or, even more important, the South American countries, which are obviously bigger, have larger markets, and are thus more viable and attractive, are now in fact pulling their capital out of the region as rapidly as they can and are reinvesting it in Western Europe and in the Asian Pacific perimeter. We are seeing a rapid turnabout in the investment strategies of larger corporations just when the actions of these companies are being closely scrutinized for the first time. Moreover, strong criticism of the multinationals is coming also at a time when the Latin Americans themselves are beginning to reverse their positions, in the sense that they (or at least their prudent and pragmatic leadership) would welcome almost any kind of investment capital, precisely because there is so much capital flight and disinvestment from the region at present.

A fifth characteristic has to do with state or government regulations of interest groups. That subject merits separate treatment by itself. Briefly stated, however, not only are we looking at political economies with limited space for the private marketplace, but also with limited space for private associational interest groups to operate. In various writings this kind of system has been called "corporatist."[3]

Most of the Latin American countries tend to have systems of limited pluralism, not necessarily the vast, hurly-burly interest-group struggle so familiar to us in the United States, with hundreds of thousands of groups and interests competing in the political marketplace. There may be only eight or nine major interests in many of the Latin American countries, and it should be emphasized that the term *interes* in Spanish means something different from the term "interest group" in the United States. The Spanish term usually has to do with a *corporate* body such as the church or the army, which is more than a mere interest group. Rather, these institutions constitute the backbone of culture and civilization, of politics and armed strength, inseparable from government and the state systems in these societies. That is quite different from our notion of interest group.

We have in Latin America not only a system of statism very strongly prevalent in the economic sphere but also a system of statism and corporatism very powerful in the political sphere as well. To organize not only a business in these countries but also a trade union is an enormously difficult process. One cannot simply go out in Latin America and organize an interest group and stage a march on the banks or other centers of power, as may happen in downtown Cambridge, Washington, Amherst, or wherever it is that interest groups organize in an ad hoc manner in this country. Rather, there is an entire and very elaborate system of licenses and permits in Latin America by which an aspiring group must satisfy state authorities before it can be duly recognized and receive its charter or before its legitimacy to function and carry out activities is recognized. Without such state recognition and the granting of "juridical personality," the group cannot bargain in the political process.

There is thus a close correlation between statism in the economic sphere and a high degree of statism, even authoritarianism, in the political sphere. Regulation of interest groups and of associability, as well as limits on the freedom of political groups to bargain politically, keep political statism, reflecting and reinforcing the economic statism, very powerful.

A sixth characteristic that we have begun to examine in a research program under way at AEI focuses on government-private cooperative ventures. These also exist in Latin America to an extent unknown in the United States; a careful examination of them would require more elaboration than can possibly be done here. The pattern is closer to that of the continental European countries than to the U.S. system.

There is not only a large degree of state ownership in the economies of these Latin American societies, but also a large degree of collaboration and cooperation in numerous joint ventures involving private capital and public capital. It is not unusual at all in Latin America these days for private capital to put up 50 percent for an investment project and state capital to put up the rest, or the ratio may be 51:49 or 49:51. The public sector in these countries is not only immense but also deeply involved in what we in the United States would think of as private sector activities. Public-private collaboration and joint ventures take all kinds of complex forms that largely do not exist as yet in this country. If one were looking for parallels, one would think perhaps of France, with its history of Colbertian, physiocratic statism, or perhaps of Italy, since both countries have long histories of state-private sector collaboration, and certainly not the laissez-faire, individualistic, private entrepreneurial capitalism of the United States. That again makes Latin American political economy quite different from that of the United States.

That brings us to a seventh characteristic of these systems—the inseparability of the private and the public domains. Those who have lived in Latin America and those who have taken Moral Philosophy 101 at Notre Dame or elsewhere know that the essential unity of the private and public spheres has a long history in Catholic political thought. In Latin America today the public and the private domains still get jumbled together in complex ways that we in this country often have difficulty comprehending. Part of this has to do, one suspects, with the historically fuzzy line between the private and the public weals, or the fact that "corruption" may mean something quite different from one society to another.

Those who grew up, let us say, in Mayor Daley's Chicago or in Boston or in other big cities with large political machines know that a chicken at Christmas time in return for a vote in November or five dollars to help a son in trouble, a man who was bailed out of jail, or someone who needs money to buy a holiday dinner for his family at Christmas time or Easter is not thought of as corruption; rather it is viewed as normal operating procedure—a favor for a favor. In Latin America this form of patronage politics often operates at the level of national affairs and throughout the system. Carried over into the national political arena, where private and public domains are often inseparable, both politically and economically, we find relatively little of what we would think of as entrepreneurial spirit. There is still that traditional Catholic hostility toward usury and investment, toward materialism and capitalism, which is present even today throughout the area. There is a certain resentment of the businessman as one who is not of noble calling, who is spending his time in demeaning pursuits rather than uplifting matters like poetry, perhaps, and other more "spiritual" and cultural pursuits.

Latin America therefore has a quite different system of political economy that we may call state capitalism. Michael Novak has written extensively about the *spirit* of democratic capitalism.[4] His writings and those of other scholars seem to indicate that the Latin American part of the world practices a form of capitalism, if it can be called that at all, quite distinct from that we are used to dealing with in the United States. If we are to make policy prescriptions regarding either the usefulness of that form of capitalism or the desirability of sweeping it away, we ought to make quite sure that we understand its nature.

Conclusions and Policy Implications

Let me draw some conclusions from this examination of economic and political statism in Latin America and in addition discuss certain implications for policy toward the region.

First, we have a set of societies—leaving aside for now national variations and immense differences between countries—in which there has been a long history of statism in the economy. This goes back, one supposes, to the Spanish medieval period; it was carried over into the New World and is reflected in a long history of mercantilism, statism, centralized bureaucracy, regulation, and quasi-feudalism, all of which are still alive throughout the area. Statism in Latin America has a long past in stark contrast to the United States.

Second, statism in the economy is closely related to statism in politics, and the two are connected in various complex ways. Again, Michael Novak has argued forcefully in various writings that freedom in the economic sphere is closely associated with freedom in the political sphere, and that these two complement each other and lie at the heart of the American political and economic experience. I suggest a corollary: statism in the economic sphere, which has been the dominant pattern in Latin America, is also related to statism in the political sphere, and those two are also equally intimately connected. This has major implications obviously for politics and economics in the region and indicates why Latin America is quite at variance with our own history and tradition in this regard. Authoritarianism, statism, semifeudalism, top-down rule may well be endemic in Latin America in both the economic and the political spheres.

Third, I want to suggest in a provocative fashion that if one is dealing with economies in which there is such a high percentage of state ownership, the stakes involved in who commands the pinnacles of these pyramids tend to be greater than in our own society. If one travels to the American Midwest, one finds it makes little difference to most people whether Jerry Ford or Jimmy Carter won the 1976 election. Some of us care about these issues because jobs and patronage as well as ideology and politics hang on the outcome of the elections— we care, but most Americans do not, with considerable reason. The United States has a tradition of a weak, laissez-faire state, of limited economic resources located in the central government, of a society in which individual initiative is celebrated. In this country, the stakes for those who win control are still relatively modest.

In Latin America, however, the fact that the stakes are higher and that such a high percentage of the GNP is concentrated in state hands helps to explain why violence may also be endemic. The competition not only for control of the state system but for the patronage, spoils, jobs, and sinecures is intense. The licenses, the permits to open a business, and the favoritism and monopolies that flow down from control of the state pyramid mean that the stakes in that part of the world are obviously considerably higher, relatively speaking, than they are in our own. That helps explain something of the degree of competitiveness and indeed the violence that exists in some of these societies and the intense rivalries for control of the central pinnacles of the state system.

Fourth, the greater statism that one finds in Latin America grows not just out of history and culture and tradition, not just out of St. Thomas or out of Suárez, let us say, but also out of the present world situation and crisis. The experience of Latin America, as well as of our own country, is that statism tends to rise during times of economic crisis. The period of the 1930s in this society as well as in Latin America was characterized by immense expansion of state power, and it is clear that the same thing is happening at present throughout Latin America in the face of another economic crisis.

It is thus not just tradition and history that help explain the level of statism that exists in Latin America but, rather, the imperatives of an increasingly interdependent and crisis-prone economic world. The downturn in the world economy over the past five years forces the state to play a stronger role in the domestic economy of all of these countries, and the recent debt crisis again forces the state to play a greater role in the management of these national economies than it might otherwise have played. Trade and planning issues devolve further power upon the state, and social turmoil tends also to increase the coercive powers of the state.

In the present crisis, therefore, on the one hand we have the need for greater private investment there; indeed it is desirable both in our view and in the view of most Latin Americans. On the other hand, we have the likelihood of greater statism on the part of governments of the area simply because of the global economic situation in which they find themselves, a situation calling forth greater regulation and greater state involvement and intervention in their national economies.

A fifth conclusion has to do with measures of the International Monetary Fund and the imposition of austerity programs in these regions. No one has any magic solutions for the debt crisis, or any ready solutions for Latin America's underdevelopment. But in the current debt situation, we have focused almost exclusively on the economic conditions involved—that is, the need to pay off the debts, the need to establish some degree of balance in the national accounts of these societies, the need for economic austerity.

We have largely ignored, though they are now becoming a matter of greater importance to us, the social and political implications of imposing IMF austerity measures, particularly in societies that are so heavily statist. In Latin America we are dealing not just with economic situations that need correcting; whole systems of national politics and national patronage are affected. In societies where the viability of the entire national system rests, to a major degree, upon patronage, the capacity to appoint to all those public sector positions not only friends and cronies of the regime in power but also its enemies is crucially important. That is, after all, the quickest and easiest way most astute Latin American politicians have found to ameliorate opposition: to put it on the public payroll. It neutralizes the opposition by giving it a stake in the very government it might otherwise oppose.

The imposition of too-tough IMF austerity measures creates the very real possibility not only that economic crises will continue to occur but also that whole systems of politics and societies will become unraveled in the process. This is especially true in systems that are so heavily dependent on state-directed policies and patronage politics for their very survival. The patient will likely remain sick, and the doctor is likely to die in the process of administering the medicine.

Finally, let me suggest that if one is dealing with societies that are heavily statist to begin with, as I have suggested the Latin American societies are, then it is a relatively easy and quick step—and we want to think of the implications of this for policy as well as for investment—from a system of state capitalism to one of state socialism. All that is required really is a shift in the political leadership at the top. We saw that in Peru in 1968 when a new generation of young military leaders seized power and said that they wished to take their country in a new nationalistic and socialist direction. One can quarrel about what the effects, results, and final impact of that revolution in Peru have been, but of the fact there was a relatively quick and easy transition to a form of socialism there can be no doubt.

The transition to socialism in Nicaragua was immensely aided by the vast proportion of the national economy already in "state" hands when Somoza, who owned roughly 50 percent of it, fled the country. We consider the Somoza regime, if you will, either a version of quasi-feudalism on the one hand or almost state- or, let us say, family-capitalism on the other. But with so much of the wealth already "nationalized" or belonging to one family, when that family was overthrown half of the national economy was inherited by the state.

The other example is Portugal, a little outside of the Latin America frame of reference but relevant as well. That is, one of the reasons that the Portuguese revolution of 1974 became so radical so quickly was that, in nationalizing the banks immediately after the revolution, the Portuguese very soon discovered that they had nationalized de facto roughly 70 percent of their national economy. Suddenly, and somewhat unexpectedly, they had this huge windfall of an immense state sector on their hands that they then called socialism, whereas before it had been called capitalism, or "state capitalism."

What I am suggesting therefore is that the transition to, and the lines between, capitalism and socialism in Latin America (at least as measured in terms of state ownership) are often very blurry indeed. We can talk about different conceptions of socialism, and one can argue that it depends, also, on who benefits from the profits of those industries that are nationalized or under state control, and obviously that is a case that can be made. The transition from the one to the other can go very quickly. One of the key implications of this statement, therefore, is that in Latin America it is a very easy transition from state capitalism to state socialism that can occur almost overnight—as in fact it has in at least four or five of the countries of the region.

We need to be well informed, therefore, as to the precise nature of the state capitalist systems in Latin America, and the major political and economic implications of those systems. Understanding the Latin American political economy in this light not only enhances our general comprehension of the area but also has major implications for policy.[5]

I do not doubt that these statist systems of political economy in Latin America need to be thoroughly reformed to be made more efficient and viable. Before plunging headlong into such a reform, however, we need to know what we are doing. We need to encourage greater freedom in these economies, greater room for private initiative and private markets; but we must recognize that doing so too precipitously may wreck the fragile economies that do exist. Some of the state enterprises undoubtedly need to be rationalized, and/or put in private hands. Such changes must come gradually and carefully, though, so that entire national systems of patronage and politics are not destroyed and whole countries are not destabilized.

We can similarly encourage the private sector in Latin America, but we must recognize that even in that area state permission is still required for the private sector or for individual businesses to operate. Whatever our wishes, the statist systems of Latin America will be with us for a long time to come.

Hence, we must proceed cautiously and prudently. We must understand Latin American realities. Reforms that are too hasty can easily result in the destabilization of the very Latin American systems we are trying to bolster.

Notes

1. Derived from William P. Glade, "Economic Policy-Making and the Structure of Corporatism in Latin America," Paper presented at the Sixth National Meeting of the Latin American Studies Association, Atlanta, Georgia, March 1976.

2. For a fascinating general discussion, see Michel Crozier, *The Bureaucratic Phenomenon* (Chicago: University of Chicago Press, 1964).

3. Howard J. Wiarda, *Corporatism and National Development in Latin America* (Boulder, Colo.: Westview Press, 1981).

4. Michael Novak, *The Spirit of Democratic Capitalism* (New York: American Enterprise Institute and Simon and Schuster, 1982).

5. AEI's Center for Hemispheric Studies is conducting a major new research project, "The State and Economic Development in Latin America," in which these themes and their implications are fully explored.

4

Systems of Interest Representation in Latin America: The Debate between Corporatist and Liberal Forms

Over the past decade Latin America has embarked on a remarkable series of transitions to democracy. In Argentina, Bolivia, Brazil, Ecuador, the Dominican Republic, Guatemala, Honduras, Panama, Peru, El Salvador, and Uruguay new, more-or-less democratic governments are now in power. Fifteen of the twenty countries and over 90 percent of the population are under democratic rule.[1] Only Chile, Cuba, Haiti, Nicaragua, and Paraguay are not governed democratically—and even Haiti may now be headed in a democratic direction. The success of these transitions so far has led some observers to conclude that this may be, at last, democracy's moment in Latin America.[2]

Democracy has not always fared so well in Latin America, and even now several of the democracies that do exist are on very shaky grounds. Doubtless several reasons can be advanced to help explain the continuing precariousness of Latin American democracy, but surely one of them is the weak legitimacy of, and continuing debate over, the system of interest representation that is to be used. Currently a liberal system of representation based on the principle of one-man-one-vote enjoys widespread legitimacy, but in Latin America's history it has not always been so. Indeed, much of Latin American history can be written in terms of the constant alternation, and continuing debate over, the liberal as opposed to the corporate or func-

Presented to the seminar "Partidos políticos y factores de poder: su inserción en un sistema democrático," sponsored by the Tinker Foundation and the University of Massachusetts/Amherst, Buenos Aires, Argentina, June 16–18, 1986. Dr. Iêda Siqueira Wiarda read and commented on an earlier version of this paper; Janine Perfit assisted with the research.

45

tional forms of interest representation. Put in other words, the debate can be seen in terms of preferences for democracy and egalitarianism on the one hand, and authoritarianism and elitism on the other. This debate is not yet over in Latin America; that helps explain why democracy there is so tenuous. In fact, Latin America continues to have strong currents and movements that are not particularly democratic, which would much prefer the reinstatement of a corporatist and nonegalitarian system or which might be willing to compromise on a mixed system that combines liberal with functional representation.[3]

The existence of these strong forces and the likelihood that they will reassert themselves at some future time obliges us to examine closely the historical and continuing debate over systems of representation in Latin America. Though this may well be "democracy's moment" in Latin America, represented by the triumph of liberal, democratic, and social-democratic institutions, historically in the region when one group or "system" has sought to govern wholly without the other or without affording it any bases of legitimacy, that has been a formula for future conflict and civil strife. It invites the other group to seek a return to power and to snuff out or again submerge the present democratic one. Hence the debate over systems of representation in Latin America is likely to go on; or perhaps there are ways (as in Mexico and Colombia) of combining and reconciling democracy and corporatism in ways that are truly Latin American, truly indigenous. Such a reconciliation might actually provide Latin America with the developmental formula for which it has been searching at least since the nineteenth century. In any case it is an important debate, with major implications, and therefore it behooves us to know more about the nature and history of the debate.

Traditional Iberic-Latin Corporatist Representation

Traditional Iberic-Latin corporatism and organic-statism derive from four main sources. The first is Biblical notions of an organic, integrated community in which all the parts are interrelated, as found for example in I Corinthians 12: "For as the body is one and hath many members, and all the members of the body, being many, are one body, so also is Christ. . . . God tempered the body together . . . that there should be no schism in the body but that the members should have the same care one for another. . . ."[4] The second is the Aristotelian notion of a society organized on the basis of its corps, communities, colleges, *états*, and associations—that is, a society organized hierarchically and in terms of its component functional parts.[5]

The third influence was Thomistic, involving the wedding of the Christian and the Aristotelian systems into a full-fledged corporatist-organic structure. St. Thomas's great contribution was to integrate Aristotle into Christian logic and metaphysics and thus to provide a logic and rationalization for state-building royal authority. It is not coincidental that the rediscovery of Aristotle and his fusion into Christian thought occurred on the eve of the growth of centralized state systems in the West (and especially in Iberia) organized on a hierarchical, corporate-functional basis. This model became the dominant one in Iberia under the Hapsburgs and was of course carried over to the New World.[6]

The fourth influence was the emerging sociopolitical systems of Iberia itself, and their bases on a structure of elites, hierarchy, and functional corporations. As the kingdoms of León, Castile, Aragon, and Portugal emerged as expanding nation-states in the twelfth through fifteenth centuries, their foundations were the organic, corporate units that then made up Iberian society. These included the towns or municipalities, the church, the military orders, other religious bodies, eventually the universities and the guilds. Some have hypothesized that because of Iberia's centuries-long effort to "reconquer" the peninsula from the Moors, its form of corporatism was more militaristic than that of other neighboring states; more intolerant, since the reconquest was a religious crusade as well as a nationalistic one; and territorial, since the reconquest gave those involved the right to the land and labor of the territories conquered as well as to political authority.[7]

Political representation, as might be expected, was similarly structured on a corporatist or functional basis. The first parliament, or *Cortes*, of which we have record in the Western world met at León in 1188. Represented there were the principal towns or municipalities of the realm. These towns were thought of as the main "corporations" of the society. Somewhat later, other corporate bodies such as the religious and military orders came to be represented alongside the towns. A good deal of the history of Iberia in these centuries can be written in terms of an emerging centralized authority or monarchy on the one hand and an emerging corporately organized associational life on the other, with the two frequently in contention.[8]

It should not be thought that these corporate bodies were democratic, by today's standards. Only certain groups were represented, not all. Second, there was in the corporate or functional idea of representation an inherent bias in favor of elites. In fact, in many such corporatist schemes there is a deliberate design to overrepresent some elite groups (the church, the army, or the nobility, for example) as a way of guaranteeing and preserving their power as against the power of the mass, which the principle of universal suffrage implies. Third, the lower classes had no representation whatsoever, except perhaps indirectly as they were represented by their "betters," in this system. It was the elites or *homens bons* who sat in parliament and *Cortes;* the so-called third estate was not present at all.[9]

Now in the North of Europe and particularly England from the sixteenth century through the eighteenth, this principle of elite and corporatist representation was locked in combat with another one that was liberal, individualistic, and nascently democratic. The apostles of the new individualistic and liberal conceptions, albeit expressed in different forms, were Hobbes, Harrington, Locke, and the French *philosophes,* especially Rousseau. But this trend toward individualism and liberalism failed to develop significantly in Spain, in part because it had no tradition there, in part because of the Counter-Reformation, and in part because of Hapsburgian and Bourbon absolutism. Only in the eighteenth and nineteenth centuries did the liberal ideas begin to take hold in Iberia and Latin America, and then, as we shall see, only partially.

Not only were the liberal ideas not allowed in, but even the limited system of corporate representation and pluralism that Iberia did have was eventually obliterated. In their drive to centralize power and consolidate their still-tenuous rule, Isabella and Ferdinand had followed a policy of luring the nobility to the royal court and, in the process, depriving them both of their lands and their corporate independence. The religious brotherhoods and the military orders were similarly subordinated to central authority in the form of an official state church and a royal army. In 1520–1521 the suppression of the *comunero* revolt meant that towns and municipalities, previously protected by organic law and charter, and *the* bases earlier of the Iberian state and society, had also lost the last vestiges of their contractually defined freedoms, or *fueros.* In addition, the insistence by the provincial *Cortes* in Spain on the preservation of the distinctive laws of the province prevented the establishment of a general or national *Cortes,* and the failure of these provincial assemblies to secure the principle of redress of grievances left the way open for further absolutism.[10]

By this point no vestige of independent self-government was left. Spain and Portugal were the havens of absolute monarchy. From time to time the doctrine of independent corporate power and autonomy was reasserted, but to little avail in the face of royal opposition. Even the eighteenth-century Bourbons, for all their lauded reforms in other areas, continued and in fact extended the trends toward centralized royal absolution. And of course it was this model, a "Hapsburgian model," of a centralized state system with no or very few independent power blocs that was carried over to the New World. There it not only persisted through three centuries of colonial rule but, because of the abundant gold and silver of the colonies to say nothing of a seemingly endless "peasant" labor supply consisting of the indigenous population, thrived and flourished, even into the independence era.[11]

Liberalism and Individualistic Representation

By the seventeenth and eighteenth centuries, the ideas of individualism, of civil society, and of democratic-representative government were becoming more widely diffused in northwestern Europe and France. These ideas were gaining a firmer basis in theology and philosophy. This was also the era in which the theory of natural rights was becoming ascendant. The value and rights of the individual had become a new focus of attention, while Luther's notion that *all* men were created equal in God's eyes was beginning to have its political as well as religious ramifications. At the same time that individualism and egalitarianism were being exalted, the moral legitimacy as well as practical utility of a society based on guilds and functional corporations was being increasingly questioned.[12]

The great innovation of seventeenth-century political theory in the "Anglo-Saxon world" (Hobbes, the Levellers, Harrington, Locke) was the emerging notion that all men are free and equal and have inalienable *individual* rights of person and property. The idea of a free and open "market society" was gradually applied in the economic sphere as in the political. Labor was brought out of the guild system and into the system of free exchange. Both the marketplace and society, including political society, were to be based on contracts entered into by free men and freely arrived at. The pressure would henceforth be great to structure all associations around mutual agreements for the exchange of goods, services, and, in the case of political groups, legal rights.[13] It became clear that applying the Anglo-Protestant idea of individualism and contract to rulership would mean necessarily the implantation of elections, limited government, and consent as constitutional norms. Representation would henceforth also be on an individualistic basis, no longer on the basis of corporate, functional, or group rights.

The seventeenth, eighteenth, and nineteenth centuries would mark the triumph of these individualistic and liberal conceptions at the expense of the organic or corporatist ones, at least in the north of Europe. They emerged triumphant in the English revolution of 1688, in the French revolution of 1789, in Holland, and in Scandinavia. In Germany the guild system and the ideal of corporate community hung on longer but eventually gave way there as well. In Spain, a country that like Germany did not experience full-fledged social revolution, the liberal ideas also seeped in but failed to achieve majoritarian support until only most recently. Indeed much of nineteenth and early twentieth century Spanish and Portuguese history can be written in terms of the alternation and virtually constant, although on-again-off-again, conflict and civil war between the earlier "Hapsburgian" and the newer liberal conceptions.[14]

In Latin America liberal and republican ideas had begun to seep in by the late eighteenth century. Ostensibly the movements toward independence in the early nineteenth century were organized around republican and democratic principles, though in actual fact these were often conservative movements aimed at substituting rule by the Crown with rule by *criollo* elites. The new constitutions written for the newly independent republics of Latin America reflected these same trends. That is, they were liberal and republican documents (often the U.S. Constitution was simply translated into Spanish and the French Declaration of the Rights of Man tacked on) superimposed upon a society that in many ways remained elitist and authoritarian.[15] This helped give rise to the supposed gap that has always existed in Latin America between "theory" (democratic) and "practice" (elitist, authoritarian).

The repudiation of Spanish and Portuguese colonial rule early in the nineteenth century meant in their former American colonies a rejection of all things Iberian or Hispanic. This included a rejection of the Hispanic university system and system of knowledge, of an official church, of Hispanic ways of thinking. It also included repudiation of the Hispanic system of representation (to the extent that had continued to exist under absolutist rule) based on corporate, functional, or group representation. In early nineteenth century Latin America, liberalism definitively triumphed—at least in its surface legal and constitutional features.

Actually, even the Latin American constitutions remained far truer to the region's historic realities than on the surface appeared to be the case. Liberalism was officially ensconced but the church and the military were frequently given a special place as almost fourth and fifth branches of government. The suffrage remained severely restricted, allowing in most countries only 1–2 percent of the population to vote. Property rights were singled out for particular legal protection. The systems of special privilege continued. Though the laws and constitutions provided for liberal and democratic rule at one level, at another they enshrined corporate privilege. Moreover the underlying structure of Latin American society, unchanged in its essentials by independence, continued to be based on oligarchic and often authoritarian principles—to say nothing of practice. Indeed, as Glen Dealy's research has shown, the Latin American "founding fathers" were by no means naive and unrealistic men imposing a set of ill-fitting liberal institutions on societies where they could not possibly take hold. Rather they were intelligent and prudent persons who sought to blend in diverse ways the legitimacy and progressive appearance of democratic institutions with the practical reality of Latin America's hierarchical and nondemocratic history.[16]

Latin American liberalism in the nineteenth century has usually been judged a failure. During the first thirty years oligarchic rule alternated in most countries with rule by men-on-horseback and the new independence armies. By the 1850s, however, the first generation of early independence leaders had passed from the scene, economic activity was revived, and some of the earlier divisive issues of the new republics (territorial disputes, church-state conflicts, issues of federalism) had been largely resolved. Some countries continued to alternate between conservative and liberal men-on-horseback, while in others (Argentina, Brazil, Chile) a liberal and republican political order was gradually established that, with various modifications and changes, lasted until the great crash of 1929–1930.[17]

Was liberalism and representative government in Latin America during this period a success? The answer is: yes and no. It also depends obviously on what we mean by "success." Certainly in looking at the limited participation and the continued instability in Latin America, some analysts have pronounced Latin American history to this point a failure. But failure can only be measured in the light of some criteria, and in this case the standards used were almost always those of U.S.-style stability and democracy. By those standards (which were also the ones most often used by Latin Americans themselves) Latin American history *was* a failure. It had failed to move forward or progress toward a stable, representative, democratic polity like the United States.

Judged by other standards, however, a more generous assessment may be possible. By these standards Latin American history may even be adjudged a "success." Certainly by the end of the nineteenth century participation, though still limited, was higher than it had been at the beginning. Elections were held—if not always regularly. Political parties had been organized—even if they did represent rival elite factions. Civil liberties were more or less respected. Latin America's associational life—groups, interests, and the like, whose absence previously had frequently been referred to as demonstrating a *falta de civilización*—was now far richer.[18] Pluralism was increasing. Though the movement was often slow, sometimes glacial, the fact is that many Latin American countries were *in the process* of becoming more representative and democratic. Even by the criteria of U.S.-style representative government, therefore, Latin America was indeed making progress.

The Corporatist Alternative

Modern representative government as it evolved over the course of the nineteenth and twentieth centuries was increasingly secular and rationalist. It was also based increasingly on egalitarianism as a principle and on the principle of universal suffrage. Modern representative government therefore demands a participatory and representative society as well.[19] None of these features would be especially welcome in Latin America.

Actually, Latin America had long had a history of antiliberal and antidemocratic sentiment and ideology. During the 1820s several countries flirted with (and Brazil actually adopted) a monarchist system. But monarchy had been generally discredited by the Spanish and Portuguese colonial experiences, republicanism was the vogue, and in the early nineteenth century no other alternative was conceivable. But by the 1830s and 1840s conservatives had begun to reassert themselves, and by the 1850s, in Mexico and elsewhere, they were back in power.

The conservative critique of liberalism in Latin America is powerful. Liberalism is faulted for its excessive individualism, which flies in the face of the historic Latin American quest for organic unity. Liberalism is also criticized for its excessive materialism, which is contrasted with Latin America's presumed spiritualism and humanism. Liberalism is further faulted for its presumed libertinism and as leading to anarchy, as contrasted with the Latin American tradition of keeping in place some controls so as not to allow offense against society or the common good. Liberalism is similarly criticized for its division of power, which diminishes the coherence and integrity of the state. And liberalism is attacked for being "Anglo-Saxon" and for not reflecting Latin American culture and traditions. Hence, it is widely suggested, liberalism does not "work" or function acceptably in Latin America.[20]

During much of the rest of the nineteenth century—and beyond—conservatives continued to vie for power with their liberal counterparts. There were liberal *caudillos* and conservative *caudillos,* liberal civilian regimes and conservative civilian regimes, as well as many mixed kinds. Most of these regimes, whether dominated by liberals or by conservatives, nevertheless came from the wealthier families, the elites and oligarchies, and they helped preserve the system of corporate privilege. Latin America continued to search for a developmental formula that was uniquely its own. Instability continued.

Toward the end of the nineteenth century a number of events occurred which not only provided the ingredients for such a hoped-for formula but also brought conservatives and liberals closer together under a common banner. Positivism, with its emphasis on order, hierarchy, discipline, and progress, provided a major ingredient in Latin America's quest to find an ideology more closely attuned to its own traditions than liberalism appeared to be. The Spanish-American War of 1898 offered a number of lessons: it rekindled Latin American sympathies for the mother country, it led to a reemphasis on the values of traditional Hispanic civilization, and it reinforced Latin America's growing fear of the United States and loathing of North American institutions, including liberalism. At the same time a new generation of Latin American intellectuals—Rodó, Martí, Montalvo—strongly criticized the United States and its institutions and drew sharp contrasts between the U.S. and Latin America. Intellectuals in the salons of Western Europe—Michels, Mosca, Sorel, Gumplowicz, Pareto—were also rife with criticism of parliamentary liberalism, a good part of which found its way to Latin America (always seeking to be *nouveau* and "with it") as well. There was, at the same time, a Catholic revival in both Southern Europe and Latin America, which not only offered a reemphasis on traditional Catholic values and beliefs but also led to the flowering of Catholic associational life: Catholic trade unions, Catholic businessmen's groups, Catholic students' associations, and so on.[21]

In the aftermath of World War I and through the 1920s these pressures began to come to a head. There were new social pressures in Latin America stemming from the middle and lower classes. The Russian revolution had accelerated the search for an alternative developmental formula. Corporatism as a manifest ideology was gaining ground in Western Europe. Finally, the great depression of 1929–1930 not only knocked the bottom out of the demand for Latin America's products but also helped precipitate a wave of coups and revolutions. Fourteen of the twenty Latin American countries underwent a profound transformation in the early 1930s. Liberalism and capitalism were bankrupt and seemed to have failed, and Bolshevism was unacceptable. That brought to prominence a "third way" that had been building strength in the hemisphere since the early part of the century: corporatism and Catholic communalism.[22]

The corporatist ideology, which built and fed upon the antiliberal, antiparliamentary currents already mentioned, was widespread in Latin America especially in the interwar period. This was a more modern form of corporatism than had been present in Iberia and Latin America historically, but it built upon these earlier traditions and a certain romantic nostalgia for them. Latin America had long been ambivalent about liberalism's efficacy and desirability, and the great depression seemed to confirm liberalism's failure. The Soviet alternative was certainly no more attractive to most Latin Americans. That left corporatism, the main idea of which had been simmering in Western Europe for over a century and which was given particular impetus by the papal encyclicals *Rerum Novarum* (1891) and *Quadregessimo Anno* (1931), as the main alternative. Note that corporatism was presented as an *alternative* to (and hence equal of) liberalism and Marxism, not a pale, retarded, or "underdeveloped" version of something else. That also appealed to increasingly nationalistic Latin Americans tired of being considered to be "without history" (Hegel), "primitive" (social Darwinists), or representing merely a "less-developed" version of the United States.[23]

Corporatism achieved widespread popularity in Latin America in the 1930s and 1940s, though the variety of its forms of expression was also considerable. In Europe, first Italy and then Portugal, and Spain at the end of the 1930s, were reconstituted along corporatist lines; corporatist systems of interest representation were also elaborated—though the actual implementation of these schemes was often delayed and uneven. The movement then spread in Latin America as well. Virtually every regime that came to power in Latin America in the 1930s, civilian as well as military, regimes on the left as well as on the right, enacted some features borrowed from the corporatist formula. These ranged from the full-fledged corporatist system of Vargas in Brazil (which, however, was only partially implemented) to the far more limited corporatist plans of a Trujillo, a Batista, or a Ubico; from the populist-corporatist schemes of an Ibañez in Chile or a Perón in Argentina to the right-wing and more bureaucratic-authoritarian forms of a Pérez Jiménez in Venezuela.[24]

Corporatism in America was never so popular, nor was it ever adopted *en toto,* as it was in Europe. Perhaps this had to do with distance, perhaps with the New World setting, perhaps with the U.S. influence, perhaps with Latin America's own preferences. Whatever the reasons, corporatism in Latin America was seldom accepted completely; rather, it was incorporated partially and in mixed forms. Some regimes, for example, simply took over the principles of hierarchy, authority, and organic unity that were strongly embedded in corporatism, and used these for their own purposes. In others the system of interest associations was restructured, usually under state guidance, direction, and control, along corporatist lines. That is, it was the state that helped create and charter new labor and other groups, that created new social security and other social programs, both as a way of recognizing labor's growing strength and of harnessing labor's potential power.[25]

Our main focus here, however, is interest representation. Nowhere in Latin America was a system of complete corporatist, or functional, interest representation elaborated let alone enacted into law comparable to Portugal's complete and all-encompassing corporatist scheme. Rather, the prevailing Latin American pattern was to adopt provisions of *partial* corporatist interest representation and to blend these somehow with the older liberal schemes. For example, in some countries such powerful corporate groups as the church, the army, the elites, and now the trade unions were accorded a special position or even functional representation within the system. In other countries plans were put forward to have one house of the legislature based on geographic representation and the other house based on functional representation. Still other countries created new corporatist institutions to go alongside the older liberal ones, and never entirely reconciled the distinct principles involved.

A favorite device was to create a separate "council of state," which existed alongside both the regular cabinet and the regular legislature, but which enshrined the principle of corporatist representation at the highest levels of the state apparatus. Ordinarily members of the council of state would include the president of the republic, the archbishop of the capital city, the rector of the national university, the heads of the three armed services, the heads of the major farmer and commercial associations, and often two or three secretaries of state of the major economics ministries. Such a council of state might serve as an informal advisory panel for the president, enabling him to tap quickly and systematically the major interests or corporate units in the nation. Hence Latin America never became fully corporatist; rather, it continued to incorporate both liberal aspects and some corporatist features of representation.[26]

It should be emphasized that corporatism in Latin America could be, and was, present in reformist, populist, and left-wing forms as well as right-wing ones, in regimes of the center, in military as well as civilian governments. Perón was a corporatist as was Vargas in Brazil.

President Lázaro Cárdenas of Mexico in the 1930s restructured the official corporately organized party of the revolution to ensure greater populist, peasant, and labor representation at the expense of business and landowning sectors; but his successors reversed that process. left-wing movements like the *Apristas* and their numerous followers in other Latin American countries incorporated some features of corporatist representation within their respective party structures, but right-wing regimes such as Stroessner's found corporatism equally attractive.[27]

Corporatism's high point in Latin America was the 1930s and 1940s, but even after World War II and into the 1950s, 1960s, and 1970s corporatism remained a major current. The outcome of World War II forced some countries to modify their corporatist institutional arrangements, substituting newer liberal forms for their older corporatist systems—but never getting rid entirely of their corporatist habits, especially as those affected labor relations.[28] And, after all, both Perón and Stroessner—manifest corporatists—came to power after World War II had already ended.

In the late 1950s and early 1960s another brief democratic opening occurred in Latin America, in part because of President John F. Kennedy and the Alliance for Progress. That wave quickly passed, however, and a new wave of "bureaucratic authoritarians" came to power, many of whom were also strongly attracted by a system of corporatist controls on labor and other groups. Hence it was not until the late 1970s that this fifty-year cycle of authoritarianism and corporatism that had begun with the crash of 1929 came to an end. At that point not only was there a new and deeper democratic opening in Latin America at the formal political level, but beneath the surface and at some very fundamental levels (unlike the situation in the early 1960s) the older system of corporatist controls and of informal functional and elite representation began increasingly to be challenged and changed.

The Democratic Resurgence in Latin America

Since the late 1970s the following countries have undergone transitions to democracy: Argentina, Bolivia, Brazil, Dominican Republic, Ecuador, El Salvador, Guatemala, Honduras, Panama, Peru, Uruguay, and possibly Haiti. The overwhelming majority of Latin American countries and peoples now live under democratic rule. The democratic trends are so widespread that many analysts are now suggesting that this may, at last, be democracy's hour in Latin America.

The societal conditions for democracy today are much more propitious than they were in the early 1960s, during the last great wave of democratic resurgence. There is at present far more affluence than there was then. The middle class is far larger. Literacy is far more widespread. The military has been thoroughly discredited by the most recent experience of these countries under armed forces' rule and is unlikely in most countries to return to power soon. The guerrilla threat seems minimal in most countries of the region, and there is similarly little sympathy for demagogic politicians. Rather, the current leadership in Latin America is quite prudent, practical, and centrist— another hopeful sign for democracy.[29]

It is not our purpose here to analyze in any detail these recent democratic trends in Latin America. What does bear emphasis, however, is how deep these trends are. For this most recent transition to democracy encompasses not just a return to democratically elected presidents and parliaments. Those are important, even fundamental steps, but they do not represent the whole story. At least as interesting is the way underlying corporatist and authoritarian features left over from the previous regimes and eras are being challenged and new, more democratic practices introduced.

In Brazil for example, not only has the country gone through a quite remarkable transition to democracy at the top levels, but at lower levels some equally spectacular changes are taking place. The whole system of corporatist labor controls left over from the Vargas era—which had remained largely intact even in Brazil's previous experiences with liberal-democratic rule—is now being abrogated and set aside. The whole licensing system whereby journalists and others were restricted and kept under wraps is being challenged. New principles of free associability are challenging the older system of state-sanctioned (and therefore usually also state-regulated and state-limited) interest groups. Genuinely grass-roots civic associations and community-based organizations are emerging nationwide, replacing the ancient Hapsburgian model with a Tocqueville-like system of free associability. Similar trends are under way in Argentina where not only has there been a dramatic changeover to democracy at the top but also new and innovative forms and systems of association and representation are being discussed.[30]

These changes offer the possibility of a transition to democracy that reaches deep into society and affects all of the national associational life, and not just the method of selecting presidents and legislators. If carried through, such changes imply far more fundamental transformation than the changes in the past that largely affected only the several elite groups. In Latin America's earlier attempts to achieve democracy, for example, it is striking that while there were some temporary (as it turned out) democratic openings at the top, there was never a thoroughgoing democratization of society. At these lower levels corporatist and authoritarian forms often remained intact. Now all that is changing. Such changes imply the potential for the liberalization and democratization of Latin American society deep down and in all its facets, not just at the top.[31] It may be if these processes continue—and there is every indication that they will—that Latin America then may finally overcome its dualism, its historic alternation and/or fusion between its corporative/authoritarian and democratic tendencies, and proceed definitively in a democratic direction. That could truly be a historic breakthrough. It would also mean that Latin America has finally resolved those age-old questions that have always plagued it: who are we as a continent, what is our destiny, are we Western or not, do we belong to the first world of developed democratic nations or to the third world? Not all the answers to these questions are in or clear as yet, but the trend is certainly toward democracy—and perhaps permanently and irreversibly so (except in some isolated instances).

Neo-Corporatism in Liberal-Democratic Societies

It is telling, and not a little ironic, that at precisely the same time in the 1970s that Latin America was beginning to move away from its authoritarian and corporatist forms, corporatism was being rediscovered as a system of sociopolitical organization in the most advanced countries of Western Europe, Japan, and even the United States.[32] Corporatism, we have found, is present not just in traditional and authoritarian regimes, but in developed, liberal, and social-democratic regimes as well. In the interdependence of the modern state, and in the formal incorporation of major interest groups into the deliberative and decision-making machinery of the modern state, a new form of corporatism has been uncovered. The questions we must ask are: is Latin America shedding its corporatist forms right at the moment that corporatism is being set forth as a hallmark of an advanced, industrial, interdependent society, such as those in Western Europe, and when corporatist interpretations have also become *de rigueur* in the social sciences? Has Latin America, in its eagerness to follow one popular *moda*—the route to democracy—in effect precipitously and prematurely cut itself off from another mark of advanced society which is similarly *de moda*, that of corporatism? Can, or should, anything be done to alter these trends and to restore some balance between these conflicting currents?

Several important distinctions must be kept in mind. The first is to distinguish between state corporatism and societal corporatism.[33]

State corporatism refers to a top-down, usually authoritarian form of corporatism, characteristic of Mussolini's Italy, Salazar's Portugal, Franco's Spain, and numerous regimes in Latin America, in which the central state controls, regulates, and usually dominates the national associational life, most often dictatorially. Societal corporatism, in contrast, springs naturally from below, represents a kind of grassroots corporatism, and reflects a vigorous and active associational life that is ultimately reflected in the interest group struggle and in the representation of interests in the state system. Leading examples would be Sweden, Austria, and, in Latin America, perhaps Mexico through the functionally organized Institutional Revolutionary party (PRI). Societal corporatism is the product of a rich associational life; state corporatism is usually the product of the absence thereof.

A second distinction is between the more traditional forms of corporatism found in the past in Latin America, and the more modern forms found in the advanced nations of Western Europe. The historic corporatism of Latin America is a reflection of that area's semifeudal past and of its roots in a medieval or pre-modern form of sociopolitical organization.[34] The best evidence for this assertion is the nature of the main corporations that exist in Latin America—such as the army, the church, and the university—all of which constitute the historic *corporations* of a quasi-medieval state. In the more advanced forms of corporatism found in Western Europe, it is no longer these historic institutions that loom large but rather the newer corporate units that are the hallmark of a modern, industrial society: organized business and organized labor. Labor and industrial relations constitute the anvil on which the structure of the modern state and society has been and is hammered out, no longer the vestigial legacies of an earlier feudal past.

A third distinction involves the causes of corporatism. In Latin America, the roots have been predominantly cultural, historical, even religious. That is, Latin American traditional corporatism evolved out of a certain history and past that was feudal or semifeudal in character, it derived in large part from historic Catholic political precepts concerning the natural and God-given form of social and political organization, and it stemmed from the particular form of the classic Hispanic state which has usually been based on a delicate balance between the central government on the one hand and its historic corporate units (such as church, military orders, and municipalities) on the other. It also grew out of efforts to control and harness the emerging social groups that were products of Latin America's modernization, primarily the trade unions. In contrast, the more modern forms of societal corporatism seem to grow out of economic interdependence, the existence of advanced planning procedures, the need for regular consultation with constituent interest groups, and hence the *incorporation* of these groups, in corporative fashion, into the numerous hearings, commissions, regulatory agencies, planning boards, social welfare agencies, trade agencies, and even legislative bodies of the modern state.[35]

Conclusion: Toward Reconciliation and Convergence

Many countries of Latin America have recently embarked on a democratic course that is both welcome and long overdue. The number of countries that have made the transition to democracy since the late 1970s is impressive and worthy of celebration.

This process neeeds to be analyzed, however, rather than merely celebrated. There is danger in the process proceding too rapidly, abruptly, and precipitously. The strong possibility exists that traditional institutions will be eliminated before new and more modern ones are sufficiently well institutionalized, and that the social and political order will hence fragment and unravel. Further, it has always been the case historically that when one faction or political movement in a Latin American country, however currently fashionable, has tried to govern without—or in defiance of—the rest of the political community, that has been a formula for disaster and maybe even civil war. Specifically in this instance we worry that in its abrupt transition to democracy, Latin America may be too precipitously discarding its older corporatist and traditional institutions—institutions that not only continue to have some viability in the Latin American context but also, in somewhat different and updated form, are the hallmarks of a modern, industrial, interdependent, and consultative polity. If Latin America wishes to advance now toward a more democratic and advanced system, and if Western Europe and other modern industrial nations constitute the model it wishes to emulate, then Latin America must also give renewed attention to its corporatist institutions and how they can be usefully transformed rather than hurriedly swept away.

The keys for understanding and coming to grips with the main parameters of such a needed transformation would seem to lie in the distinctions offered earlier. First, Latin America needs to move progressively from an older form of state corporatism to the newer societal kind, where a genuine, grass-roots, and hence more democratic and participatory associational life is encouraged and institutionalized. Second, Latin America needs to evolve from its older quasi-feudal system of corporatism, where only some elite and privileged groups are organized and represented and where the system is strongly imbalanced, to a newer form of genuine interest group competition and pluralism in which the more modern corporative groups (business and labor) are more or less equally represented. Third, Latin America needs to move from its older form of culturally based corporatism to a newer one based on greater economic interdependence, regular consultation with all the sociopolitical groups affected by government decisions, and even the incorporation of these groups into the state system.[36]

In our current enthusiasm for democracy in Latin America, I am worried that what may be sacrificed are the threads, the infrastructure, the historic corporative and associational ties that help hold the societal fabric together. We need to be supportive of democratic transitions while also being cognizant of the need both to keep the society from being irrevocably torn apart and to transform the historic civic, corporative, and associational life into a more open and more modern form. There are numerous examples in Latin America of how these old and new structures can be combined and reconciled in viable forms to help bridge the often-wrenching transition from traditional to modern.[37] These include functionally representative councils of state that exist alongside democratically elected representative bodies; two-house legislatures with one house based on geographic and popular representation and the other based on some other, perhaps partially functionally grounded criteria; a political party system like Mexico's that incorporates all the nation's major corporate groups into a single official party, while also allowing great freedom and even the existence of opposition parties; or the Colombian or Venezuelan systems which have institutionalized the principles both of democratic alternation between the two main parties in each country *and* of the incorporation of a modern interest group system into these parties.

It would seem that in these ways Latin America can both continue and expand its democratic openings while at the same time preserving the continuity and web of associations that Tocqueville and a long list of distinguished political analysts before and since recognized as so necessary for stable, democratic rule. In the process of resolving these issues Latin America may derive one further advantage, that of finding and fashioning the developmental model for which it has been searching for nearly two hundred years that eclectically borrows the best and most useful of imported institutions and blends these with indigenous features and practices into a formula that is uniquely its own and that reflects Latin America's own distinct realities. That is a process and undertaking worth putting more thought and effort into.

Notes

1. A useful compendium of data is in U.S. Department of State, *Democracy in Latin America and the Caribbean* (Washington, D.C.: Government Printing Office, 1984).

2. For a general discussion see Kevin Middlebrook and Carlos Rico, eds., *The United States and Latin America* (Pittsburgh, Pa.: University of Pittsburgh Press, 1986), especially the articles by Margaret Crahan, Guillermo O'Donnell, and the present author.

3. For an earlier discussion see Howard J. Wiarda, ed., *The Continuing Struggle for Democracy in Latin America* (Boulder, Colo.: Westview Press, 1980).

4. I Corinthians 12:12–31 (American Standard Edition).

5. Antony Black, *Guilds and Civil Society in European Political Thought from the Twelfth Century to the Present* (Ithaca, N.Y.: Cornell University Press, 1984).

6. Richard M. Morse, *El espejo de Próspero: Un estudio de la dialéctica del Nuevo Mundo* (Mexico: Siglo Veintiuno, 1982).

7. Gaines Post, *Studies in Medieval Legal Thought: Public Law and the State, 1100–1322* (Princeton, N.J.: Princeton University Press, 1964); Post, "Roman Law and Early Representation in Spain and Italy," *Speculum*, vol. 18 (April 1943), pp. 211–32.

8. Evelyn Stefanos Procter, *Curia and Cortes in León and Castile, 1072–1295* (Cambridge: Cambridge University Press, 1980).

9. The topic has been dealt with in more detail previously by the author in *Corporatism and Development: The Portuguese Experience* (Amherst, Mass.: University of Massachusetts Press, 1977).

10. G. Griffiths, *Representative Government in Western Europe in the Sixteenth Century* (Oxford: Clarendon, 1968); also E. H. Kontorowicz, *The King's Two Bodies: A Study in Medieval Political Theology* (Princeton, N.J.: Princeton University Press, 1957).

11. On the differences between Iberian and Latin American corporatism see Lyle N. McAlister, *Spain and Portugal in the New World, 1492–1500* (Minneapolis, Minn.: University of Minnesota Press, 1984).

12. Black, *Guilds and Civil Society,* Part II.

13. The classic literature includes A. H. Birch, *Representation* (London: Pall Mall Press, 1971); Heinz Eulau and John C. Wahlke, *The Politics of Representation* (Beverly Hills, Calif.: Sage Publications, 1978); Ferdinand Aloys Hermens, *The Representative Republic* (Notre Dame, Ind.: University of Notre Dame Press, 1958); J. Roland Pennock and John W. Chapman, eds., *Representation* (New York: Atherton, 1968); and Hannah F. Pitkin, *The Concept of Representation* (Berkeley, Calif.: University of California Press, 1967).

14. Stanley G. Payne, *A History of Spain and Portugal* (Madison, Wis.: University of Wisconsin Press, 1973).

15. James Busey "Observations on Latin American Constitutionalism," *The Americas,* 24 (July 1967), pp. 46–66.

16. Glen Dealy, "Prolegomena on the Spanish American Political Tradition," *Hispanic American Historical Review,* 48 (1968), pp.37–58.

17. Tulio Halperin Donghi, *The Aftermath of Revolution in Latin America* (New

York: Harper, 1973); Roberto Cortés Conde, *The First Stages of Modernization in Spanish America* (New York: Harper and Row, 1974).

18. For the experience of one not atypical country see H. Hoetink, *The Dominican People, 1850–1900: Notes for a Historical Sociology* (Baltimore, Md.: Johns Hopkins University Press, 1982); and E. Rodríguez Demorizi, *Sociedades, Cofradías, Escuelas, Gremios y otros Corporaciones Dominicanas* (Santo Domingo: Educativa Dominicana, 1975).

19. Harvey C. Mansfield, "Modern and Medieval Representation," in Pennock and Chapman, eds., *Representation*.

20. Howard J. Wiarda, "Corporatist Theory and Ideology: A Latin American Development Paradigm," *A Journal of Church and State*, 20 (Winter 1978), pp. 29–56.

21. William Rex Crawford, *A Century of Latin American Thought* (Cambridge, Mass.: Harvard University Press, 1961); Miguel Jorrín and John D. Martz, *Latin American Political Thought and Ideology* (Chapel Hill, N.C.: University of North Carolina Press, 1970); and Howard J. Wiarda, *The Brazilian Catholic Labor Movement* (Amherst, Mass.: University of Massachusetts, Labor Relations and Research Center, 1969).

22. Michael Novak, *Freedom with Justice: Catholic Social Thought and Liberal Institutions* (New York: Harper and Row, 1984).

23. James Nestor Moody, ed., *Church and Society: Catholic Social Thought and Movements, 1789–1950* (New York: Arts Inc., 1953).

24. James M. Malloy, ed., *Authoritarianism and Corporatism in Latin America* (Pittsburgh, Pa.: University of Pittsburgh Press, 1977).

25. Howard J. Wiarda, "The Corporative Origins of the Iberian and Latin American Labor Relations Systems," *Studies in Comparative International Development*, 13 (Spring 1978), pp. 3–37.

26. The Paraguayan Council of State is an example of this kind of structure.

27. Malloy, *Authoritarianism and Corporatism*, for chapters on the various countries.

28. Kenneth P. Erickson, *The Brazilian Corporative State and Working Class Politics* (Berkeley, Calif.: University of California Press, 1977).

29. The author is completing a major project on this theme for the Twentieth Century Fund, tentatively entitled *The Democratic Revolution in Latin America: Implications for United States Policy.*

30. For example, Hilda Sábato and Marcelo Cavarozzi, *Democracia, Orden político y parlamento fuerte* (Buenos Aires: Centro Editor de America Latina, 1984).

31. Daniel Levine, ed., *Churches and Politics in Latin America* (Beverly Hills, Cal.: Sage Publications, 1980); also Brian H. Smith, *The Church and Politics in Chile: Challenges to Modern Catholicism* (Princeton, N.J.: Princeton University Press, 1982).

32. Philippe C. Schmitter and Gerhard Lehmbruch, eds., *Trends Towards Corporatist Intermediation* (Beverly Hills, Calif.: Sage Publications, 1979); and Wiarda, "The Latin Americanization of the United States," *New Scholar*, 7 (1978), pp. 51–85.

33. Phillippe C. Schmitter, "Still the Century of Corporatism?" in Frederick

Pike and Thomas Stritch, eds., *The New Corporatism* (Notre Dame, Ind.: University of Notre Dame Press, 1974).

34. Black, *Guilds and Civil Society.*

35. Andrew Shonfield, *Modern Capitalism: The Changing Balance of Public and Private Power* (London: Oxford University Press, 1965).

36. For the need to reconcile these trends with democracy see Robert Dahl, *Polyarchy: Participation and Opposition* (New Haven, Conn.: Yale University Press, 1971); and Grant McConnell, *Private Power and American Democracy* (New York: Vintage, 1966).

37. For further elaboration see Howard J. Wiarda, *Corporatism and National Development in Latin America* (Boulder, Colo.: Westview Press, 1981).

PART TWO

Criticism, Issues, and Agendas

5

Can Democracy Be Exported?
The Quest for Democracy
in U.S. Policy toward
Latin America

Can democracy be exported? Should the United States support democracy in Latin America (and presumably elsewhere) when it has
the opportunity? Which are the democratic forces in Latin America,
and could they be assisted by the United States? If so, how? What are
the constraints and limits on U.S. assistance to democratic regimes
and movements in Latin America? Is this a period of "opening"
(*abertura*) for democracy in Latin America, and how might the United
States assist its development? These are the questions explored in this
chapter.[1]

It must be stated at the outset that it is unlikely that the United
States can "bring" or "teach" democracy to Latin America. It is doubtful that U.S.-style democracy can be exported, or even that Latin
America (allowing for country variations and historical swings in
democracy's popularity) wants it, at least all that much. It is also
uncertain that democratic forces in Latin America can more than
marginally be helped by the United States. In addition, there are
numerous constraints and limits on the U.S. capability to assist democratic regimes and democratic movements in the region. Not only is it
unlikely that U.S. efforts in this area can be very successful, but there
are also strong possibilities that Latin America's development prospects might be harmed by such initiatives. Indeed, it is not clear that
asking whether democracy can or should be exported is asking the
right question about U.S.-Latin American relations.[2]

From Kevin Middlebrook and Carlos Rico, eds., *The United States and Latin
America* (Pittsburgh, Pa.: University of Pittsburgh Press, 1985); also published
as Occasional Paper No. 157, Woodrow Wilson International Center for Scholars, The Smithsonian Institution, Washington, D.C. (1984).

The Democracy Agenda

The "realism versus idealism" debate in U.S. foreign policy—of which the current discussion of U.S. efforts to promote human rights and democracy abroad is the most recent manifestion—has been long and arduous. Realists argue that the United States must defend not principles but national interests or that "we have no friends, only interests."[3] Idealists favor a policy that goes beyond "mere" national interest and incorporates as well a concern for international morality and ethics, including democracy and human rights.[4] In this debate, both sides have sometimes caricatured the arguments of the other.

In fact, U.S. policy has been more complex, incorporating ingredients from both the realist and the idealist schools of thought—and often denying a contradiction between them. George Kennan, long identified with the realist or pragmatic school, sees the support of democracy as part of a hard-headed defense of U.S. national interest.[5] And Henry Kissinger, a leading theorist and practitioner of *Realpolitik*, has similarly come to view the defense of human rights as part of the U.S. national interest.[6] The real question is not national interest versus morality, but how to combine and reconcile the two considerations to achieve a judicious balance.

The issue by now, however, is murkier and more complicated. The United States has had considerable experience—not all of it successful—with efforts to promote U.S.-style democracy and human rights abroad. There are strong interests, vested and otherwise, at stake. The democracy and human rights agenda has also expanded (under the impact of the cold war and other pressures) to encompass motives and objectives not contemplated in earlier discussions. Some of these agendas are apparent or acknowledged. Others are not. In addition, the issue has become politicized: powerful lobbies are involved, and the question has become a heated issue in domestic politics and election campaigns.

The combination of factors (some not always complementary), motives, justifications, and pressures involved in the democracy debate includes the following:

1. *Cold war strategy:* Political democracy (for example, elections) is the one dramatic, visible thing that the United States stands for that the Soviet Union and the so-called people's democracies do not. This may in part explain the strong U.S. commitment to elections in El Salvador and elsewhere. The promotion of democracy is thus part of a larger cold war strategy directed primarily at the Soviet Union and its allies.[7]

2. *Foreign policy considerations:* The promotion of democracy is often viewed by the United States not just as an end in itself in chronically unstable countries in Latin America but also as a means to secure even more basic U.S. interests, such as order and stability. In some instances, these core U.S. interests can best be served by promoting democracy; in other circumstances, however, the promotion of democracy may not be perceived as serving these more fundamental U.S. interests.[8] Whether the United States opts to promote democracy in a given instance may depend on such circumstances, especially on pragmatic considerations that may or may not lead to democratic outcomes.

3. *Hegemonic considerations (or "democracy as a smokescreen"):* On numerous occasions a policy of pursuing democracy has been used as a smokescreen for other, less glorious policy goals. Under the guise of pursuing democracy, the United States has frequently intervened in Latin America, used it for self-serving purposes that have little or nothing to do with democracy, imposed U.S.-preferred solutions upon it, and sometimes used "democracy" as a cover for maintaining U.S. dominance in the area. In this way, democracy has served sometimes as a major means to increase U.S. influence in Latin America. Latin American countries have not always been convinced, however, that these policies are beneficial to them.[9]

4. *Political factors:* Promoting democracy abroad is often useful in domestic politics. Both Congress and the bureaucracy favor democracy as a foreign policy goal, and no major interest group could be opposed. Because politicians from all parties can agree on democracy as a policy goal (if on little else), there are no electoral costs incurred by favoring it. The public (or at least its opinion leaders) and U.S. allies are also supportive. Thus promoting democracy abroad is almost irresistible from a domestic politics perspective—although the results may often leave much to be desired.

5. *Democracy and human rights lobbies and constituencies:* These include some research institutes, church groups, labor organizations, academic associations, and Latin American exiles. Many of these groups and lobbies genuinely favor democracy and human rights on the basis of principle. Some combine this interest with other agendas, including political goals, private ambitions, and power seeking. Democracy and human rights are no longer (if they ever were) simply a matter of individual preference and noble purpose; they have become a raison d'être of major interest groups and professional lobbies with a considerable range of motives, for both good and ill.

6. *Ethnocentrism:* U.S. notions of democracy usually reflect North American institutional arrangements and may not always be relevant

to Latin America. U.S. observers, for example, often depict the political process in Latin America as a dichotomous, either/or "struggle" between dictatorship and U.S.-style democracy. This is a biased, narrow, and ethnocentric formulation that distorts our understanding, closes off other possibilities, and blinds U.S. observers to Latin American realities. But perception such as these do shape much of the political discussion in the United States regarding Latin America.[10]

7. *Latin America as an experimental laboratory:* The United States does not follow a policy of promoting democracy in the Soviet Union, China, or Saudi Arabia. Are there special reasons why it does so in Latin America? The willingness of the United States to experiment politically in the region is in part related to the fact that Latin America is a low foreign policy priority. The United States generally does not perceive the region to be of crucial importance; Latin American countries cannot retaliate; and therefore it is safe to use the region as a laboratory for policy experimentation.[11]

8. *The missionary tradition:* U.S. citizens believe that democracy is good and that it is good for all peoples—the Churchillian notion that democracy is the worst form of government, except for all others. From this perspective, the United States has an obligation to export democracy (missionary style) to less fortunate "developing" peoples. The Carter administration's human rights campaign was heir to this manifest destiny phenomenon—the idea of spreading U.S. expertise and institutions to the rest of the world, the naive if idealistic Wilsonian view of "making the world safe for democracy."[12]

9. *Soul-satisfaction:* The United States also promotes democracy abroad because U.S. citizens, particularly political activists, feel good about it. To stand for democracy is soul-satisfying in a personal and collective sense. Democracy and human rights seem almost to be a new form of religiosity and "true belief" around which to rally in an age of secularity.

10. *La moda:* Apart from the intrinsic value of democracy, supporting democracy in its more advanced and esoteric form is often thought to be (especially in some academic, church, exile, and literary circles) chic, stylish, and "with it." Without belittling what are in many cases good intentions, the current fashion in favor of more radical forms of democracy is in part a reflection (by some U.S. and Latin American intellectuals) of the desire to be stylish. The problem is that policy makers, politicians, the general public, and the countries to which the United States might seek to export these ideas may not always be receptive to them or to the policy prescriptions associated with them.

Of course, many people (including this author) are in favor of promoting democracy and human rights both in the United States and in Latin America. The purpose of presenting this list of motives is not to demean democracy or those struggling to achieve it. This examination does show, however, that the issue is more complex than is often thought; that it is not just a matter of moral good versus moral evil; and that a variety of political, cold war, private, and other agendas and ambitions are also involved.

Is Latin America Democratic—And Does It Want to Be?

The popular image of Latin America held by many U.S. citizens is that it is a continent seething under the tyranny of seemingly endemic oligarchies and repressive military dictatorships. If only these dictatorships can be removed or overthrown, the argument runs, then the natural democratic inclinations that have been suppressed under right-wing and oligarchic rule may find fruition. This view is a happy, optimistic, and poetic one, but it does not always reflect Latin American reality.

That the United States focuses on democracy and the struggle for democratic ideals does not necessarily mean that Latin Americans similarly clamor for democracy. U.S. observers often *assume* that this is the case, but few bother to examine the evidence. The evidence is decidedly mixed. Four measures are used here to demonstrate this ambiguity: Latin America's constitutional and legal traditions, survey research results, voting returns, and patterns of legitimacy. The issues are complex, and the discussion must necessarily be brief and therefore somewhat incomplete.

Latin America evidences two quite distinct traditions with regard to constitutional and legal precepts. There is no single Lockean democratic tradition with the support of the majority, as in the United States. Rather, two currents have consistently been present, existing side by side and often alternating in power. The first is liberal, democratic, and republican; it is enshrined in many articles in the laws and constitutions of the region. This tradition has been present since the Latin American countries achieved their independence in the early nineteenth century and, in many cases, simply translated the U.S. Constitution into Spanish. However, the precepts inscribed in these Latin American constitutions have always been viewed as ideals to strive for, not necessarily as operating realities.[13]

There is a second tradition inscribed both in laws and constitutions and in actual practice. It is hierarchical, authoritarian, and nondemocratic, and its roots antedate the liberal tradition to the period of Spanish colonial rule. This tradition is reflected in the privileged position afforded the Catholic church in Latin American society; the extraordinary powers granted to the executive, who can rule almost as a *de jure* dictator; the special status given to land and wealth; and the position of the armed forces as virtually a fourth branch of government, authorized constitutionally and by "organic laws" (or by hallowed custom) to play a major, moderating political role. These (and other) hierarchial-authoritarian features frequently enjoy as great a degree of legitimacy as do the liberal-democratic ones. The two traditions coexist, with neither necessarily or consistently dominant.[14]

Survey research results are a second indicator of this heterogeneous set of beliefs. If one asks Latin Americans which form of government and what kinds of institutions they prefer, the answer is, overwhelmingly, democratic ones. That is, Latin Americans prefer—at least in the abstract—checks and balances, an independent legislature and judiciary, a free press, human rights, elections, an apolitical military, and so forth. These responses lend support to the thesis that democracy is not alien to Latin America and that the political arrangements Latin Americans prefer are much like those found in the United States.[15]

If one probes deeper, however, the responses are less clear cut. Latin Americans also favor strong executive leadership, which may come at the expense of an independent congress or court system. There is sympathy, under crisis circumstances, for limiting freedom of the press and other basic political rights. Considerable skepticism exists in Latin America about how well democracy works in the region, at least in its Anglo-American forms in the face of the endemic violence, conflict, *falta de civilización,* weak civic institutions, and powerful centrifugal forces that from time to time tear the Latin American nations apart. Considerable sympathy exists for authoritative if not authoritarian rule, particularly in periods of stress and as long as a mild authoritarianism does not degenerate into tyranny (as it did under Trujillo and the later Somozas).[16]

Similarly ambiguous attitudes regarding democracy have been manifest in many Latin American countries. The 1983 election that brought President Raúl Alfonsín to power in Argentina is particularly instructive. This election and Argentina's return to democracy have been rightly celebrated. But such sentiments should not cloud Argentina's more complex political realitites. In the weeks before the election, a nationwide survey showed 86 percent of the Argentine people in favor of democracy. Nonetheless, the same survey showed that less than half the population favors democracy's necessary institutional arrangements: only 46 percent of those surveyed supported political parties, and only 40 percent held a favorable opinion of trade unions. When asked what form of democracy they preferred, moreover, 84 percent of those surveyed responded "strong government." These responses clearly reveal a double loyalty: support both for democracy and for its Bonapartist forms. These are the "forked trails" (as they were labeled by the Argentine social scientist who conducted the survey, Natalio Botana) open to the country: broad support for a democratic opening, but widespread concern and skepticism rearding what that process will unleash—and, therefore, a concurrent preference for authoritative if not authoritarian government. Argentine citizens want democracy, but in an orderly and probably organic form. If democracy proves chaotic, the authoritarian solution may reappear as what Botana called a "wicked necessity." He concluded: "There is conflict between two trends and, perhaps, two traditions. Neither has been able to assert itself definitely in Argentina."[17]

Voting returns provide a third indicator of these mixed beliefs. The analysis here must be incomplete, but several examples are relevant. In the Dominican Republic in 1966, the conservative and authoritarian Joaquín Balaguer easily defeated socialist Juan Bosch in the presidential election, even though it was widely assumed that the U.S. millitary intervention in 1965 would provoke a radical nationalist electoral response favoring Bosch. In 1986 Balaguer again defeated a more democratically inclined candidate. In Chile before the 1973 military coup, voting returns consistently showed an electorate almost equally divided among rightist forces, centrist parties (chiefly the Christian Democrats), and the socialist-communist popular front. The November 1982 electoral results in Brazil could be interpreted to show the country almost evenly divided between supporters of the existing authoritarian military regime and those opposed to it. Even in beleaguered El Salvador in 1981, the U.S.-favored centrist Christian Democrats could manage only 40 percent of the vote, and they lost to a coalition of conservative and rightist forces. In 1984 the Christian Democrat candidate won the presidency, but the candidate representing unabashed authoritarianism, Roberto D'Aubisson, won 46 percent of the vote in an election generally regarded as open and fair.

One should not read too much into these examples, but electoral returns do show what U.S. citizens often find surprising—the continued strength of the Latin American right, traditional caudilloism, and authoritarianism even in an era that is almost always referred to as change-oriented and revolutionary. Labeling such rightist sentiment the result of "false consciousness" is too simple an explanation. The fact is that electorally (and in other ways as well) many Latin American societies are deeply divided among their historical authoritarian and conservative, liberal, and more recent socialist tradi-

73

tions. The clashes among these traditions—which are not just differences among rival party platforms but among wholly different perspectives and world views—help explain present instability in the region and the existence of what the longtime Latin Americanist Kalman Silvert called a "conflict society."[18] In short, it is clear that electoral preferences in Latin America are not unambiguously liberal, democratic, or leftist. The situation is much more complex.

The fourth point concerns democratic legitimacy and the means to achieve it. In the United States elections are the only legitimate route to power. In Latin America, elections are not the one route to power; other routes are also open.[19] These may include a skillfully executed coup d'état, a heroic guerrilla movement that holds out against all odds and finally seizes power, a well-planned protest movement, a general strike, or a street demonstration that succeeds in toppling a minister or perhaps even a government. Actions such as these not only are widely admired, but also have the potential to help a regime that comes to power through nonelectoral means to achieve the legitimacy it may initially lack. The "populist" regimes of Omar Torrijos in Panama and René Barrientos in Bolivia are cases in point. Democratic elections offer one route to power, but in Latin America there are also other means to achieve both legitimacy and democracy.

These comments are not meant to imply that if Latin Americans had their choice, they would not—at least theoretically—choose democracy. In fact, democratic sentiment is vigorous throughout the region. But it is not the only widespread sentiment, and in a number of countries it may not even be the majority sentiment. Especially as one probes beneath the surface, Latin Americans' doubts and fears concerning democracy's viability or their own nations' capacity for democratic politics become clear.[20] Thus the answer to the question "Is Latin America democratic, and does it want to be?" is ambiguous: many Latin Americans want democracy, but many do not; some Latin Americans (primarily in older generations) want a democracy structured largely in terms of U.S. institutional arrangements, but others (the rising younger generations) prefer their own indigenous forms (populist or other kinds). Any effort by the United States to export or encourage democracy in Latin America must come to grips with these differences.

The Problems and Consequences of a Foreign Policy Oriented toward Promoting Democracy

The historical record offers little cause for optimism or enthusiasm regarding vigorous new U.S. efforts to promote democracy in Latin America. This record merits a brief review.

Commodore Cornelius Vanderbilt, his agent William Walker, and the latter's "merry" bunch of filibusterers were no doubt sincere in believing that, by taking over Nicaragua in the 1840s and holding elections in which U.S. citizen Walker was "elected" president, they brought the benefits of democratic civilization to that poor, benighted land. Sam Houston and others were also probably genuinely convinced that depriving Mexico of half its national territory and ultimately absorbing it into the United States would be infinitely better *even for the Mexicans* than continued rule by the mercurial López de Santa Anna. The former slaveholders who sought to annex or control Cuba, Hispaniola, Puerto Rico, and other islands after the Civil War were also convinced that U.S.-style "democracy" was good for our "little brown and black brothers" throughout the Caribbean.[21]

Similarly, the Spanish-American War of 1898 was in part rationalized on the basis of the presumed superiority of U.S. democratic political arrangements to "Catholic-inquisitorial" Spanish institutions. Under the same aegis, the United States acquired Puerto Rico as a protectorate and attached the Platt Amendment to the Cuban constitution, giving the United States virtual carte blanche to intervene in Cuba at any time. When Theodore Roosevelt, William Howard Taft, and Woodrow Wilson dispatched U.S. occupation forces to Haiti, Cuba, the Dominican Republic, Nicaragua, and Panama, they also believed that these actions were part of a larger mission to make the world safe for democracy. However brief and one-sided, this background survey provides ample reason to be skeptical regarding the presumed benefits to Latin America of U.S. efforts to encourage "democracy" in the region.[22]

Setting the Limits of Permissible Behavior: The Post-World War II Period. At the end of World War II, the United States displaced both Germany and Great Britain to achieve unquestioned hegemony in Latin America. With the war over, the United States viewed Latin America attractively as a vast reserve of untapped resources and potential markets. Gaining access to those markets, however, required a diminution in Latin America's system of economic statism, cartels, monopolies, and other controls. The United States therefore exerted pressures for economic liberalization (reduced state economic controls), which carried with it the need for a certain degree of political liberalization. In 1946–1947 (before the onset of the cold war) the United States insisted on new elections in several countries, and it exerted strong pressures on several populist leaders to resign from office. Among those leaders forced from office or pressured into taking unwelcome actions were Vargas in Brazil, Morínigo in Paraguay, and Perón in Argentina.[23]

The immediate post–World War II period in U.S.–Latin American relations was important beyond its specific time because it largely determined the future range of permissible options for Latin American political behavior. Latin America was forced to choose between "dictatorship" (statism, neocorporatism, neomercantilism, and so forth)—which the United States would no longer countenance—and U.S.-style democracy, which was not entirely compatible with the region's history and traditions. Whatever the original intention, Latin America was subjected to far greater U.S. economic penetration in the name of democracy. In addition, forcing the Latin American countries to choose a form of democracy for which they were ill suited, the United States effectively ruled out both a Latin American form of democracy (for example, Vargas-style populism) and various intermediate political arrangements (for example, combined civil-military regimes). Latin American politicians have always had a flair for improvising such arrangements, which might have better enabled these nations to manage the wrenching transition to modernity that they had recently begun. By insisting on democracy (and only its U.S. variant), the United States helped precipitate wild swings of the political pendulum in Latin America, leading to the kinds of imbroglios that the United States now confronts in Central America and elsewhere.[24] This is not the only reason for Latin America's post-World War II political instability, but it was certainly a major contributing factor.

Kennedy and the Alliance for Progress. John F. Kennedy and his Alliance for Progress are widely admired for supposedly ushering in a new era in U.S.-Latin American relations. There *were* changes in the personal qualities for which the U.S. president was noted in Latin America (including his youth, his vigor, his idealism, his Catholicism, his beautiful and artistic wife, and so forth); changes in the means used to pursue basic U.S. interests (stability and anticommunism would be achieved by aid to liberal democrats rather than to dictators); and changes in personnel appointments within the U.S. Department of State.[25] But there were also important continuities. The basic elements of U.S. policy remained constant: stability, anticommunism, hegemony, and political-economic-military penetration.[26]

But it is specifically the issue of democracy that is relevant here. Once again, the record was mixed. Kennedy supported Latin America's democratic left during the first part of his presidency, but his attitude toward these groups cooled considerably toward the end of his brief tenure. Although Kennedy favored democrats, he was also reluctant to undermine or remove dictators unless assured that a

Castroite takeover would not occur. He showed reserve regarding wobbly democrats like Bosch in the Dominican Republic, and he eventually chose the lesser evil of military juntas there and in Honduras rather than risk weak, ineffectual democrats unable to deal with guerrilla threats.[27] The United States helped some of these democrats come to power, but it often failed to come to their assistance when they were threatened by military coups. Nor did the dramatic and highly publicized U.S. efforts in Peru in 1962 to reverse a coup and ensure democratic rule succeed. If anything, these efforts harmed U.S.-Peruvian relations in the long run and probably led directly to the confrontation between the United States and Peru that occurred in the late 1960s. In summary, one would be hard pressed to conclude that U.S. efforts to promote democracy under Kennedy and the Alliance for Progress were very successful. In fact, a strong case could be made that these efforts were counterproductive and that they helped precipitate a wave of antidemocratic coups that swept Latin America (Argentina, the Dominican Republic, Honduras, Peru, Brazil) in the early and mid-1960s.

Carter and Human Rights. The Carter human rights campaign also produced decidedly mixed results. There is no doubt that, as a result of the campaign, some people were not tortured; some liberties were preserved; some people were released from jail; and some restraints were placed on military repression. These are not small accomplishments, particularly from the point of view of the individuals and groups affected.

The costs incurred and the damage done were also considerable. Some of the human rights activists' actions were unrefined, heavy-handed, and counterproductive. By engaging in wholesale condemnations of entire nations, regimes, and military establishments as human rights violators (as in the cases of Brazil and Argentina), they insulted national sensibilities and often forced public opinion—which otherwise would have been opposed to or neutral toward these regimes—to rally behind repressive governments. Such unrefined condemnations blurred the differences between the repressive forces in the Latin American militaries and more democratic elements, obliging the latter to defend the military institution as a whole. The differences between honest and well-meaning governments and their out-of-control security forces were also blurred, at the cost of antagonizing or sometimes undermining the former.

The Carter human rights campaign needlessly alienated important countries such as Argentina, Brazil, and Chile, and it produced few changes in the behavior of these countries' governments. Nor was

77

the policy evenhanded. Right-wing dictatorships were condemned, but leftist dictatorships did not receive the same attention. Ethnocentrism was also strong. The human rights campaign in Latin America was often viewed as an extension of the civil rights struggle in the southern United States in the 1960s. The criteria for judging human rights violations were exclusively U.S. criteria; little interest in or comprehension of differences in Latin American values was shown.[28]

Even the greatest success story of the Carter administration's campaign for democracy—the U.S. political and diplomatic intervention in the 1978 Dominican presidential election—was not the unqualified success that the action's defenders claim. In the face of blatant ballot tampering by the military, the Carter administration acted to ensure an honest vote count—thereby securing victory for Antonio Guzmán. Intervention of this kind may have produced a beneficial result, but it was intervention nonetheless—and not much different from countless other U.S. intrusions into Latin American countries' internal affairs. Furthermore, because of the Carter administration's actions, Guzmán became known in the Dominican Republic as "Jimmy Carter's and Cyrus Vance's boy," dependent upon them and presumably certain to fall when they left office. In the end that did not happen. But there is no doubt that U.S. actions strongly reinforced the dependence of the Dominican Republic and its government on the United States. Whether that is good or bad is irrelevant here. The point is that this most recent U.S. intervention in the Dominican Republic was not quite the shining, unambiguous achievement that it is sometimes held to be.[29]

One need not exaggerate these failures, self-deceptions, hypocrisies, and limited and ambiguous accomplishments in order to make the main point: past U.S. policies to promote democracy and human rights in Latin America have not been unqualified successes. For reasons to be explained in the next section, such efforts are likely to be even more problematic in the future. In fact, a close examination of the historical record would leave one skeptical that promoting democracy was ever a primary U.S. objective or that it is soon likely to become one. If, as most analysts would agree, the major goals of U.S. policy toward Latin America have been stability, anticommunism, and access to the region's markets and resources, promoting democracy has been chiefly a means to achieve those ends. Its greatest importance has been as an instrument to be employed under the right conditions (and only in some administrations) to help secure the higher-priority goals of stability and anticommunism.[30]

This argument does not, however, rest only on the conclusion that U.S. efforts to promote democracy in Latin America have not been very successful. In some cases these initiatives were actually *harmful* in the long run. The reasons for this negative assessment can be summarized briefly as follows.[31]

- Immense amounts of money, time, and resources have been wasted, with but very modest results. Taxpayer and congressional support for such activities has been squandered. The widespread popular notion is that in seeking to promote democracy abroad, the United States may be chasing chimeras.
- The effort has produced a host of foreign policy setbacks, unanticipated consequences, and sheer disasters. The simple listing of these reverses in just one country—for example, the Dominican Republic—would fill more than the remainder of this chapter.[32]
- U.S. attempts to promote democracy abroad have helped perpetuate and reinforce condescending, superior, and patronizing attitudes toward Latin America. The notion is still widespread in both government circles and popular opinion that "the United States knows best" for Latin America.
- The emphasis on democracy has also perpetuated misleading conceptual models for understanding Latin America. By focusing attention on the supposed "struggle for democracy," U.S. citizens often fail to appreciate the complexity of events in the region. The emphasis on democracy has contributed to a misunderstanding of many developing nations and of the real dynamics of change in Latin America.[33]
- The stress on democracy also encourages U.S. interventionism and proconsularism. Although the United States generally acts with the best of intentions, it sometimes attempts to run some Latin American countries from its embassies. There is considerable reason to be suspicious of such U.S. interventionism, whether it comes from "bad" agencies such as the Central Intelligence Agency or "good" agencies such as the Department of State or the Agency for International Development.
- The democracy that the United States espouses always seems to conform to its own notions of democracy, not to Latin America's. The United States stresses elections, political parties, apolitical trade unions, apolitical armed forces, and so forth. Latin American forms of democracy—emphasizing populism, organicism, the accommodation of new "power contenders," corporatist representation, and societal pluralism and shared power—are seldom given serious attention.[34]
- By emphasizing democracy so strongly in rhetoric and in policy pronouncements, the United States has limited Latin America's

choice to a false dichotomy: democracy or dictatorship. It rules out the various intermediate solutions that Latin Americans themselves have historically demonstrated a remarkable capacity for fashioning. It also means that the United States has a certain responsibility for causing political instability in Latin America, the prevention of which is one of the pillars of U.S. policy toward the region. Rather than allowing these countries to settle more or less naturally on some middle ground, the United States has sometimes imposed two extreme options on the region, neither one of which is always appropriate or especially comfortable.

• Finally, the U.S. emphasis on democracy has undermined various traditional institutions (patronage networks, religious agencies, family and clan groups, and so forth) that might have helped Latin America make the difficult transition to modernity, while failing to create viable structures to replace them. In this way the United States has helped create the very problems and institutional vacuums that U.S. policies were ostensibly intended to prevent.[35]

On balance, U.S. efforts to promote democracy in Latin America have produced mixed results. There have been successes as well as failures. Neither outcome ought to be emphasized at the expense of the other.

Nonetheless, the troubling questions raised here are seldom considered in policy discussions in the United States. The lessons of the past are forgotten or unlearned. Policy is often based on romantic hopes and wishful thinking rather than on an examination of the historical record. Past experiences have had very little effect on U.S. perceptions of its various campaigns to export democracy to Latin America. Yet U.S. citizens are often so committed to the democracy agenda (albeit for diverse reasons and motives, as suggested earlier) that they would prefer not to deal with the more difficult questions of whether the United States should become involved in these efforts at all, or to what extent, or whether such actions are helpful or harmful. Inattention to the negative consequences of these policies is particularly poignant and troubling now, because the U.S. government is poised on the threshold of a new attempt to promote democracy abroad. The Reagan administration has created the National Endowment for Democracy to implement a pro-democracy program abroad, but the implementation of the program has frequently been strongly criticized.[36] It is necessary to interject some realism into this discussion based on the historical evidence—a perspective that is woefully lacking in all the current proposals. At the same time, it is important to consider new realities in the United States, in Latin America, and in U.S.-Latin American relations.

New Realities and New Directions

The previous sections of this chapter examined democracy in Latin America and U.S. efforts to promote democracy in the region in largely theoretical terms—whether such efforts are desirable, what the motivations are for pursuing this course, what the prospects are for achieving this goal, what the historical record shows, and so forth. The discussion now turns to the newer *realities* in Latin America, in the United States, and in U.S.-Latin American relations. Few of these factors augur well for U.S. efforts to promote democracy in the hemisphere.

The first issue with which the United States must come to terms is that in recent years Latin America has become increasingly independent, nationalistic, and assertive. This is less true in the smaller, more dependent countries of Central America and the Caribbean than in the larger countries of South America, but the trend is manifest throughout the region. Therefore Latin American countries are less willing to accept U.S. advice, including advice on the issue of democracy. Most Latin American countries are willing to look to Western Europe for advice or models to emulate, but they turn less and less to the United States. Latin America (at least most of the region) seeks to reduce or modify its dependence on the United States, not to increase it. This is the case regarding not just economic issues, but cultural and political questions as well. It is unrealistic to expect that this trend will be reversed and that Latin America will suddenly (or even gradually) look again to the U.S. political system as the model to follow. Too much has changed in Latin America in the past twenty years (as well as in the United States) for that to be possible.[37]

A second, related new reality is the situation in the United States itself. In comparison with the prevailing situation twenty years ago, the United States is now a diminished presence in Latin America. This is not to say that the United States is unimportant or that it does not continue to have great influence in the region. But many aspects of the U.S. role have changed considerably. United States foreign assistance to Latin America has declined; there are far fewer U.S. diplomatic personnel in the field; and, except in the special case of Central America, U.S. military missions are greatly reduced. The hotels in Latin America are filled not with U.S. businessmen but with West Germans, Japanese, French, Spaniards, Italians, Scandinavians, East Europeans, Russians, and Chinese. These are the countries that now often win the contracts for dams, highways, port facilities, and development projects, rather than the United States. Together these changes mean a greatly reduced U.S. presence in Latin America in a wide variety of speheres, with a concomitant lessening of U.S. influence.

Moreover, this decline in U.S. hegemony and influence is unlikely to be reversed soon. Opinion polls show that the U.S. public is overwhelmingly opposed to foreign aid, a sentiment that is certain eventually to be translated into congressional votes.[38] Those who would promote a stronger U.S. role in support of democracy in Latin America must ultimately ask themselves what means will be available to implement such a strategy. Where are the foreign assistance funds comparable to those available under the Alliance for Progress to give the United States the leverage it needs to carry out a foreign policy promoting democracy? Where is the necessary commitment on the part of the public, the Congress, or the presidency? Where is the Peace Corps–like enthusiasm for this cause, the willingness to go "any distance" (as John F. Kennedy described it)? And what are the realistic possibilities of asking U.S. citizens to suffer further unemployment in order to give Latin American manufacturers increased access to U.S. markets? The fact is that the domestic infrastructure and support for a major new U.S. initiative to promote democracy in Latin America do not exist. The resources, commitment, and the public and official support for such acitivities are simply not present in the United States today.

A third new reality, related to the first, concerns Latin America's increasing assertion of its own indigenous models of development and democracy.[39] Latin American nations increasingly wish to develop autonomously in the political arena as well as in the economic sphere, independent of U.S. wishes and preferences. Thus U.S. citizens must face the unsettling fact that democratic forces in Latin America may not want U.S. assistance even if it is proffered. Latin American countries may wish to fashion their own forms of democracy, but they are less and less inclined simply to imitate the United States. Whether the United States is capable of dealing with this new situation is uncertain.

The problem is complicated by the fact that many Latin Americans (especially an older generation that is now fading away) still look to the United States, including the U.S. political model, for guidance and direction. They also believe in the institutional mechanisms that characterize U.S.-style democracy: political parties, separation of powers, competitive elections, and so forth. Given a choice, and all other things being equal, many of these Latin Americans would probably prefer competitive elections and U.S.-style democracy.

But all other things are not equal. First, as previously noted, there are other legitimate routes to power in Latin America besides elections, and democracy itself is often of tenuous legitimacy. Second, Latin Americans have traditionally meant something different by "democracy" from what U.S. citizens do. Whereas U.S. citizens emphasize the procedural dimensions of democracy (elections and so forth), Latin Americans are more inclined to judge a regime democratic (regardless of its route to power) that governs for, and in the name of, the common good; that is broadly representative of society's major interests; that evidences a degree of populism and nationalism; that promotes economic and social development; and that is not brutal or oppressive. In short, the meaning of democracy may differ considerably in different parts of the hemisphere, with Latin America following a tradition that is closer to French, Spanish, and Italian models than to the Anglo-Saxon tradition.[40]

Furthermore, the United States must come to terms with some of the newer and innovative democratic forms in Latin America that have experienced notable growth in the past decade. These include community self-help groups, consciously nonpartisan movements for political reform, neighborhood-based and popular organizations, and nascent human rights and reform groups seeking to strengthen the rule of law.[41] In all the discussion emanating from the United States concerning the need to strengthen democracy in Latin America, almost nothing has been said about any of the newer, *Latin American* forms of democracy that exist outside standard U.S. terms of reference and the customary framework of U.S.-style institutions.

A fourth factor concerns the severe downward turn of the world economy beginning in 1979 and its implications for democracy in Latin America. This issue can be approached in terms of the U.S. economy and the U.S. capacity and willingness to provide assistance to Latin America, from the perspective of worldwide economic conditions and what effect they have in Latin America, or from the view of the depressed Latin American economies themselves. From whatever vantage point, the prospects for democracy are hardly encouraging.

The facts are quite obvious. The global economy has been in the midst of the worst depression since the 1930s. Oil prices have fallen, at least temporarily, but the impact of earlier price increases on Latin America was (and remains) devastating. The U.S. economy has also encountered serious problems. Even a major U.S. economic recovery may be insufficient to produce renewed growth in Latin America. The strong protectionist sentiment in the United States is not propitious either for Latin American export possibilities or for necessary U.S. foreign assistance programs, such as the Caribbean Basin Initiative.

None of these economic conditions is encouraging to the cause of democracy in Latin America, nor do they help established democracies in the region to survive.

Economic conditions in Latin America are terribly depressed. The boom years of the 1960s and early 1970s are over. Because the economies in the area are stagnant or contracting, the traditional Latin American means (not altogether undemocratic) of responding to change—accommodating new power contenders that agree to abide by the established rules of the game—cannot work.[42] In the present prevailing economic circumstances, there are no new resources to distribute to emerging groups. Given rising expectations, competition for control of the fewer resources that do exist becomes intense, polarized, and violent. Thus it is easy to understand why political challenges to the status quo in Latin America (where economic conditions have been even more depressed than in the United States) have been so intense. Liberal-pluralist democracy is difficult to sustain under such conditions, and even more difficult to renew or create anew. The major victim of the worldwide economic downturn in Latin America may be the very democracy the United States would hope to stimulate.

Fifth, the United States must consider why some Latin American regimes have in fact chosen democracy. The motives are complex, but not all of them have to do with a strong commitment to democracy. For example, it is clear that for some regimes a new opening to democracy has been dictated not so much by a firm or enduring commitment to democracy per se but by a discrediting of the established bureaucratic authoritarian model. Rather than have the blame for economic and other policy failures fall entirely on the ruling military or military-cum-civilian groups, the incumbents opted to step aside for a time and allow eager civilian groups and political parties to share responsibility. This was clearly the motivation behind the recent so-called democratic *aberturas* in Honduras, Peru, and Bolivia, where the military had been thoroughly discredited by charges of graft, inefficiency, and repression, and where continued military rule would only further embarrass and debase the armed forces. In Argentina, military mismanagement and brutality were sufficiently exposed that it was no longer advantageous for the armed forces to stay in power. In Brazil, too, the generals opted for a democratic opening only after the glory of the vaunted "economic miracle" began to fade and new challenges confronted continued military rule.[43]

Of course, these and other cases of political transition require more detailed analysis than is possible in this chapter and the factors involved are not so simple as indicated here. But in many cases the dominant motives clearly were not a strong commitment to democracy, but rather the military's fear of further discrediting of the military institution. This also implies that the commitment to democracy in these countries may not be especially strong. Indeed, it may well be reversible in Bolivia, Peru, and other countries where recently established democracies are already in trouble. It is hard to believe that the transition from authoritarianism to democracy in Latin America (the recent subject of many conferences and much wishful thinking) is really firm, unilinear, and irreversible.

A related question concerns who in these several Latin American countries initiated the democratization process. The sources are sometimes difficult to identify, but in general these processes were initiated as an elite response to changed circumstances, not as a result of much popular clamor or grass-roots pressures from below. Of course these two dimensions are often interrelated, and one could argue that elites act only when they are pushed or threatened from below. But that does not appear to be the case in this instance. Instead, there is strong evidence that change was initiated primarily from above. Although this issue cannot be fully resolved here, there is room for considerable doubt regarding both the degree of elite commitment to democracy and the depth of commitment in the society at large.

Why national elites want democratization is also an important question.[44] Although these groups are accomplished at voicing the slogans of representative government, many civilian politicians in military-dominated countries leave the strong impression that they have other agendas besides democracy. What often comes through most clearly in interviews with these politicians is not so much a firm commitment to a democracy that serves the public purpose, but rather a democracy that serves private well-being. Civilian politicians in these countries are united on few issues, but the one goal they do seem to have in common is a desire to reoccupy the ministry, sub-ministry, government corporation, or autonomous agency positions—and to regain the opportunities that go with these positions—from which military rule has long deprived them. If this impression is well founded, it is the basis for considerable skepticism regarding the underlying motives for some efforts at democratization.

Another aspect of democratization in Latin America merits close examination: the political and partisan use of this process. Some Latin American opposition groups, for example, have used the democratization issue both to strengthen their position and to undermine their own government. This result may be well and good in some cases, but not necessarily in all. Why should one opposition movement become the recipient of U.S. funds and favors and not others? Does a particular opposition group really have the popular support it claims, and does it deserve the assistance that outside groups may therefore give it? Is the opposition's claim to democratic values really merited? Does the opposition's claim to democratic legitimacy necessarily outweigh that of the government it seeks to replace? These are complex questions that can only be answered in individual circumstances. But they do indicate that the issues are not always clear cut and that on numerous occasions partisan priorities are served rather than broader public interests.

In an overall examination of Latin American regimes' movement toward democracy, what is striking is the degree to which these have been autonomous Latin American choices, not U.S.-inspired decisions. There may be some congruence of interests on the democracy agenda, and in some cases a push by the United States or a deftly administered aid program has been crucial in tipping the balance toward democracy. But the real story, even with these qualifications and reservations, has been Latin America's efforts. In fact, U.S. commitment and assistance to emerging Latin American democracy has historically been quite limited. Thus some modesty is required in an assessment of U.S. influence, capacities, and accomplishments in promoting democracy in Latin America.[45]

The sixth factor to consider concerns U.S. domestic politics, especially the ways in which it impinges on U.S. efforts to promote democracy in Latin America. Reviewing recent U.S. efforts to export democracy does not leave one overly confident of future success in this area. U.S. foreign policy goals in the region have traditionally included political stability, access to markets, support for anticommunism—and occasionally democracy insofar as it serves these other goals, which have often been considered more important.[46] Democracy as a policy goal has been pursued only up to the point at which more fundamental U.S. strategic interests are affected. One must wonder, for example, how interested the United States would be in democracy in Nicaragua if the Sandinista government suddenly (and unexpectedly) renounced Marxism, expelled Cuban advisers, and realigned itself with the United States.

Moreover, the democracy that the United States envisages and will accept looks remarkably like the U.S. system. Ethnocentrism is still present within the U.S. government, despite protestations from some officials that this has changed and that "they [the Latin Americans] know how."[47] To the extent that U.S. foreign policy favors democracy at all, the emphasis is on U.S.-style political institutions, such as political parties, elections, and so forth. Democracy on Latin

America's own terms—involving populism and power sharing, new community-based organizations, and institutional arrangements other than those familiar to the United States—has not yet been seriously considered.[48]

Then, too, the kind of democracy that the United States can and will officially support will almost certainly be a reflection of U.S. domestic pluralism and interest group politics. Business groups will insist that the private sector be given a major role; labor groups will claim a similar privilege concerning labor relations; the Democratic and Republican parties will each want to create and assist like-minded groups abroad; church and human rights groups will exercise veto power over human rights policy; the Cuban exile community will demand veto power over U.S. relations with Cuba; and so forth. Every special interest involved will seek a role in policy formulations, and no administration will be able to resist these pressures. Observers who search for a coherent, sustained, integrated, nonfragmented definition of the kind of democracy the United States will export, as well as for some recognition of Latin America's own special needs, definitions, and preferences in these matters, are certain to be disappointed.[49]

Finally, one must recognize that any U.S. program to promote democracy abroad is certain to be partisan and to be regarded as such. The plan announced by President Reagan in early 1983 was strongly criticized because it channeled aid and contracts chiefly to groups thought to be conservative.[50] Although this program may demonstrate a certain bias, it is difficult to believe that a Democratic administration would not also—and equally lamentably—award those same contracts to *its* friends and supporters. In either case, partisan rather than public purposes will be served. Democracy in Latin America will once again be an accidental by-product of (or perhaps victimized by) such domestic U.S. political considerations.

Conclusions and Implications

To the somewhat rhetorical question posed in the title of this essay, "Can democracy be exported?" the answer must be no. It is not possible for the United States to *export* democracy to Latin America or to other areas. The United States can hardly shape (much less determine) the political preferences and institutional arrangements of other countries.

But perhaps the title asks the wrong question. Perhaps the issue is not whether democracy can be exported, but whether this is one of those periods in Latin American history when democracy could grow and develop. Is Latin America at the end of a bureaucratic-authoritarian epoch and on the threshold of a democratic one? Are the forces and currents now present in Latin America propitious for democracy? Is this democracy's historical "moment" in Latin America? If so, what should and can the United States do to assist and encourage this presumed transition to democracy? Are there elements of congruence between U.S. foreign policy and Latin America's recent movements toward democracy? Should the United States support democracy in Latin America when it has the opportunity to do so?[51] What specific actions should the United States take?

To begin, it is necessary to strike a balance between observers who are entirely cynical about democracy's future in Latin America and those who are excessively enthusiastic. There *are* new democratic trends in Latin America. With great care, empathy, prudence, and a sustained, coherent policy, these trends might be encouraged and developed. With sensitive foreign policy officials, the judicious use of assistance funds, and a sense of restraint and modesty as to what the United States can accomplish, the United States can and should aid Latin American democracy. Some tasks can be accomplished unilaterally, while others require multilateral cooperation. Several different approaches and techniques are available.

One should oppose a loud new official *campaign* in favor of democracy, however, especially if it is characterized by the missionary zeal so typical of such efforts. U.S. pressure is unlikely to work and may backfire.[52] Hopes and expectations in favor of democracy should not be raised too high. One should be skeptical that this is democracy's "moment" in Latin America, that the moment will be long lasting; it may have already passed in some countries. One must caution against the belief that Latin America is clamoring for democracy (especially U.S.-style democracy) or that the Latin American countries cannot resolve their own problems in their own sometimes incompletely democratic ways. One must also recognize that U.S. domestic public opinion and the U.S. Congress are not enthusiastic about new aid programs; that worldwide economic depression augurs ill for new democratic openings: that trade protectionism is strong and will further hurt Latin America's economic prospects; that special interests will undercut or capture parts of any such democracy program; that diverse motives and ambitions are at work in this area; that much of Latin America may reject U.S. initiatives; and that the United States rarely understands and cares about Latin America sufficiently to help fashion an indigenous democracy for the region rather than a system based patronizingly and condescendingly on its own preferred political arrangements. The "new realities" in Latin America, in the United States, and in inter-American relations make a U.S.-sponsored effort to promote democracy in the hemisphere problematic at best.

In conclusion, it is important to note a series of dilemmas that must be resolved if democracy is to be promoted in Latin America. First, the issue of idealism versus realism in U.S. foreign policy is still a concern. Is the United States really trying (in El Salvador and elsewhere) to promote democracy, or is it simply protecting its own interest?

Second, are the differences between U.S. and Latin American preferences for—and understandings of —democracy reconcilable? In ostensibly promoting democracy abroad, does the United States fully understand what it is doing?

Third, limits and constraints on U.S. actions in this area must be recognized. The United States must appreciate what it can and cannot do in Latin America, as well as the difference between good intentions and complex realities.

Fourth, there are difficult problems of consistency and double standards, of reconciling democracy and human rights concerns with strategic and other U.S. interests, and of whether to treat all countries equally in this regard (that is, whether to be concerned with democracy in Cuba or Nicaragua as in Chile or Guatemala).

Fifth is the problem of achieving U.S. goals for democracy in Latin America without the implication of blatant interference in the internal political affairs of other countries.

Sixth, the United States must also reconcile domestic political considerations with the realities of other countries—especially the awareness that what is advantageous in the United States may not be realistic elsewhere. Latin America has often been an unfortunate laboratory for U.S. social and political experiments that frequently produce unforeseen consequences.

Finally, the United States should not pursue efforts to promote democracy so zealously that it overlooks the nuances, combinations, and heterogeneous patterns that are the real world of Latin American politics.

It is doubtful that the United States can reconcile these various dilemmas and pursue a policy to promote democracy in Latin America that is rational, coherent, and sustained over a relatively long (twenty-year) period. On this issue as on others, the United States must recognize severe limits on the possibilities for its policy. The United States must have modest expectations and recognize the strong constraints on what can and cannot be accomplished. The United States should pursue a policy that is realistic, prudent, enlightened, pragmatic, and based on some understanding of and empathy for Latin America—a policy that is not overzealous in any aspect, including its pursuit of democracy.[53] This would seem to be an appropriately modest agenda. But given the pressures in which U.S. foreign policy now operates, and the special conditions of U.S.–Latin American relations within that broader context, this may be all that one can reasonably hope or expect.[54]

Postscript: Toward a Positive Democracy Agenda

It is clear from the foregoing that I am skeptical and somewhat doubtful about U.S. efforts to promote democracy abroad. Above all, I think we must guard against a loud and energetic missionary-style *crusade*, in favor of democracy. I recognize the domestic urges and pressures that propel us in that direction, but I would hope these could be channeled, controlled, and directed toward a more modest, circumscribed, and realistic U.S. policy. I believe it important for the United States to stand for and to be a symbol, even a beacon, of democracy; but I suspect a major campaign to export democracy will not work and may well produce deleterious consequences.

Hence I would like to suggest that U.S. efforts to promote democracy be considered not as a grandiose design but as a series of more modest, rather traditional policies which, if sustained over time and in succeeding administrations, may be realizable. The elements of such a program might encompass the following:

1. A vigorous publication program to spread American ideas, writings, constitutional and political precepts, technological discoveries, and social science innovations abroad. If we do not do this, we will be overwhelmed by the flood of Marxist-Leninist literature that is available, free or at low cost, to emerging opinion leaders in other nations.

2. A vigorous translation program, aimed at the same goals and objectives. Such a program should not only bring our classics to other nations but also make their best work available to us. Perhaps then we can begin to learn from them instead of always trying to "teach" them something.

3. Expanded student exchanges. The Soviets and East Europeans are now doing at least as much as we are in the area—and perhaps much more. We may well "lose" an entire generation of young Latin Americans.

4. Lectures, exchanges, and aid to study centers in Latin America aimed at increasing their understanding of us and of our institutions, which is at least as weak as our understanding of them and their institutions.

5. Expanded cultural exchanges, at all levels. We must continue what we are now doing in this area—but much more of it and with greater imagination and sensitivity to innovative thinking in various areas. An example of such a useful and imaginative program is the week-long seminars organized by John Belcher in the Dominican Republic to bring American ideas in history, the social sciences, law, film, and other subjects to young Dominican opinion leaders.

6. Expanded radio broadcasts abroad, presenting serious discussion and not just partisan pronouncements.

7. A greatly expanded fellowship program to bring more young Latin Americans to this country. Our follow-up on this and other exchanges needs to be greatly improved.

8. A strong human rights policy, but one that is even-handed and moderate and that weighs other U.S. interests and is attuned to national and regional variations in the meanings and priorities of human rights.

9. Some modest aid, under open, not covert, auspices, to Latin American journals, reviews, and study centers to help promote democratic "openings" and a more democratic political culture.

10. Some aid, again under the right auspices, to parties, unions, and other groups with which we can work. Such a program is fraught with possibilities for disaster, and one should not be optimistic that these will be avoided. Nevertheless, a sensitive and informed strategy in this direction may produce positive results.

11. More assistance to international conferences such as that held in 1982 under White House auspices on free elections. It was a huge success that produced a host of beneficial, though not yet fully visible, consequences.

12. Some modest nudges and pushes by the U.S. government to encourage democracy in Latin America. Such nudges (political, diplomatic, economic, sometimes even military), while also fraught with dangers, can be decisive under certain circumstances.

13. A research project to support investigations of Latin American forms of democracy, how they differ from our own, what the differences mean for the kinds of institutions we can expect, and what the implications of such indigenous routes to development may be for policy. This is precisely the kind of innovative study that, as suggested earlier, we need to undertake.

We should thus refrain from a loud and overly vigorous crusade in favor of democracy. It will not work, and Latin America may not want it.

There is, however, much we can do at a more modest level that is positive and realistic and that has strong possibilities for success.

From both an individual and an organizational point of view, I think it is important for us to support programs that have a reasonable chance of success rather than those that do not. Our strategies in this area must therefore be based on realism rather than on the romance and wishful thinking in which we too often engage, and they must be restrained and prudent and within the range of realizable possibilities. An agenda has been suggested that meets these criteria. Such a strategy, to be optimally successful, should be coupled with an overall policy toward Latin America that is similarly based on restraint, modesty, good neighborliness, and prudence. It should take cognizance of the new realities in Latin America and in U.S.–Latin American relations, and it should be grounded in a realistic assessment of what the United States can and cannot do in that area of the world.

Notes

Peter Bell, Margaret Crahan, Kevin J. Middlebrook, and Iêda Siqueira Wiarda offered helpful comments on an earlier version of this chapter. However, the views expressed are the author's own.

1. See also Howard J. Wiarda, ed., *The Continuing Struggle for Democracy in Latin America* (Boulder, Colo.: Westview Press, 1980), especially the editor's introduction and conclusion. On the same theme, see Frank Tannenbaum, *The Future of Democracy in Latin America* (New York: Knopf, 1974).

2. For an elaboration, see Howard J. Wiarda, ed., *Politics and Social Change in Latin America: The Distinct Tradition*, rev. ed. (Amherst: University of Massachusetts Press, 1982), and Wiarda, *Corporatism and National Development in Latin America* (Boulder, Colo.: Westview Press, 1981).

3. The quotation has been attributed to John Foster Dulles. The foremost representative of the "realist" approach is Hans J. Morgenthau, *Politics Among Nations: The Struggle for Power and Peace*, 5th ed., rev. (New York: Knopf, 1978).

4. Reinhold Niebuhr, *Moral Man and Immoral Society: A Study in Ethics and Politics* (New York: Scribner's, 1932), and Ernest Lefever, *Ethics and United States Foreign Policy* (New York: Meridian Books, 1957).

5. George F. Kennan, *The Cloud of Danger: Current Realities of American Foreign Policy* (Boston: Little, Brown, 1977).

6. Henry Kissinger, "The Realities of Security," 1981 Francis Boyer Lecture on Public Policy, in *AEI Foreign Policy and Defense Review*, vol. 3, no. 6 (1982), pp. 11–16.

7. Theodore P. Wright, Jr., *American Support of Free Elections Abroad* (Westport, Conn.: Greenwood Press, 1980).

8. James Kurth, "The United States, Latin America, and the World: The Changing International Context of U.S.-Latin American Relations," in Kevin J. Middlebrook and Carlos Rico, eds., *The United States and Latin America* (Pittsburgh, Pa.: University of Pittsburgh Press, 1985); see also the report of Susan Kaufman Purcell's remarks on this issue, in Lisa L. Condit, "Rapporteur's

Report on the Inter-American Dialogue Workshop on United States–Latin American Relations in the 1980s," Woodrow Wilson International Center for Scholars, Latin America Program, Washington, D.C., January 21–22, 1983.

9. See the fascinating cable by Ambassador Spruille Braden (soon to become even better known—or infamous—through his opposition to Argentina's Juan Perón), "Policy Respecting Dictatorships and Disreputable Governments" (Havana, April 5, 1945), Department of State, Document No. 711.00/4-545. An excellent book on this theme is Michael Grow, *The Good Neighbor Policy and Authoritarianism in Paraguay: United States Economic Expansion and Great-Power Rivalry in Latin America During World War II* (Lawrence, Kans.: University of Kansas Press, 1981).

10. Wiarda, *The Continuing Struggle for Democracy,* "Conclusion."

11. These points are elaborated in testimony delivered at the time of the Falklands/Malvinas crisis in 1982: Howard J. Wiarda, "The United States and Latin America in the Aftermath of the Falklands/Malvinas Crisis," *Latin America and the United States after the Falklands/Malvinas Crisis: Hearings Before the Subcommittee on Inter-American Affairs of the Committee on Foreign Affairs, House of Representatives, Ninety-Seventh Congress, Second Session, July 20 and August 5, 1982* (Washington, D.C.: U.S. Government Printing Office, 1982), pp. 22–42, 77–82.

12. Larman C. Wilson, "Human Rights in United States Foreign Policy: The Rhetoric and the Practice," in Don C. Piper and Ronald J. Terchek, eds., *Interaction: Foreign Policy and Domestic Policy* (Washington, D.C.: American Enterprise Institute, 1983), pp. 178–208; Joshua Muravchik, *The Uncertain Crusade: Jimmy Carter and the Dilemmas of Human Rights Policy* (Lanham, Md.: Hamilton Press, 1986).

13. James L. Busey, "Observations on Latin American Constitutionalism," *The Americas,* vol. 24, no. 1 (July 1967), pp. 46–66.

14. Glen C. Dealy, *The Public Man: An Interpretation of Latin American and Other Catholic Countries* (Amherst, Mass.: University of Massachusetts Press, 1977); Claudio Veliz, *The Centralist Tradition in Latin America* (Princeton, N.J.: Princeton University Press, 1980).

15. The literature on this point is vast; particularly useful is Enrique A. Baloyra and John D. Martz, *Political Attitudes in Venezuela: Societal Cleavages and Political Opinion* (Austin, Tex.: University of Texas Press, 1979).

16. Veliz, *The Centralist Tradition;* Dealy, *The Public Man;* Wiarda, *Corporatism and National Development.*

17. Natalio R. Botana, "New Trends in Argentine Politics," paper presented at the Southern Cone Seminar, Washington, D.C., June 5–6, 1983.

18. Kalman H. Silvert, *The Conflict Society: Reaction and Revolution in Latin America* (New York: American Universities Field Staff, 1966); John Mander, *The Unrevolutionary Society: The Power of Latin American Conservatism in a Changing World* (New York: Knopf, 1969).

19. For a conceptual overview, see Charles W. Anderson, "Toward a Theory of Latin American Politics," Occasional Paper No. 2, the Graduate Center for Latin American Studies, Vanderbilt University, Nashville, Tenn., February 1964.

20. For a sensitive treatment of these themes, see Richard Nuccio, "The Family as Political Metaphor in Authoritarian-Conservative Regimes: The Case of Spain," Occasional Papers Series No. 9, Program in Latin American Studies, University of Massachusetts, 1978.

21. See the two-volume study by Lester D. Langley, *Struggle for the American Mediterranean: United States-European Rivalry in the Gulf-Caribbean, 1776–1904* (Athens, Ga.: University of Georgia Press, 1976) and *The United States and the Caribbean in the Twentieth Century* (Athens, Ga.: University of Georgia Press, 1982). The term "little brown and black brothers" is used advisedly to denote the paternalism and racism then strongly prevalent.

22. See Reginald Horsman, *Race and Manifest Destiny: The Origins of American Racial Anglo-Saxonism* (Cambridge, Mass.: Harvard University Press, 1981).

23. Grow, *The Good Neighbor Policy.*

24. Howard J. Wiarda, "Corporatism and Development in the Iberic-Latin World: Persistent Strains and New Variations," *The Review of Politics* (January 1974), pp. 3–33; reprinted in Fredrick B. Pike and Thomas Stritch, eds., *The New Corporatism* (Notre Dame, Ind.: University of Notre Dame Press, 1974).

25. Based on a personal communication with former Assistant Secretary of State for American Republics Affairs Edwin M. Martin, who is writing a book on the subject; January 18, 1983.

26. For elaboration on this point, see Howard J. Wiarda, "The United States and Latin America: Change and Continuity," in Alan Adelman and Reid Reading, eds., *Confrontation in the Caribbean Basin: International Perspectives on Security, Sovereignty, and Survival* (Pittsburgh, Pa.: University of Pittsburgh, Center for Latin American Studies, 1984), pp. 211–25.

27. Karl Meyer, "The Lesser Evil Doctrine," *The New Leader* (October 14, 1963), p. 8.

28. Muravchik, *Uncertain Crusade.* Also see Howard J. Wiarda, ed., *Human Rights and U.S. Human Rights Policy: Theoretical Approaches and Some Perspectives on Latin America* (Washington, D.C.: American Enterprise Institute, 1982).

29. Michael J. Kryzanek, "The 1978 Election in the Dominican Republic: Opposition Politics, Intervention and the Carter Administration," *Caribbean Studies* (April–July 1979), pp. 51–73.

30. Howard J. Wiarda, *In Search of Policy: The United States and Latin America* (Washington, D.C.: American Enterprise Institute, 1984).

31. More extended treatments are in Howard J. Wiarda, "The Ethnocentrism of the Social Sciences: Implications for Research and Policy," *Review of Politics* (April 1981), pp. 163–97; and "Toward a Non-Ethnocentric Theory of Development: Alternative Conceptions from the Third World," *Journal of Developing Areas* (July 1983), pp. 433–52.

32. John Barlow Martin, *Overtaken by Events: The Dominican Crisis from the Fall of Trujillo to the Civil War* (New York: Doubleday, 1966); for another perspective, see Howard J. Wiarda, *Dictatorship, Development and Disintegration: Politics and Social Change in the Dominican Republic* (Ann Arbor, Mich.: Xerox University Microfilms, 1975).

33. See Howard J. Wiarda, *Politics and Social Change in Latin America*, especially Introduction.

34. The concept is defined in Charles W. Anderson, "Toward a Theory of Latin American Politics."

35. The point is elaborated in Wiarda, *Politics and Social Change in Latin America*.

36. The outlines of the program were reported in the *Washington Post*, February 24, 1983.

37. See James R. Green and Brent Scowcroft, eds., *Western Interests and U.S. Policy Options in the Caribbean Basin* (Boston: Oelgeschlager, Gunn and Hain, 1984).

38. John E. Reilly, "The American Mood: A Foreign Policy of Self-Interest," *Foreign Policy* (Spring 1979), pp. 74–86.

39. These concepts are elaborated in several writings by the author, especially, "Toward a Non-Ethocentric Theory of Development."

40. Howard J. Wiarda, "Democracy and Human Rights in Latin America: Toward a New Conceptualization," *Orbis* (Spring 1978), pp. 137–60.

41. Margaret E. Crahan, personal communication, February 9, 1983; see also her chapter, "Human Rights and U.S. Foreign Policy: Realism Versus Stereotypes," in Middlebrook and Rico, eds., *The United States and Latin America*.

42. Anderson, "Toward a Theory of Latin American Politics." For an application of Anderson's model to the crisis in Central America, see Howard J. Wiarda, ed., *Rift and Revolution: The Central American Imbroglio* (Washington, D.C.: American Enterprise Institute, 1984), "Introduction."

43. Douglas A. Chalmers and Craig H. Robinson, "Why Power Contenders Choose Liberalization: Perspectives from Latin America," paper presented at the 1980 annual meeting of the American Political Science Association, Washington, D.C., August 18–31, 1980; Richard Sholk, "Comparative Aspects of the Transition from Authoritarian Rule," Latin American Program, Working Paper No. 114 (Washington, D.C.: Woodrow Wilson International Center for Scholars, 1982).

44. Chalmers and Robinson, "Why Power Contenders Choose Liberalization."

45. Sholk, "Comparative Aspects." These comments are also based on Ronald C. Schneider's analysis of the Brazilian *abertura,* as presented in a series of discussions at the Center for Strategic and International Studies, Georgetown University, Washington, D.C., 1982–1983.

46. Langley, *Struggle for the American Mediterranean* and *The United States and the Caribbean*.

47. After the title of the volume prepared by the Inter-American Foundation, *They Know How* (Washington, D.C.: U.S. Government Printing Office, 1977).

48. See the references given in notes 24, 31, 37, and 40.

49. This paragraph was written before the establishment of the National Endowment for Democracy, the agency created to carry out the new democ-

racy agenda. As predicted, the endowment has a corporatist structure: business and labor are both represented, as are the two major U.S. political parties. For early congressional and other critical comments on the plan, see the *Washington Post*, February 24, 1983, and February 27, 1983. For contrasting views, see David D. Newsom, "Can Democracy Be Promoted around the World?" *Christian Science Monitor*, November 24, 1982, and the materials prepared for the American Enterprise Institute–Department of State "Conference on Free Elections," Washington, D.C., November 4–6, 1982, at which a variety of divergent democratic conceptions were presented. Perhaps the best statement on what one might call the "indeterminateness" of U.S.–Latin American policy is Richard J. Bloomfield, "Who Makes American Foreign Policy? Some Latin American Case Studies," paper presented at the Center for International Affairs, Harvard University, March 1972.

50. *Washington Post*, February 28, 1983, and March 3, 1983.

51. Peter Bell, former president of the Inter-American Foundation, has suggested this approach.

52. See former Undersecretary of State David D. Newsom's interesting qualifications in his essay "Pressure," *Christian Science Monitor*, February 23, 1983.

53. I have presented such a "prudence model" of U.S.–Latin American relations in Wiarda, *In Search of Policy*, chapter 8.

54. For a similar statement, see Paul E. Sigmund, "Latin America: Change or Continuity," *Foreign Affairs* (1981), pp. 629–57.

6

The Problem of Ethnocentrism in the Study of Political Development: Implications for U.S. Foreign Assistance Programs

The body of literature dealing with what is called "political development" has recently come under severe attack.[1] Once the dominant paradigm within the field, the political development approach is now being strongly criticized from diverse viewpoints. The criticism that is our focus here is the charge that political development has been conceived in almost exclusively Western (Northwest European and North American) terms—that is, that the categories and understandings of political development are derived ethnocentrically from the Euro-American experience and have no or little relevance to the non-Western world.

This charge is especially serious from several vantage points. First, it has major implications for the third world: whether the development process is universal, whether third world nations are in essence but pale and retarded versions of the Western model, whether they will repeat the experience of the early developers, or whether they will fashion an indigenous model of development—or perhaps some blend of the Western and the indigenous. Second, it has important ramifications for the social sciences, most of the concepts of which are based on the Western developmental experience and which may or may not be relevant to the third world. And third, it has important implications for the nations that provide foreign assistance, chiefly the United States but increasingly those of Western

Presented at the Thirteenth World Congress of the International Political Science Association, Paris, July 15–20, 1985; published in *Society* (1987).

Europe, involving the relevance for the third world of the development models and programs they seek to export.

This chapter explores the problem of ethnocentrism in the study of political development. It is part of a larger project examining both Western and non-Western theories of development.[2] This work suggests that the models of development most familiar in the literature are all derived from the Western experience, of a particular time and place, and therefore have but limited relevance to today's third world nations. The study emphasizes the efforts of various third world areas to devise indigenous models of development or to blend these with the Western and presumably more universal models. It suggests that Western foreign assistance programs, largely based on the older ethnocentric understandings, have seldom been successful; yet it concludes not very optimistically that because Western policy makers, regardless of party, generally lack the comprehension and knowledge base to understand the third world on its own terms, in its own language, and in its own cultural and institutional terms, the mistakes of the past are likely to be repeated.

In other works the author has dealt with the ethnocentric assumptions of the social sciences,[3] as well as with the effort by third world leaders to articulate and fashion an indigenous developmental model.[4] He has considered this issue as it affects human rights and U.S. human rights policy[5] and has examined the revived effort to export democracy abroad,[6] the ethnocentrism of U.S. economic assistance programs,[7] expectations regarding the political role of the middle class, the armed forces and "professionalization,"[8] and the model of trade unionism the United States has tried to implant abroad.

This chapter concentrates on a series of other, but closely related, development assistance efforts: agrarian reform, community development, the U.S.-sponsored law and development program, and family planning. All of these programs derive from the same ethnocentric assumptions; together they help form a social and political history of developmentalism. We discuss the common intellectual and programmatic assumptions of all these efforts as well as third world attempts to devise its own developmental paradigms. Our criticisms of the ethnocentrism of the Western approaches are not limited to the United States but encompass the major European donors as well. Finally, we deal with the politics of the developmentalist approach and why it will be such a difficult paradigm to change or supersede.

Three brief additional introductory points need to be made: (1) Our conclusion is that the often misguided and misdirected developmentalist programs analyzed here grow chiefly out of naiveté and wrong assumptions, not from venality, malevolence, or "imperialism." The U.S. development assistance programs are generally based not on evil scheming but on good intentions gone awry for various reasons. (2) One must ask from where, other than from their own experiences, the Americans or the Western Europeans could have drawn their developmentalist models. We fault them here for their biases and ethnocentrism, but realistically it is unlikely that any models other than their own could have been used. (3) For the record, the third world's lack of understanding of the United States is often at least as great as ours of it. We concentrate here on our lack of understanding, but its also requires attention.

Development and Developmentalism: The U.S. Approach

The literature of development and the practice of developmentalism as an approach to alleviating underdevelopment were uniquely American phenomena, although scholars and political leaders from other areas accepted and participated in the formulation of this approach. It was uniquely American in that it was extremely optimistic, it derived from the American experience of development (Lockean liberalism, pluralism, and the like), it was largely written by Americans, it reflected a long American "missionary" tradition of bringing the benefits of our civilization to other lands, and it became an integral part of U.S. foreign policy toward the third world, particularly Latin America.[9]

The development literature and developmentalism were not abstract intellectual formulations confined to the academy. Rather these ideas had both direct and indirect influence on policy. Through the incorporation into the Kennedy administration of intellectuals associated with developmentalist themes, such as Walter W. Rostow, McGeorge Bundy, John Kenneth Galbraith, Adolph Berle, Arthur Schlesinger, Jr., and Lincoln Gordon, the ideas of developmentalism were often translated directly into policy.[10] Indirectly, the development literature also had major influence: as developmentalism became something of the leitmotif of the 1960s, the thing to do, and the basis of U.S. policy toward the third world, the ideas of the leading theorists of development were gradually infused into the bureaucracy. This came about through conferences organized by the Agency for International Development (AID) and the Department of State to which the developmentalist intellectuals were invited and through the widespread dissemination of their ideas through the universities and among university-trained technocrats of development. Although government officials may not have known specifically that they were implementing Walter Rostow's or S. M. Lipset's ideas, for a long time these ideas had immense influence on U.S. foreign assistance programs. And they continue to have great influence in many government circles today.

Two themes particularly command our attention here—both deserving of more serious attention in book or doctoral dissertation form. The first is the need for a social and political history of the idea of development itself, tracing the reasons for its rise in the 1950s and 1960s and its gradual decline in the 1970s and 1980s.[11] The second is a history of the rise and fall of various developmental panaceas—agrarian reform, community development, infrastructure development, family planning, basic human needs, the democracy agenda, private-sector initiatives—that have been proffered by the developmentalist school over the years, the elevation and then abandonment of various development ideas, their origins intellectually and politically, and their fates when tested against the hard realities of third world and non-Western areas. Some introductory notes for constructing such a history of these several developmental initiatives are offered in the following pages.[12]

Agrarian Reform. Any discussion of agrarian reform in the third world must recognize that it is a part of a larger scheme to promote economic development, to build a stronger middle class, and, from the point of view of its U.S. sponsors, to reduce or eliminate the appeal of radical groups. Agrarian reform must be looked at, thus, in the broader context of the U.S. effort to fashion a Marshall Plan-like assistance program for the third world, one component of which was designed for the rural sector.[13] Rostow's significantly titled *The Stages of Economic Growth: A Non-Communist Manifesto* provided the intellectual rationalizations for such an effort.[14] He argued that the stages of economic growth outlined in his book were universal, that all societies went through the same processes, that the United States was the most advanced nation and therefore provided the model for others, that the United States should assist the third world in its growth, that the funds thus generated would "trickle down," that by our assistance a middle-class society would be created that looked just like our own—stable, politically moderate, socially just, etc. We have dealt critically with Rostow's arguments in other writings[15] and need not repeat those arguments here. Our point in raising the issue, which we hope can be conceded, is to show that agrarian reform was merely one aspect of a much larger assistance program that had at its base a definite political agenda.

There is nothing wrong with agrarian reform per se. In fact, under the proper circumstances agrarian reform and other social assistance programs such as community development, law and development, and family planning are valuable and necessary. These programs, however, need to be evaluated in the context from which they emerged and in terms of the particular biases of the U.S. officials who formulated them. In doing this we seek not to tear these programs down but to provide a basis to refashion and foment them in ways that make them culturally and socially relevant to the societies where they are applied, so as to enable them to "take" and to have more lasting effects than they have in the past.

Agrarian reform, as part of a broader U.S. assistance program, was viewed as an extension of the Rostow analysis to the third world countryside. It was aimed, especially in Latin America, at creating a rural middle class where none had existed before. According to much lore and popular literature, the Latin American countryside was characterized by immensely large landholdings (*latifundia*) and dominated by a rapacious oligarchy, more interested in exploiting the peasants and using land as a symbol of social status than for greater production. By dividing up the land, the argument ran, the back of this quasi-feudal system could be broken, the oligarchy destroyed, and a new class of medium-sized rural landholders created. Because they would own their land and thus have a stronger stake in their futures, these new middle-class family farmers would be loyal to the system and no longer prey to the appeals of either fascism or communism. Agrarian reform thus stood as the rural counterpart to what overall U.S. economic assistance was designed to create in urban areas: a prosperous middle class that could serve as a bastion of democracy, stability, and anticommunism.[16]

As a form of social engineering, agrarian reform originated in the postwar U.S. occupation of Japan and in the Nationalist occupation of Taiwan. Initially, virtually everyone involved in the U.S.-promoted agrarian reform programs in Latin America had first learned their lessons through experience in Japan and Taiwan. Indeed, Japan and Taiwan served as the models for the programs in Latin America. Scholars are still discussing, however, whether or to what degree the programs in Japan or Taiwan may be termed successes.[17]

I believe the successes in these two countries outweigh the failures. But one must doubt the appropriateness of applying the Japanese or Taiwanese models to Latin America where the conditions are entirely different. Far more open space exists in Latin America, which gives agrarian reform less immediacy there; there is no occupation army to enforce the program as there was in Japan and Taiwan; the Latin American ethos, behavior patterns, social structure, and attitudes toward land are quite different from those in the two Asian nations.

Although the model for the agrarian reform program came from Japan and Taiwan, the real example was the United States. Agrarian reform in Latin America and other third world areas derived from a rather idealized version of the family farm in the American midwest or New England.[18] That farm was medium sized, neither too big nor too small; it was managed by self-sufficient yeoman farmers who were educated and used the most modern techniques; these farmers were active participants in local government and town meetings; and they were politically moderate, not subject to the appeals of radical ideologies of left or right.

Leaving aside for now the questions of whether the portrait of the American farm and farmer painted above was accurate, whether the family farm was really the rock of stability it was imagined to be, or even whether the family farm has any future in America, one must question the applicability of this model in Latin America and other third world areas. The differences between the United States and these other areas seem more significant than the similarities. The social structures are entirely different (there is no rural middle class in most of Latin America), the class and ethnic differences are large, the economies are quite different (capitalist versus neomercantilist), the political structures are different, and so is the political culture. These differences are so pronounced that it seems far-fetched and beyond the realm of possibility to expect a North American rural structure ever to be transplanted into Latin America.

The U.S. effort to bring agrarian reform to Latin America and the rest of the third world was born of the cold war and launched in the wake of the "great fear" following the Cuban Revolution that all of Latin America was about to repeat the Cuban experience.[19] Agrarian reform was in part a cold war strategy initiated in some desperation and without the prospects and possibilities having been thoroughly thought through. The arguments seemed so plausible: American technology and funds would help the Latin American nations achieve democracy, development, and stability through the reform of the rural sector. At the time, no one paid much attention to the impossibility of the U.S. transferring its institutions to societies where they did not fit, or fit only imperfectly. After all, John F. Kennedy was in office, the United States was at the height of its power and influence, optimism and hope ran high, Vietnam and Watergate had not yet occurred, and the United States still seemed to be both the policeman and the inspiration to the world. Only later would we see why the program not only did not work but could not work.

Agrarian reform, however, was not a program the Latin Americans could just take or leave; rather the adoption of an agrarian reform law was the condition by which a country qualified for Alliance for Progress assistance.[20] Hence most of the Latin American countries dutifully enacted an agrarian reform law. But since their hearts were not really in it, or because they soon developed other priorities, relatively little in the way of agrarian reform was ever implemented. Some peasants received titles to land under the program, but in no country was the structure of rural life fundamentally affected by the U.S.-inspired agrarian reform efforts.

To be fair, it must be said that there are various forms of agrarian reform. The one at which the United States is most successful involves technical assistance, farm credits, agricultural extension, and the like. None of these involves changing the pattern of ownership; instead they provide aid to those who already own land. One must also distinguish between an agrarian reform carried out for economic purposes versus one carried out with social or political goals in mind. The conclusion of the experts is that in general agrarian reform does not make sense economically because it causes production to fall, at least initially; whether agrarian reform makes much sense sociologically or politically is a bit more difficult to determine. It could be argued that agrarian reform has helped buy the United States some time and perhaps some limited stability in Latin America, but the revolutions in Nicaragua and El Salvador and the unrest in many other countries seem to indicate that it was not enough.

Eventually the United States itself lost interest in agrarian reform—except in emergency cases like El Salvador where it may have come too late. The results were generally disappointing, the Latin American governments were not very cooperative, and other agendas came to the fore. Agrarian reform was the great developmentalist panacea of the 1960s, but by the 1970s there were other concerns.

Overall—and whatever one's private and political sentiments about agrarian reform—what most impresses this observer is: (1) the political agenda and cold war considerations that undergirded the U.S. agrarian reform efforts; (2) the strong influence on these programs of the Japanese and Taiwanese experiences, which had little relevance for Latin America; (3) the implicit reliance on the U.S. family farm model as a model for Latin America; (4) the grounding of these programs so heavily in U.S. political assumptions; and (5) the naiveté and lack of knowledge or sophistication about Latin America of so many of the U.S. officials and technicians involved in the program.

With such pervasive ethnocentrism characteristic of so many aspects of the U.S. efforts to export agrarian reform, it is small wonder that the program produced limited results.

Community Development. The social and political history of community development runs remarkably parallel to that of agrarian reform. Both programs flourished in the early 1960s. Both emerged as major public policy agenda items during the presidency of John F. Kennedy. Both were products of what has been called the "Peace Corps mood"[21] of those times—that is, the urge not just to study development but to bring its agreed-upon benefits to less-favored lands. But by the end of that decade both programs had faded. Neither disappeared entirely, but neither enjoyed the levels of enthusiasm and support that characterized the earlier halcyon and optimistic years.

The community development programs of the 1960s grew directly out of the U.S. programs of the same name and era. In Latin America and elsewhere in the third world a large share of the program was actually carried out by U.S. Peace Corps volunteers. In addition, there was a cottage industry of community development experts, all trained in the United States, deriving their models from the United States, and often closely connected with the U.S. civil rights movement and with other forms of political activism.[22] In the Latin American countries where there was no or little community development, the United States proceeded, as it did with agrarian reform, to create a special agency within the host country government structure to administer the program.

As with agrarian reform, community development programs are valuable and necessary. The problem is not community development but the models used and their appropriateness in a non-Western, partially Western, or third world context.

Community development was the special preserve of the Peace Corps. A considerable literature developed out of the Peace Corps experience dealing with community development. Some of this literature even had more ambitious general and theoretical pretensions. In their training programs, Peace Corps volunteers "majored" in community development. The Peace Corps' definition of community development however, was often quite rudimentary: building latrines, digging ditches, organizing various self-help projects, and teaching what was called organizational literacy, which meant the basic organizational principles of running a meeting, talking in order, contacting a local official or congressman, forming a cooperative, or lobbying local authorities for housing materials, well-drilling equipment, sewers, roads, and electricity.[23]

These Peace Corps activities were generally harmless, and sometimes something positive was accomplished, although over the long term the advantages of Peace Corps service were probably greater for the volunteers themselves (in learning a new language and culture) than for the host community. One problem was, again, the model with which the volunteers had to work.

That model was derived almost entirely from the U.S. experience. The community-based, grass-roots, self-help programs the Peace Corps initiated came from the North American experience grounded in the tradition of the New England town meeting and local self-governance. It was based on a liberal, Lockean, Jeffersonian notion of direct and participatory democracy that had almost no basis in Latin America. The base historically of the Latin American systems is not Lockean but derived from the organic monism and unity of Saint Thomas and Suárez, or perhaps in updated secular form from Rousseau. Lockean liberalism, as we saw in the previous chapter, is a relatively recent implant historically in Latin America, and in most countries it remains a decidedly minority strain.[24]

The other major problem had to do with the structure of Latin American local government. Local government in Latin America is patterned after the French system. Almost all power is concentrated in the central state and its agencies. Local governments have almost no independent authority. They have almost no power to tax, to set policy, or to initiate new programs.[25] Organizations and services that in the United States are administered at the local level—schools, utilities, health care, police, water supplies, sewers, etc.—are in Latin America handled at the national level. The national government and its ministries determine education policy, health policy, and so forth. Hence even if the Peace Corps volunteers could convince local authorities that they needed roads or well-drilling equipment or virtually anything else, the local government had no funds, no authority, and no requisitioning power to get any of those things done. The result was a great deal of unhappiness on all sides.

The response took various forms. The United States helped create in several Latin American countries a national Office of Community Development that would help organize and facilitate these activities. These agencies were staffed, funded, and run almost entirely by the United States—or by Latin American nationals trained in the United States. To compound the problem, these agencies served to further centralize already highly centralized countries. In many instances they even took away the slight local power that existed.[26]

The Peace Corps volunteers were also frustrated. In some notorious early cases they all but took over the local communities to which they had been assigned. At least one was elected mayor of his town, a

105

perfectly rational step from the point of view of local townsfolk who believed they would get more for their community that way, but unacceptable to Peace Corps officials who rightly pointed out to this particular volunteer that he was there to help at the local level, not take over. Many volunteers put the lobbying and political organizing skills they had learned in the United States to work by leading demonstrations, marching on town hall, or leading delegations to the capital city to push for their particular projects. Again, Peace Corps officials had to suggest that such activities, heretofore largely unheard of in Latin America, were not quite what they had in mind by "community development." After considerable comings and goings, many volunteers ended up teaching English at the local level, a useful contribution to be sure, but far removed from the more grandiose designs of community development theory.[27]

These comments are not meant to imply that either the Peace Corps or community development is a bad idea. Their accomplishments have been many and significant. But the model of community development used was flawed, perhaps mortally so, from its inception. It was (1) based on a set of liberal Lockean U.S. political perceptions and understandings about participatory government that had very little relevance in Latin America; (2) grounded on the model of a decentralized political system that was entirely at variance with Latin America's centralist tradition;[28] and (3) responsible for producing the opposite effect from that intended: greater centralization often at the expense of local units. By the end of the 1960s the community development panacea had also run its course.

The Law and Development Program. Compared with these others, the U.S.-sponsored program on law and development in Latin America was quite modest. Nevertheless it was cut from the same cloth as those previously discussed and exhibited the same biases.[29]

In a manner remarkably parallel to that of a myriad of other U.S.-conceived programs fashioned in the early to mid-1960s, the law and development program was an effort to use U.S. legal expertise and methods to benefit third world development. In part it reflected the aspiration of American lawyers to enjoy the same travel and consulting opportunities that economists, sociologists, and political scientists had;[30] but more fundamentally it reflected the belief among lawyers that they too had major contributions to make to third world development.

The problem, however, was that it was exclusively American concepts and models that underpinned and defined the program. The model used was an idealized vision of law and the lawyer (pragmatic, omnicompetent, problem-solving) in U.S. society. No attention was paid to Latin American law or legal precepts. They were in fact to be swept aside as "traditional" in favor of the new American conception. In addition, the program was strongly conditioned by strategic purposes and cold war considerations that detracted from its focus on law and development. It was bolstered, as were the other programs already discussed, by a Marshall Plan–like vision and by confidence that American know-how would make the program work. As James Gardner has written, the program was fatally flawed from the beginning.[31]

It relied exclusively on an American conception of legal culture. It was based on and tried to implant an American system of legal education; it used the case method; it was grounded in American legal thought; it employed the Socratic dialogue of U.S. law schools; it taught the adversarial approach of U.S. law; and it was policy- and issues-oriented as in the American political system. The U.S. model these legal advisers sought to export also contained a benign view of the state—that it was or would be liberal, pluralist, developmental, impartial, and progressive—which soon ran head on into the authoritarian statism of Latin America.[32]

The program was initiated on the basis of U.S. notions of political democracy, liberal capitalism, and anticommunism. There is nothing wrong with these values; one must question, however, their relevance to Latin America in the same terms that U.S. citizens would understand them. U.S. lawyers intended to help engineer freer and more democratic societies in Latin America. They viewed Latin America as not having viable institutions of its own, and hence as a social laboratory for a U.S.-based program of law-and-development assistance. The program had as its goal the advancement and implanting of a particularly American legal model. As one writer put it, the program was a "tropical New Deal."[33]

According to Gardner the U.S. lawyers and law schools who were part of the law and development program in Latin America were poorly equipped by training or background for their assignments. Typically, they had no understanding of the local language, customs, or law. They were culturally unaware, sociologically uninformed, and ethnocentric, consistently viewing Latin America in the U.S. self-image. They found, apparently to their surprise, that the goals and methods of the United States, which they assumed to be universal, were not necessarily shared in the third world. They found the local legal cultures resilient and resistant to change. Many apparently lacked the tact to deal with their local counterparts. Despite their almost crusading zeal and their frequent ineptitude and insensitivity in dealing with local practices, they—or at least the program's administrators—soon realized the model was inappropriate. The overall result, by common consensus of both the host countries and the program's U.S. administrators, was failure.

The problem is that the Latin American legal tradition is entirely different from that of the United States.[34] It is based on a code or civil law tradition, not on a common-law tradition as in the United States. Most of the U.S. lawyers involved in the program knew that, but they were not aware of the wide-ranging ramifications of this distinct jurisprudential tradition. At a most basic level, it is doubtful that this tradition in Latin America is even compatible with a law-and-development orientation. The Socratic method is of little use in a system based on rote memorization. The use of cases is not appropriate in a context where the role of the judge is to find the applicable provision of the code, not to induce a general principle from a series of cases. The system of law school training in Latin America and even the role of the law school teacher is entirely different from the U.S. system. In addition, Latin America has little judicial review. Rather like the French systems these are administrative states, bureaucratic states, grounded on a system of state positivism, not on U.S.-style separation of powers and interest group pluralism. Furthermore, prior to plunging headlong into the field, the U.S. assistance teams received almost no preparation, no grounding in Latin American law, and conducted no studies of the implications of bringing an American legal system in intimate contact with an undeveloped Roman-Iberian one. As a result the program had what Gardner calls "unexpected vulnerabilities," even in those countries of Latin America (Colombia, for example) that were most democratic and therefore closer to the American system.[35]

In conclusion, three aspects of the law and development program especially command our attention. The first is that although neither the Latin American governments nor their lawyers or law schools especially wanted the program, the United States sent it anyway. The law and development program was like many U.S. programs then and now: it was grounded on the notion that "we (North Americans) know best," not "they (Latin Americans) know best."[36] The Latin Americans not only had different expectations of the program but they knew from the beginning that it would not work in their context. Bringing in a program anyway where it was considered folly and known ahead of time, by the locals if not by the Americans, that it would not work was highly insensitive and ethnocentric.

Second, one is struck by how closely this program complemented and reinforced other U.S. ideas about foreign aid. The program was entirely grounded in the American experience with little

reference to Latin American realities. It viewed Latin American realities with considerable disdain, its legal institutions as a "problem to
be overcome." Since Latin America's history had been, by common
U.S. understandings, a "failure" and its institutions unresponsive and
dysfunctional, it was believed they could be cavalierly discarded in
favor of a presumably better model. Attempting to recast Latin America in the U.S. mold, without consideration for the possible viability of
indigenous institutions, the program was doomed to be a failure. The
strong criticisms leveled by Gardner are equally applicable to the
other assistance programs here described.

Third, the program had a not very thinly disguised political
agenda. Though small in comparison with other programs, it was
neither harmless nor benignly neutral. The program was to be an
agent of advanced, even radical change. It was designed to break
down the existing legal system of Latin America and to substitute
another, more progressive one. When the program failed, Latin
America's own traditional legal system had been severely damaged.
The notion that we and our assistance programs could attempt to
replace the legal systems of other countries with our own reflected the
height of arrogance, to say nothing of misguidance, blindness, and
shortsightedness.

Family Planning. Family planning was to the late 1960s and early
1970s what agrarian reform and community development had been to
the early 1960s: the great panacea that would solve all of Latin America's problems. Such "true believer" attitudes may be useful when
recruiting new supporters for the programs envisioned, but in foreign
policy it can easily become a formula for disaster.[37]

The language used here in describing family planning and population control activities is sometimes harsh, but the author himself is
sympathetic to family planning. To the extent that these are effective
and well-run programs that reflect the wants of the local population,
he is supportive of them. The problem here as elsewhere is not the
promotion of family planning but rather the particular model used by
the United States to export it.

Perhaps the most successful early family planning programs took
place in Taiwan.[38] A significant decline in birth rates began there in
1951 and, after a brief interruption, continued from 1955. Many of the
experts in family planning and population control began by studying
the Taiwanese model. Other places where efforts to reduce fertility
have attained at least the appearance of success include Puerto Rico,
Jamaica, Singapore, South Korea, and Thailand. The experience of
these societies has been carried over to the rest of Latin America.[39]

It has never been made entirely clear, however, whether the decline in the birth rate in these societies was due to the actual program to induce smaller families or to "natural" changes in the society itself. But leaving that aside for now, it is clear that the societies from which the population model derives may not be entirely representative of the rest of the third world. Taiwan, Puerto Rico, Jamaica, Singapore, South Korea, and Thailand have characteristics in common that may make them atypical of much of the developing world. All are relatively small, homogeneous, stable, and generally well administered, so that the substantial financial assistance from the U.S. government and the population agencies could be put to good use. These countries are also among the most advanced of the developing nations, typically already making the transition to a developed economy. Nor could it be said that Jamaica, with its high literacy rate and Westminster political institutions, or Puerto Rico, with its special relationship (and outlet for surplus population) to the United States, are typical of the rest of Latin America. As demographer and population expert William Peterson has written, Taiwan is not India, and Puerto Rico is not Mexico or Brazil.[40] Nevertheless, despite its ill fit, the model used in those countries served as the basis for the family planning programs in Latin America.

The Latin American programs have been designed, launched, inspired, funded, and in large part administered from the United States; but considerable pains have been taken to disguise that fact. First, much of the funding has been channeled through third-party agencies to disguise the extent of the U.S. involvement. Second, various fronts have been set up to make it appear particularly in the early stages as though it is a private association that is supporting the program, not the U.S. government. But when an agency receives, directly or indirectly, 90–95 percent of its funds from the U.S. Agency for International Development, we are probably safe in considering it a front agency. Third, care has been taken to find local doctors and concerned citizens in the countries affected so as to provide the appearance of local control, even though the funding and much of the direction may come from outside.[41]

Family planning and population control have been brought to the third world by a somewhat secretive and back-door route. Only the general picture is provided here.

First, a group of doctors are found, usually gynecologists and health care specialists, who receive specialized training in the United States and begin to talk about and publicize population-related topics in the Latin American target countries: abandoned children, illegal and dangerous abortions, crowding, population growth rates that exceed economic growth, and so forth. They provide a climate conducive to initiating family planning activities. Then, typically, a private family planning association is formed consisting of these same doctors, demographers, and interested persons. U.S. aid is provided, usually funneled initially through private agencies. A pilot program of family planning clinics, more publicity, and a government lobbying effort are initiated. In the third stage, the government of the Latin American country, through its health or social assistance ministry, is persuaded to take over an existing program of family planning and to incorporate it into its nationwide system of maternity and child health care. This step makes the program eligible for large-scale foreign assistance from AID, the United Nations, the Pan American Health Organization (PAHO), and others. At that stage the program is, presumably, well established, on its way, and on its own.[42] These often secret strategies have frequently generated resentment in the third world and have made the population programs objects of suspicion or hostility.

While these maneuverings to establish population programs were under way, no one had bothered to check with Latin America to see if it wanted family planning. The case being made here is complicated by the fact that survey data indicate Latin Americans *do* overwhelmingly want to limit family size and want to have fewer children. Moreover, most influential groups in society—the army, the elites, even some sectors of the church—now see the need for some form of family planning. The problem is that they often see the issue differently from the population control donor agencies. The "population problem" in Latin America is often defined differently from country to country, but it is usually put in terms of dealing with the problem of abandoned children, of illegal and often dangerous abortions, of resettlement of population and colonization, of squaring population growth with social and economic growth and ensuring the former does not outstrip the latter.[43] The donor agencies, however, barely give lip service to these Latin American concerns. Their overriding concern has been to limit population growth. The major population agencies are hence insensitive to Latin American wishes in this area. But unless population programs are carried out in accord with the wants of the host countries, they are unlikely to be successful.

There are at this stage so many problems with the population programs that in these few pages about all one can do is mention them. First, the model may not be appropriate: what worked in Taiwan or even in Puerto Rico is unlikely to work in Peru or Colombia. Second, the three-stage plan for population policy development noted above can be and has been, in various countries, stalled at any one of several points; there is nothing inevitable or unilinear about the model. Third, while population growth rates are falling in Latin America, we are still not sure—as we are still not sure for Taiwan—whether this is due to natural causes (rising literacy, better education, urbanization, greater numbers of women in the work force) or to the efforts of the family planning agencies. Resolving that issue before plunging ahead would seem to be important.

Fourth, there are major problems with the population agencies responsible for carrying out these programs. Their accounting methods often leave much to be desired: some have been guilty of doctoring population statistics to suit their own purposes; some have presented misleading information to the U.S. Congress and to AID, and some have violated the spirit, if not the letter, of U.S. law. There are now clear legal guidelines prohibiting the use of U.S. government funds in support of, for example, abortion services; yet some of the population agencies have continued to provide abortion information and equipment—though under pressure from Washington they have been discouraged from direct involvement in actual abortion services. In addition, the population agencies are full of globalists and generalists, and their knowledge of particular regions has often been minuscule. Indeed, since the population problem is global and the solutions universally applicable, in their view, there is no need to acquire specialists or expertise in specific culture or geographic areas.

Fifth and most important is the true-believer syndrome. The population issue is defined differently in Latin America, but it is very difficult to convince the population control advocates—the true believers—that the difference is important and should be given serious consideration. They see the population problem as a world problem demanding immediate and emergency measures, and they see it as unidimensional: there are too many people. Since it is an emergency problem, they do not feel time and energy should be wasted paying attention to cultural differences across continents or to the nuances of individual nationalistic preferences. It is hard for these true believers to comprehend that once the demographic facts are presented that everyone would not see the solution in the same terms. They may give limited attention to the broader and more intricate Latin American views of the problem, but basically their concern is global population *control* first and foremost. They may even be right, but it is unlikely they will ultimately win the "war" in Latin America, which is becoming increasingly nationalistic, assertive, and resentful of outsiders—without taking into account Latin America's own perception and definition of the problem.[44]

In the case of population policy it is not so much an American model that is being exported. Although Americans have served as the architects of the program, the United States itself has no national population policy, yet we insist that the Latin American countries adopt one, again as a condition of foreign aid or, it is strongly suspected, World Bank subsidies. U.S.-inspired, it is nevertheless a *global* model that is being exported, a perception of spiraling population growth that must be checked at all costs worldwide through the use of a plan of action applicable universally and emanating from the United States. Peterson concludes,

> Those (population) analysts in each social discipline who have attempted to transcend the bounds of a single case have very often erred on the side of too facile generalization, and repeatedly we have been put to the task of freeing our thoughts from one or another monistic bond—in earlier generations racial or geographic determinism and, more recently, their economic or demographic analogues. How much of a guide is the past development of advanced countries for mapping the future modernization of presently backward areas? In some overall sense, obviously, the world is becoming more homogeneous, and it is just this metamorphosis that we mean by modernization. But to assume the details of the process must follow a known course, or that the homogenization must eventually eliminate all fundamental differences, is to commit the most egregious error of comparative analysis.[45]

European Ethnocentrism: How Different?

This chapter is mainly concerned with the ethnocentrism of U.S. models of development and foreign assistance programs. A brief digression may, however, be useful at this point to analyze Western European developmental models and the assistance programs based on them. For the fact is that European ethnocentrism with regard to the third world may be at least as great as that of the United States. Both areas are products of a particularly Western tradition, history, and orientation that, albeit with somewhat different emphases, they have sought to export to the third world.

If anything, the Europeans may be even more ethnocentric than their U.S. counterparts, particularly with regard to Latin America. The United States has worried about, struggled, and dealt with Latin America for a long time. We do not always do well by that area, but we do have a solid core of people (journalists, scholars, public officials) who know the languages and the region. This is less true for the Western Europeans. Latin America is geographically distant, and

113

historically they have not paid the area much attention. The number of Europeans who have been there, speak the language, and know the region is slight. If a personal note may be interjected, since the Central American crisis developed, I have had through my Washington office many Western European journalists, academics, television crews, and parliamentary delegations who find it useful to stop in the U.S. capital before proceeding on to Central America. It is striking that the attitudes of some of them toward Latin America are as patronizing and superior as, and sometimes considerably stronger than, those of Americans.[46]

Ethnocentric attitudes are similarly reflected in Western Europe's foreign assistance programs toward the third world. One must distinguish among countries because the thrust of their foreign aid programs toward the developing nations varies considerably.[47] In all cases, however, the main focus of their foreign assistance mirrors their domestic politics, as it does in the United States. Austria, with no strong colonialist tradition, has few substantial ties with the third world, has provided little aid, and has made little substantive contribution to the North-South dialogue. Britain under Prime Minister Margaret Thatcher is a staunch defender of free trade and economic liberalism, views aid as an instrument of its foreign policy, puts Britain's self-interests above the needs of poverty-stricken people and nations, and has not supported the New International Economic Order (NIEO). Denmark, however, has sided with the NIEO on ideological grounds but has provided few binding contracts. Denmark stresses the development of the third world on the same basis as Danish internal development: through solidarity, under state control, and by means of a welfare ideology.

West Germany has been, like Britain, against the NIEO and a powerful defender of economic liberalism. Germany stands for a strong free-market ideology in the third world, as it does at home. Economic liberalism and a free-market system are closely associated with the postwar German economic miracle; hence Germany (consistently under the Christian Democrats and usually under the Social Democrats) associates itself with the old international economic order, not the new.

France has postured as a friend of the third world and has supported the NIEO but has been very nebulous with regard to specific third world demands. Its policy is aimed at making trading partners out of the third world, and its economic doctrine is rather like its domestic orientation: it falls somewhere between a free-market and a planned economy.

Norway and Sweden proclaim their internationalism and support for the NIEO and the third world. In their aid doctrines they envisage a future world welfare state—rather like their own. Their aid programs, in contrast to Britain's or Germany's, are strongly idealistic: they claim to provide aid not out of self-interest but from the point of view of solidarity with the poor countries. The Swedish and Norwegian aid programs reflect their egalitarian ideologies: they wish to transfer their own domestic welfare state to the global level. In both countries, as in the United States, there is a quasi-missionary fervor to their assistance: they want to bring their progressive values to the rest of the world. This attitude is based on considerable self-content with their own society and its accomplishments. Their posture is to be as progressive internationally as they are domestically. Along with Holland, which shares this orientation, the Scandinavian countries alone have reached the level of foreign assistance (0.7 percent of GNP) recommended by the United Nations as the goal for official development assistance.

Yet there is a Janus face to this image of progressivism and idealism, as well as a certain naiveté. The Scandinavian countries are integrated, well-governed, and extraordinarily cohesive societies culturally, racially, politically, religiously, and ideologically; it is unlikely that the consensus they have been able to achieve on welfare statism could be repeated in very many third world societies. Moreover, if Swedish, Danish, Norwegian, or Dutch NIEO policy is judged on the basis of the internal costs these countries have borne, the record of achievements is quite limited. They have been, in this sense, "free riders," supporting third world demands as long as they incur no substantial political or economic costs. When the world economic downturn took place in the early 1980s, these countries had no trouble emphasizing their commercial relations with the third world along with their more idealistic face.

The United States, Britain, and West Germany have been most hostile to the NIEO agenda; the Scandinavian countries and Holland have been most supportive. There is, thus, a significant correlation between an advanced social welfare program at home and a high level of foreign aid. The high-foreign-aid countries have "sold" these programs to their domestic populations on the argument that if one favors the welfare state at home one should also support foreign aid to the third world. In the recent economic downturn, however, even the Scandinavian countries have reexamined their policies and have begun to look at aid programs case by case.[48]

Overall, the Western European aid programs are just as ethnocentric as the U.S. programs. The Scandinavian countries and Holland have sought to transfer a model of the advanced European welfare state to the third world—a model that looks, unsurprisingly, just like their own. Conversely, Britain and especially Germany have sought to export a model grounded on economic liberalism and laissez faire—similarly based on their own experiences. France has been an apostle of its own form of statism and neomercantilism. All of them have assumed, as has the United States, that the Western experience should provide the model, that with the proper amount of aid deftly applied the third world can also aspire to the Western example, and that the developing nations are but pale and retarded versions of the already developed countries who may one day be able to repeat the Western experience. Western Europe places no more emphasis on indigenous third world institutions and models of development than does the United States, and the notion that the third world knows best what will work for it is just as unacceptable to the European way of thinking as it has been so far to the American. In both the United States and Western Europe ethnocentrism remains powerful.

Given that European ethnocentrism toward the third world is at least as strong as the North American, the European criticism of U.S. policy toward the third world is that much more difficult to understand. The Europeans argue that the United States does not understand the third world, but it is difficult to demonstrate that their own comprehension is any greater. The criticism has been especially strong with regard to U.S. policy in Central America. Without going into any details here, let it simply be suggested that Western Europe understands Central America no better than the Americans do and probably less so; that Western Europe has the luxury of being able to criticize policies in a region that is so far distant from Europe that whatever the outcome (and unlike the United States) Western Europe will be virtually unaffected; that many Europeans have consistently misrepresented the U.S. position as chiefly seeking military solutions and seeing the conflict in an East-West dimension (neither of which reflects actual U.S. policy); and that Americans in general are becoming rather tired of both the criticism and the holier-than-thou attitudes assumed by many in Western Europe.

Conclusions

Ethnocentrism is strong in all aspects of U.S. foreign policy toward the third world—and in the policies of Western Europe as well. All these policies are based on and derive from the peculiarly Western experience with development and therefore are of limited relevance to the third world. That is, they are based on a particular and rather

116

special experience with development, of a particular time and period of development, whose economic, sociological, and political laws may not apply in the third world—or apply only partially and incompletely.

Whether one is talking of agrarian reform, community development, law and development, or family planning and population control, or in other contexts of economic development strategy, military modernization, the democracy agenda, human rights concerns, trade unionism, or any one of countless other programs, the problems have been remarkably parallel. They were all born of a particular Western experience of development; they are based on Western assumptions about the modernization process, which were then overgeneralized to the rest of the world; and they have not adequately taken into account local and indigenous institutions and methods.

It is easy to understand why we use models we are familiar with to understand other areas of the world and therefore why our ethnocentrism is so pronounced; but we must also be aware of the consequences of ethnocentrism. The U.S. policy failures are by now so numerous and the third world resentments so strong that the retort "let us do it our way" is becoming widespread. The third world is increasingly rejecting the models and recommendations imposed by the West and is more frequently searching for and asserting indigenous models and institutional arrangements more attuned to its own preferences, histories, and methods.

It will be a long time, however, before the policies based on the developmental assumptions of the past will change. These assumptions are strongly entrenched in the foreign assistance bureaucracies; and we know that once a policy consensus on these or any other issues is reached it is very difficult to alter. Change will be difficult because these assumptions about agrarian reform, community development, the role of the middle class, and so on, are closely associated with the history, culture, and ethos of the Western countries. They are deeply embedded in our educational system, our values, and our civic consciousness and ideology and will not be changed quickly or easily. Current policies are a product of a powerful social science tradition that sees the Western nations as most developed and hence leading the way and providing the example for the less-developed countries to follow.

Change will be difficult to achieve also because in political Washington it is the image, the brief phrase, the lowest common denominator that usually counts in policy making; a new premise for formulating policy argument is often difficult to establish. It is hard enough in Washington to get a consensus on such programs as agrarian reform and family planning; recommendations for greater refinement and adaptations to diverse local conditions are difficult to convey to lawmakers or the public—and may have the political side effect of scuttling a whole program or making it impossible to get through Congress. For these and other reasons, it will likely take considerable time, perhaps a generation, for the changes suggested here to reach fruition, for us to become less convinced that our own model is universal and for us to take seriously the efforts of various third world peoples to chart and institutionalize their own developmental routes.[49]

The implications of the trends discussed here are that the already developed donor nations will have to reorient their assistance programs if they are to succeed in the third world of the future. They will have to pay attention to local wants and aspirations. They will have to come to grips with models of development different from the Western one. Far better and more thoroughly than in the past, they will have to learn the languages, cultures, and institutional procedures of various third world areas. They will have to accept the notion that the third world may know best what is good for itself. The donor nations will have to empathize and listen seriously to the third world for the first time and be prepared to support some of its notions of development. In the Islamic world, in Africa, in Asia, and in Latin America the sense is now almost universal that the Western models, in their several varieties, have not worked very well, and therefore a social science and model of development more attuned to local ways will have to be created. Efforts are now under way in various areas of the third world to fashion such indigenous models or to achieve a better blend and fusion between imported and indigenous ones.[50]

It is likely that this will be the next great innovative frontier in the social sciences and in development and foreign assistance research and theory. Foundations, research institutes, and some within the academy—to say nothing of the third world itself—are all moving in this direction. It is time for political development theory also to rethink its earlier premises and assumptions, all based strongly on the Western experience, and to move toward greater cultural relativism and an understanding of the third world on its own terms. Once this revolution in the social sciences and in development theory has taken place, it may be that the foreign assistance programs emanating from the Western nations can also be reoriented.[51]

But if past experience is a guide, it will likely take at least ten years (we are already halfway through the generation change referred to earlier, marking a move away from the earlier developmental literature) before these newer models of development, based on a more

118

accurate portrayal of third world realities and institutions, are reflected in more realistic development assistance programs. It is, nevertheless, important to begin making the case now, both for educational purposes and because one may still hope to convince policy makers that the success of their development programs must finally depend on their being adapted to the realities of distinct third world areas. Success, after all, ultimately determines the nature and size of the American commitment to such programs.

Notes

1. Among others, see P. T. Bauer, *Dissent on Development* (Cambridge, Mass.: Harvard University Press, 1976); Reinhard Bendix, "Tradition and Modernity Reconsidered," *Studies in Society and History* IX (April 1967), pp. 292–346; Ronald H. Chilcote, *Theories of Comparative Politics* (Boulder, Colo.: Westview Press, 1981); Philip Coulter, "Political Development and Political Theory: Methodological and Technological Problems in the Comparative Study of Political Development," *Polity* V (Winter 1972), pp. 344–42; Clement Dodd, "Political Development: The End of an Era," *Government and Opposition*, VIII (Summer 1973), pp. 367–74; C. D. Hah and J. Schneider, "A Critique of Current Studies of Political Development and Modernization," *Social Research*, XXXV (Spring 1968), pp. 130–58; Robert T. Holt and John E. Turner, "Crises and Sequences in Collective Theory Development," *American Political Science Review* LXIX (September 1975), pp. 979–95; Samuel P. Huntington, *Political Order in Changing Societies* (New Haven, Conn.: Yale University Press, 1968); Mark Kesselman, "Order or Movement: The Literature of Political Development as Ideology," *World Politics* XXVI (October 1973), pp. 139–53; Philip Melanson and Lauriston King, "Theory in Comparative Politics: A Critical Appraisal," *Comparative Political Studies* IV (July 1971), pp. 205–31; Dean C. Tipps, "Modernization Theory and the Comparative Studies of Society: A Critical Perspective," *Comparative Studies of Society and History* XV (March 1973), pp. 199–226; Howard J. Wiarda, ed., *New Directions in Comparative Politics* (Boulder, Colo.: Westview Press, 1985); Peter Winch, *The Idea of a Social Science and Its Relation to Philosophy* (Atlantic Highlands, N. J.: Humanities Press, 1970).

2. A larger work examining both Western and non-Western theories of development is forthcoming from the American Enterprise Institute for Public Policy Research. The volume will contain selections covering all third world areas.

3. Howard J. Wiarda, "The Ethnocentrism of the Social Sciences: Implications for Research and Policy," *Review of Politics* XLIII (April 1981), pp. 163–97.

4. Howard J. Wiarda, "Toward A Non-Ethnocentric Theory of Development: Alternative Conceptions from the Third World," *Journal of Developing Areas* XVII (July 1983), pp. 433–52.

5. Howard J. Wiarda, "Democracy and Human Rights in Latin America: Toward a New Conceptualization," *Orbis* XXII (Spring 1978), pp. 137–60.

6. Howard J. Wiarda, "Can Democracy Be Exported? The Quest for Democracy in United States Latin America Policy," in Kevin Middlebrook and Carlos Rico, eds., *The United States and Latin America* (Pittsburgh, Pa.: University of Pittsburgh Press, 1985).

7. Howard J. Wiarda, "At the Root of the Problem: Conceptual Failures in U.S. Central American Relations," in Robert Leiken, ed., *Central America: Anatomy of Conflict* (New York: Pergamon Press, 1984), pp. 259–78.

8. Howard J. Wiarda, "The Armed Forces and Politics in Latin America: The Role of the Military in the New Democratic Era," *Harvard International Review* (May/June, 1986).

9. Robert Packenham, *Liberal America and the Third World: Political Development Ideas in Foreign Aid and Social Science* (Princeton, N. J.: Princeton University Press, 1973).

10. See especially Walter W. Rostow, *The Stages of Economic Growth* (Cambridge: Cambridge University Press, 1960); and Seymour Martin Lipset, *Political Man: The Social Bases of Politics* (New York: Doubleday-Anchor, 1959).

11. An earlier effort is Robert A. Nisbet, *Social Change and History: Aspects of the Western Theory of Development* (London: Oxford University Press, 1969).

12. The analysis offered is based on field work and interviews in the Dominican Republic, Mexico, Brazil, Venezuela, and Central America from 1962 to the present.

13. See in general Clarence Senior, *Land Reform and Democracy* (Gainesville, Fla.: University of Florida Press, 1958); and T. Lynn Smith, ed., *Agrarian Reform in Latin America* (New York: Knopf, 1965).

14. Rostow, *The Stages of Economic Growth.*

15. Howard J. Wiarda, *Corporation and National Development in Latin America* (Boulder, Colo.: Westview Press, 1981), chapter 5.

16. Gifford Rogers, *Agrarian Reform Defined and Analyzed* (Santo Domingo, Dominican Republic: International Development Services, Inc., 1964).

17. Ibid. Based also on interviews in Washington, D.C., with the officials involved in these early agrarian reform efforts.

18. Senior, *Agrarian Reform;* and Smith, *Agrarian Reform.*

19. After the title of the book by John Gerassi, *The Great Fear in Latin America* (New York: Macmillan, 1963).

20. Frances M. Foland, "Agrarian Reform in Latin America," *Foreign Affairs* XLVIII (October 1969), p. 97.

21. The phrase is Gabriel Almond's, *Political Development* (Boston: Little, Brown, 1970), Introduction.

22. James W. Green, "Local Responsibility in the Dominican Republic: A Report of a Short Investigation into Local Government, Community Development, Cooperatives, and Agricultural Extension" (Santo Domingo, Dominican Republic: Mimeographed copy of report prepared for AID, July 27, 1965); and Richard V. Bernhart, "Dominican Community Development Program" (Santo Domingo: Mimeographed copy of report prepared for AID, February 2, 1965).

23. Frank P. Sherwood, *Institutionalizing the Grassroots in Brazil: A Study in Comparative Local Government* (San Francisco: Chandler, 1967); also Arpad Von

Lazar and John C. Hammock, *The Agony of Existence: Case Studies of Community Development in the Dominican Republic* (Medford, Mass.: Fletcher School of Law and Diplomacy, 1970). This second citation is a particularly devastating critique of the community development programs.

24. Richard M. Morse, "The Heritage of Latin America," in Louis Hartz, ed., *The Founding of New Societies* (New York: Harcourt Brace and World, 1964).

25. Carlos Mouchet, "Municipal Government," in Harold E. Davis, ed., *Government and Politics in Latin America* (New York: Ronald Press, 1958), pp. 368–92.

26. See Howard J. Wiarda, "The Dominican Fuse," *The Nation* CCVI (February 19, 1968), pp. 238–40, as well as the letter to the editor and the author's response in the issue of May 6, 1968.

27. These statements are based on extensive field work in the Dominican Republic in 1962, 1963, and 1964–1965, and also on the author's contract and consultancy work with the Peace Corps, 1963–1966. Although she was not a Peace Corps volunteer, Lisa Redfield Peattie in *A View from the Barrio* (Ann Arbor, Mich.: University of Michigan Press, 1968) has many poignant comments to make about the U.S.-sponsored community development program.

28. Claudio Veliz, *The Centralist Tradition in Latin America* (Princeton, N. J.: Princeton University Press, 1980).

29. For a thorough and scholarly study that recounts the social and political history of the law and development program, see James A. Gardner, *Legal Imperialism: American Lawyers and Foreign Aid in Latin America* (Madison, Wis.: University of Wisconsin Press, 1980).

30. Ibid., Introduction.

31. The analysis in this and succeeding paragraphs follows closely that of Gardner.

32. Ibid., pp. 4–6, 9, 38, 61, 67, 247.

33. Ibid., pp. 68, 229.

34. John Henry Merryman, *The Civil Law Tradition* (Stanford, Calif.: Stanford University Press, 1969). For one volume in the field that did describe these differences, see Kenneth L. Karst and Keith S. Rosenn, *Law and Development in Latin America* (Berkeley, Calif.: University of California Press, 1975). See also, Howard J. Wiarda, "Law and Political Development in Latin America," *American Journal of Comparative Law* XIX (Summer 1971), pp. 434–63.

35. Gardner, *Legal Imperialism*, p. 210.

36. From the volume *They Know How . . .: An Experiment in Development Assistance* (Washington, D.C.: Government Printing Office for the Inter-American Foundation, 1977).

37. Eric Hoffer, *The True Believer: Thoughts on the Nature of Mass Movements* (New York: Harper, 1961).

38. We do not yet have a social and political history of family planning programs comparable to Gardner on law and development. We need an insider account by someone in the Ford Foundation, the Population Council, the Population Crisis Committee, or the U.S. Agency for International Development. We await the memoirs of one of those dozen or so key persons who has been influential in designing and implementing population policy

over the past quarter century. The closest is the volume by N. J. Demarath, *Power, Presidents, and Professors* (New York: Basic Books, 1967).

39. William Peterson, *Population*, 3rd ed. (New York: MacMillan, 1975), chapter 16.

40. Ibid., p. 651.

41. Howard J. Wiarda, "The Politics of Population Policy in the Dominican Republic," in T. McCoy, ed., *Dynamics of Population Policy in Latin America* (Cambridge, Mass.: Ballinger, 1974), pp. 293–322; see also, with Iêda Siqueira Wiarda, *The Politics of Population Policy in Brazil* (unpublished ms., 1974).

42. Aaron Segal, *Politics and Population in the Caribbean* (Rio Piedras, Puerto Rico: Institute of Caribbean Studies, University of Puerto Rico, 1969).

43. Iêda Siqueira Wiarda and J. F. Helzner, *Women, Population and International Development* (Amherst, Mass.: International Area Studies Programs, University of Massachusetts, 1981).

44. Howard J. Wiarda and Iêda Siqueira Wiarda, "Population, Internal Unrest, and U.S. Security in Latin America," in J.V.D Saunders, ed., *Population Growth in Latin America and U.S. National Security* (Boston: Allen and Unwin, 1986).

45. Peterson, *Population*, pp. 559–60.

46. For a more thorough discussion, see Howard J. Wiarda, *In Search of Policy: The United States and Latin America* (Washington, D.C.: American Enterprise Institute for Public Policy Research, 1984).

47. The analysis here and in subsequent paragraphs is drawn from the excellent comparative treatment of European foreign assistance programs in Helze Ole Bergeson, et al., eds., *The Recalcitrant Rich: A Comparative Analysis of the Northern Responses to the Demands for a New International Economic Order* (New York: St. Martin's Press, 1982). See also Bruce Dinwiddy, ed., *Aid Performance and Development Policies of Western Countries: Studies in U.S., U.K., EEC, and Dutch Programs* (New York: Praeger, 1973); see also Dinwiddy, ed., *European Development Programs: The United Kingdom, Sweden, France, EEC, and Multilateral Organizations* (New York: Praeger, 1973).

48. I am indebted to my colleague at the University of Massachusetts, Eric Einhorn, an expert in Scandinavian social policy, for his insights on these themes.

49. For some further comments see Howard J. Wiarda, *Ethnocentrism in Foreign Policy: Can We Understand the Third World?* (Washington, D.C.: American Enterprise Institute for Public Policy Research, 1985).

50. I have tried to chart these changes in Latin America, as well as the complexities involved, in my *Corporation and National Development in Latin America*, as well as in *Politics and Social Change in Latin America: The Distinct Tradition*, second revised edition (Amherst, Mass.: University of Massachusetts Press, 1982).

51. Four major problems come immediately to mind—dilemmas that cannot be resolved here but which will be discussed in a future essay on this theme: (1) Are there still universals in the development process and, if so, what are they and how do we go about implementing and bringing about their more positive ends and features? (2) How do we make wise decisions in

our foreign policy if not from the matrix of our own experience and under-standing? (3) Where do we limit the cultural relativism implied here—that is, once we are agreed that Hitler and Bokassa are unacceptable, what do we do about the tougher cases: Pinochet, Marcos, South Africa, Zia, the Ayatollah, and Central America? (4) Suppose we heed the admonitions offered here—and then find that there are no third world models of development worth hanging our hats on? How then do policy makers make decisions and carry out policies for these countries?

7

Population, Internal Unrest, and U.S. Security in Latin America

Population policy is a controversial subject in the United States, which is going through one of the periodic, highly emotional and deeply divisive debates about it that has raged over the past twenty-five years. Population policy is controversial not just because it relates closely to the abortion issue—about which feelings are very strong and which politicians of all stripes would just as soon stay away from—but because it touches on deeply felt personal, ideological, and social science belief systems. It is also a political issue, not necessarily or always a moral or a technical one—a fact that is sometimes lost on population policy advocates.

Population policy, as noted in chapter 6, has perhaps more "true believers"—that is, persons who are so deeply committed to it that for them it has become a system of beliefs and an ideology—than any other foreign public policy area. The true believers in population policy think that once the demographic "facts" are presented, any thinking person will reach the same conclusions they have regarding the need for population policy; and they are often bewildered, dumbfounded, and angered when this does not happen. There are far more true believers in population policy, for example, than in agrarian reform, infrastructure growth, community development, basic human needs, or any of the other developmental panaceas that have been offered to the third world in the past quarter century. Perhaps that has something to do with dramatic book titles such as the *Population Bomb*,[1] perhaps with the way statistics are highlighted relating population growth to per-capita income, perhaps with the universalist notions that are often assumed in the fields of demography and sociology, perhaps with our own sense of urban blight and cramped

Published in John V. D. Saunders, ed., *Population Growth in Latin America and U.S. National Security* (Boston: Allyn and Unwin, 1986). Dr. Iêda Siqueira Wiarda is coauthor of this chapter.

124

space and the projection of these to other nations, perhaps even with the character and closely inbred nature of the population policy "establishment." Whatever the precise causes, the true-believer syndrome is strongly present among population policy advocates.

The opposition has often been equally vehement, emotional, and ideological, condemning family planning and population control programs in the harshest of terms. One suspects that the extremism of the one side plays on and reinforces the extremism of the other. Surely in all the heat and controversy that has been generated, there must be a middle ground, room for a prudent and realistic population policy program. That is at least the assumption on which this chapter proceeds.

Background: The Problem and the Debate

The Problem: Demographic Trends. Current demographic projections for the Western Hemisphere indicate that if the present population growth rates remain unchanged, the population of the Western Hemisphere will have increased by 42 percent between 1981 and 2001.[2] Translated into numbers of people, that means an increase of 263 million. Of this total, using current rates of increase, the United States and Canada will see an increase of 38 million by 2001, while the increase in Latin America will be 225 million—six times larger. The most dramatic population increases during this period are projected in Mexico and Central America—the countries nearest to the United States, the sources of most of the illegal migration to the United States, and the countries in the region currently of most concern to U.S. foreign policy. While the U.S. population will increase by only 15 percent by the end of the century, Latin America's will increase by over 60 percent. Table 7–1 shows these dramatic changes.

By 2001 the population of Latin America will be approximately twice that of North America. Brazil will have a population of close to 200 million by the turn of the century, and Mexico will grow to 113 million—a population almost half that of the United States but on only one-fifth the national territory. The population of the Central American countries will be similarly burgeoning. Meanwhile, as table 7–2 indicates, the percentage of the U.S. population relative to the rest of the world, and particularly with regard to Latin America, will have declined dramatically. By the year 2000, the U.S. population will be only 4.4 percent of the world's population, down from 5.3 percent in 1975 and from 6.1 percent in 1950. By 2025 the U.S. share will be only 3.8 percent. Meanwhile, Latin America's share will have increased

TABLE 7-1
WORLD POPULATION AND AVERAGE ANNUAL RATES OF GROWTH BY CONTINENT, 1950–2000

Region	Midyear Population (millions)								
	1950	1960	1970	1975	1980	1985	1990	1995	2000
World	2,549	3,035	3,703	4,082	4,451	4,845	5,258	5,702	6,152
Africa	222	278	358	409	472	548	636	738	850
Asia	1,410	1,685	2,111	2,361	2,591	2,833	3,081	3,351	3,620
Latin America	166	218	286	324	363	407	455	505	557
North America	166	199	226	239	252	264	277	287	297
Europe and Soviet Union	572	640	703	728	750	770	788	803	815
Oceania	12	16	19	21	23	24	26	28	30

Region	Average Annual Rate of Growth (percent)							
	1950–60	1960–70	1970–75	1975–80	1980–85	1985–90	1990–95	1995–2000
World	1.7	2.0	1.9	1.7	1.7	1.6	1.6	1.5
Africa	2.2	2.5	2.7	2.9	3.0	3.0	3.0	2.8
Asia	1.8	2.3	2.2	1.9	1.8	1.7	1.7	1.5
Latin America	2.7	2.7	2.5	2.3	2.3	2.3	2.1	2.0
North America	1.8	1.3	1.1	1.1	1.0	0.9	0.8	0.6
Europe and Soviet Union	1.1	0.9	0.7	0.6	0.5	0.5	0.4	0.3
Oceania	2.3	2.1	1.9	1.3	1.5	1.4	1.3	1.2

NOTE: Total of regional population may not add to world population totals because of rounding.
SOURCE: *World Population: 1984* (Washington: U.S. Dept. of Commerce, Bureau of the Census, November 1984), p. 2.

TABLE 7–2
RELATIVE POPULATION SHARES FOR SELECTED COUNTRIES AND
REGIONS, 1950–2025
(percent)

Country/Region	1950	1975	2000	2025
China	26.8	22.9	20.5	17.9
India	14.0	15.2	15.7	14.6
Africa	8.9	10.1	14.3	20.1
Latin America	6.6	7.9	9.0	9.6
Europe	15.6	11.6	8.4	6.4
USSR	7.2	6.2	5.1	4.5
United States	6.1	5.3	4.4	3.8
Rest of world	14.8	20.8	22.6	23.1
Total	100.0	100.0	100.0	100.0

SOURCE: *Estimates and Medium Variant Projections, United Nations Assessment* (UN: 1983)

from 6.6 percent in 1950 to 7.9 percent in 1975 to 9.0 percent in 2000 and to 9.6 percent in 2025. At the same time, food output in Latin America has been going down.

Based on these projections it can be surmised that population growth in Latin America will have serious political, economic, social, strategic, and other implications not just for that area but also for the United States. The work force in Latin America, for example, will double and in some countries triple without the remotest prospect that local industries or agriculture will produce the jobs to absorb the surplus manpower. Unemployment and underemployment, already severe throughout the hemisphere, will increase. Agricultural production will not be able to meet the food needs of the population. Pressures on utilities and basic services, especially in the area's mushrooming cities, which are almost unmanageable already, will increase dramatically. Pressures to emigrate will be immense in Central America, particularly toward the United States. Social unrest will surely grow. The level of tension, violence, and conflict will increase. Social and political systems are likely to unravel under these pressures, and revolution and increased international conflict will result. All these prospective changes carry profound implications for the United States and for U.S. foreign policy.

U.S. Attitudes and Policy. U.S. attitudes and policy with regard to Latin America's population increase have gone through various changes since the 1960s. We began that decade with John F. Kennedy's Alliance for Progress. Almost no attention was paid in that program, or at any time earlier, to the dramatic increases in Latin America's population or to its implications for U.S. policy. By the mid-1960s, under Lyndon Johnson and with Robert McNamara's influence, the population problem in Latin America was being viewed as a crisis. That perspective carried over into the 1970s, although the emphasis under the Nixon, Ford, and Carter administrations was not quite so strong. Other endeavors—providing basic human needs and ensuring human rights—were supplanting population control efforts as new panaceas and preoccupations.[3]

Today we have almost returned—at least rhetorically—to the posture of the 1950s. That is, Latin America is frequently viewed in the United States as still having vast empty spaces and as requiring larger internal markets for future economic growth. A larger population is seen as a plus for economic development, not a negative.[4] We are thus dealing with the population problem in Latin America by denying it exists; indeed population growth is frequently viewed as advantageous rather than deleterious. The population problem in Latin America has been defined in almost exclusively economic terms. Practically no attention is being paid to the social, political, and strategic implications of unchecked population growth. Furthermore, almost no consideration is being given in the United States to Latin American ideas about population policy, which as we shall see have changed rather dramatically since the 1960s.[5]

The political climate in the United States and in Washington with regard to population policy has undergone a significant transformation. Few politicians want anything to do with population policy—and certainly not as sponsors of new bills dealing with the issue—because of the costs that will accrue electorally. The pro-life movement is stronger and more aggressive than it was before, scientific research has demonstrated that such devices as the IUD may be essentially abortive, which thus makes it harder for politicians to support population control programs, the political tides in this country are running conservative, and the time does not seem to be propitious for new thrusts in the direction of larger and innovative programs. Yet, population policy goes on, despite the rhetoric and often with expanded budgets.

Latin American Perspectives. Attitudes and the political winds in Latin America regarding population policy have followed an opposite trajectory from those in the U.S. In the 1960s the opposition to family planning was strong principally from nationalists, the military, the church, the right, and the left.[6] Today, much of Latin America has gravitated to a position, not unlike that of the United States in the 1960s, of support for family planning programs but with several modifications.

First, too rapid population growth is now widely viewed in Latin America as aggravating the problems of development and putting severe strains on services and facilities: housing, land, health care, water resources, social services, and the political system. Second, all the surveys we have on Latin America show a growing preference for smaller families. This is especially true in the cities where "more hands in the field" is not a compelling argument and where a point of diminishing returns has been reached in terms of numbers of children desired. The desire to limit family size is particularly strong among women. Third, both civilian and military elites in Latin America have come to the conclusion that unchecked population growth and hence an uneducated, alienated, unemployed "mass" in the area's capital cities spells disaster in the long run for the society and nation. Moreover, they have come to believe that unless something is done about the population problem, chaos is likely in the short run in the form of food riots, mass protests, and general discontent that may produce the destabilization of the government in power at the moment.[7]

In general, the following may be said about developments in the population policy area in Latin America over the past twenty years: First, most countries of the area now have, more or less, an official statement that family planning should be available but that it should be voluntary. Second, most of the activities in the family planning area in Latin America are still carried out by private agencies or by private groups now operating in and through public agencies. Third, in several countries, such as Colombia or Mexico, the government has become quite active in family planning, providing not just an official statement of support but also information and services. Colombia, known as the most Catholic country in Latin America, has not only major research and training activities but also an extensive program (albeit unofficial and privately financed) for abortion services. Fourth, a few countries such as Chile have actually regressed in terms of family planning programs, going from a situation of well-run and extensive services prior to 1973 to the present situation of official denouncement by the Pinochet regime. Despite various *pronunciamientos* concerning family planning, other countries—Bolivia for example—have changed little over twenty years. Fifth, even in those countries where an official statement has been made in favor of family planning and some limited services are available, family planning ranks low on the list of national priorities and therefore seldom receives concerted governmental attention.[8]

129

Most Latin American groups remain divided on the population issue, but there has been change over time. In most countries the military has shifted from a pronatalist position to one of concern for the burden of unchecked population growth and the instability that may result. The Roman Catholic Church is divided on the issue. Many clerics are liberal on economic issues but quite conservative on family planning, although some priests and nuns have been supportive. Actually, what the church says about the issue does not matter much because the demand to control family size is so great and most Latin Americans will decide to practice some form of birth control regardless of what the church says. The church's position has prevented some governments from doing more officially, and some already weak governments have decided to ignore the issue to avoid a fight with another potential opposition force. But by and large the church has not been as vocal as might be expected on this issue, and some clever governments have learned they can go forward with family planning as long as they do not make it a public issue that needlessly antagonizes the church.[9]

Leftist groups have been deeply divided. The Marxist argument is that the problem is poor distribution of resources, not unchecked population growth. The radical left accepts the notion (also accepted, ironically, by the United States two decades ago, though from different perspectives) that larger numbers of starving babies and unemployed young people will fuel the revolutionary fires later on. But sometimes female Marxists see their male counterparts as excessively *macho* and complain that that is the real reason their comrades are against family planning. The traditional right in Latin America has in the past been opposed to family planning programs but, like the military, has come to see the explosive and revolutionary potential of unchecked growth. Latin American intellectuals are divided on the issue as are most women's groups, though the latter tend to argue family planning services should be available as an option and that population is as much a woman's personal problem as any other.[10] Several of the private family planning organizations in Latin America have been discredited for providing insufficient medical backup and inadequate health care coverage as well as for engaging in some questionable practices; but in many Latin American countries they are the only organizations providing family planning services.

Overall, there remain deep divisions in Latin America over population policy, though the clear trend is toward greater acceptance of the need for voluntary family planning services closely attuned to the particular needs of individual countries. Furthermore, the divisions are not always what one might expect. Some priests have been very active and vocal in supporting family planning services. The military in most countries has not been overly concerned with the issue except as it sees the effects of unchecked population growth on internal security and stability. Women have tended to look at it as an issue of family and personal health influencing the numbers of mouths to feed or hands to work, and not so much as a national issue. There are, in short, different perceptions by different groups in Latin America as well as distinct understandings from country to country of what the "population problem" is.[11]

Population and Internal Unrest in Latin America

This chapter is chiefly concerned with the largely unexplored area of population and internal unrest in Latin America and the implications of this for U.S. foreign policy. Other issues—the effect of population on family size, for example, or on economic growth, or the rights of families and mothers to choose—are also important. This chapter focuses, however, on the strategic and policy implications of unchecked population growth. The following topics are relevant in a discussion of population and internal unrest in Latin America: the relation between size, crowding, and internal tension; the changing age profile of Latin America and whether younger means more radical; the pressures on land and agriculture brought on by increased population growth; the effects of urbanization and immigration and of cities that have grown beyond the size of livability or governability; the prospects for increased emigration and spiraling refugee problems; the prospects for economic growth or, alternatively, contraction and negative growth; rising social tensions, riots, and revolutionary activities; the unraveling of political systems; and, finally, war, both civil and international. The combined effect of these forces oblige one to consider more seriously than in the past the effect of Latin American population growth on security and stability issues in the hemisphere, and hence on U.S. foreign policy.

Size, Crowding, and Internal Tension. The relations between size, crowding, and internal tensions are complex and not entirely clear in the literature. Virtually all the scientific work that has been done relating crowding to tension and to increased level of violence derives from studies of animal behavior. Those studies do show a close relationship between crowding and violence, but the relationship is usually indirect. That is, one cannot say that crowding is a direct cause

131

of violence. But crowding does provide conditions and a context in which tension, violence, and various forms of aberrant behavior are more likely to occur.[12]

Of course not all propositions need to be scientifically proven for them to be valid. In this case common sense may be as valid a guide as the, admittedly, inadequate scientific evidence available. We know, for example, that Latin America, like the United States, no longer has virtually unlimited frontiers. There are no more vast empty spaces amenable to new settlements or an abundance of untapped lands on which the nation's malcontents, or its excess population, can begin new lives.

Although the man-to-land ratio is not as high in Latin America as in India or China, for example, or even in Western Europe or the United States (see table 7–3), that fact is often misleading. Most of the unused land in Latin America is unusable, either so steeply mountainous or having such dense jungles with such thin topsoil (as in the Amazon Basin, for instance) that it cannot support even the most meager level of subsistence. The frontiers that do exist in Latin America (western Brazil, the Colombian and Venezuelan *llanos*) have been claimed and settled in the past thirty years, there is precious little new land left, and hence the "escape valve" of the frontier is virtually nonexistent.[13] If there is a parallel in the United States, it is that we also can no longer advise "go West young man." The disappearance of frontiers from our own nation has led to a sense of crowding and absence of escapes, as well as to a new preoccupation with immigration to the United States and with securing our borders. Massive, uncontrolled immigration to the United States is producing the same kinds of worries and problems as excess population growth produces

TABLE 7–3

POPULATION, AREA, AND DENSITY FOR SELECTED COUNTRIES AND REGIONS

Country/Region	Population	Area (Sq. Km)	Density
United States	213,121,000 (1975)	9,363,353	24
South America	195,000,000 (1971)	17,834,000	11
India	547,367,926 (1971)	3,280,483	168
Europe	466,000,000 (1971)	4,936,000	94
China	853,000,000 (1976)[a]	9,560,990	89

a. Estimate.

SOURCE: United Nations, *Demographic Yearbooks* and *The International Geographic Encyclopedia and Atlas* (Boston: Houghton Mifflin, 1979).

in Latin America: too many people; too little space; crowding; tension; high unemployment, especially among the poor; few opportunities for release; and ultimately rising crime and violence.

These conditions are particularly acute in Latin America's teeming, exploding (and explosive) cities. Metropolises like São Paulo and Mexico City have grown to 16 or 17 million, almost twice the size of New York City, which once was the world's largest. Cities like Lima or Bogotá, not quite so large, have also seen their populations double in the past two or three decades. The same is true of capital cities in the smaller countries: Santo Domingo, with 300,000 people in 1950, now has over a million, some of the most horrible slums anywhere in Latin America, and virtually unmanageable problems. In all the capitals of Latin America social services are breaking down, there is no water or sewage system for over half the urban dwellers, unemployment and underemployment are rising, crime and violence are spreading, and food riots and other forms of rioting are now frequent. The food riots in Santo Domingo in the spring of 1984 made national headlines in the United States, but the spreading riots and conditions of abysmal poverty in other cities have not.[14]

No one knows or can define precisely what the upper limits of city size are. We do know that cities such as Bogotá, São Paulo, and especially Mexico City are breaking down, crumbling, and becoming unlivable. Pollution, crime, disintegration, and violence are becoming endemic. These cities are no longer manageable. We read now of the phenomenon of "ungovernability" in the advanced industrial nations, but that is nothing compared with the increasing ungovernability of most Latin American capital cities. The relations between size, crowding, and domestic tension and violence may be indirect and the evidence may not yet be all in, but in Latin America it seems plain and visible for all to see.

Age: Does Younger Mean More Radical? In virtually all the countries of Latin America half the population is under eighteen years of age (see table 7–4). In some of the countries half the population is under fifteen. The cause of these astounding figures is, of course, continued high birth rates accompanied by major improvements in infant and child care and in public health measures such as immunizations. The implications for politics and foreign policy of these figures are enormous.

In all countries there has been a quantum increase in what is called the dependency ratio. The dependency ratio is a figure that compares the economically active and productive population with the economically inactive or dependent population. Throughout Latin

TABLE 7–4
POPULATION UNDER FIFTEEN YEARS OF AGE, 1982

Region	Percent of Population
Africa	45
Latin America	39
Asia	37
Oceania	29
North America	22
Europe	22
World	35

SOURCE: United Nations, *Demographic Yearbook, 1982.*

America this ratio has been increasing steadily in recent years—that is, fewer and fewer productive persons are being called upon to support more and more nonproductive ones. The rising dependency ratio has created increased tensions in recent years, as an ever larger burden is being placed on governments and productive persons to carry the burden of an enormously large youth population on their shoulders.

There is mixed evidence on the relationship between youth and radicalism. In Latin America virtually an entire generation and more of university-trained young people is Marxist. Figures indicate that whereas in the United States only 2–3 percent of the college-age population could be classified as activist in a political sense, in Latin America the figure may be 40–45 percent. Of course the figures need to be broken down further: state universities tend to be more radical and politicized than private ones in Latin America; the law and arts and letters faculties tend to be more activist than those in engineering or other technical fields. Moreover, student politics in Latin America is way to the left of what it would be in the United States. Socialism occupies the middle of the political spectrum, with social democracy on the right; there are no groups of what Americans would call conservatives on most Latin American campuses. Part of the ideology of these young persons is virulent anti-Americanism.[15]

The implications of these disaffected young persons' coming to power are enormous. Only in part is their radicalism diluted by working in the government. In some countries this age group that has grown up since the 1960s is already in low-level government positions. Within five or ten years they will be in the cabinet or the presidency. And that is only the first wave. The generation that is presently under fifteen is likely to be even more embittered, more radical, and more anti-American than its older brothers and sisters. Already, because of the suspicions and hostility, it is more difficult for American foreign service officers to work cooperatively with their Latin American counterparts than it was in the 1960s. In the future these problems will multiply, for among the younger generation the strong residue of trust, admiration, and good will that used to exist toward the United States is no longer present.

Illustrative of these themes is the Nicaraguan Revolution. In our preoccupation with the political and ideological aspects of the revolution, we tend to forget that it also marked a sharp generational change. Both the Somoza regime and its more moderate opponents represented one generation; the Sandinistas represent a whole new age group that has come to power. In 1979 most of the *comandantes* were in their late twenties or early thirties; the revolution's strongest supporters are also found at the younger end of the age spectrum. That is why the Sandinistas lowered the voting age for the 1984 election from eighteen to sixteen—because they knew their vote margin would thereby be increased. If Nicaragua is at all indicative of what will happen politically when this younger generation rises to power (and many professional Latin Americanists think that it is), then the implications for U.S. foreign policy and security interests are enormous.[16]

It is not likely that there will soon be a wave of Nicaraguas sweeping over Latin America—although in quite a few countries radical change led by these new generations can be expected. What is more likely is that demagogic politicians and political movements will seize upon the frustration and radicalism of the youth for their own purposes. The spectacle of young high school and university students, or unemployed recent graduates, leading protest marches of recent migrants, or urging peasants to take the agrarian reform laws long on the books but often unimplemented into their own hands by seizing private landholdings, is now common in Latin America. These are, again, indirect effects of spiraling population growth rather than direct ones. The governments in power where such "direct action" takes place do not consider population growth per se to be the culprit but instead blame a malevolent opposition using the "marginals" (as the urban and rural unemployed are often called) as shock troops. In response the government usually reasserts authoritarian controls instead of addressing the root causes of rebellion, which lie in overpopulation, poverty, marginality, unemployment, and the like. In either case, if the revolution succeeds or if the government overreacts, U.S. foreign policy interests will be hurt.

Pressures on the Land and Agriculture. Latin American landholding has long been characterized by latifundia on the one hand (large, often unproductive estates) and "minifundia" on the other (small holdings that are too small to be economically viable). To these twin problems, which still exist in all the countries of the region, have now been added some newer ones.

First, there is widespread abandonment of the land as people leave the rural areas and flock to the cities. However awful the conditions are in the city slums, the possibilities and opportunities there are infinitely greater than in the countryside. Indeed, the most ambitious and energetic tend to abandon the *campo*, leaving behind children, the infirm, and old people. Whole villages have been emptied of able workers and field hands, and agriculture has been neglected.

Second, food production in most Latin American countries has not kept up with population growth. In fact, population growth is considerably outstripping new agricultural production. Moreover, most of the new agricultural production that has been created in Latin America has been oriented toward production for a world market, not home consumption. One can talk all one wishes about comparative advantage and the benefits of global divisions of labor, but while foreign trade is increasing, most Latin American rural populations are becoming worse off rather than better off. Agricultural and once self-sufficient countries are being forced to import basic foodstuffs at, for them, very high prices that the poor cannot afford. Subsistence agriculture was not very profitable, but at least it enabled many to eke out a meager subsistence and to feed their own families. Today, these peasants are being forced off their lands and into the less fertile hillsides, often falling across that thin but deadly barrier separating subsistence from starvation. Under such conditions it is not unexpected that they would migrate massively to the cities—or that they might be lured by radical causes. The violent, destructive Mexican revolution of 1910 provides an early case in point.[17]

In the past, increases in food production in Latin America were mainly due to bringing more unused lands under cultivation. Now, however, unused land is becoming more and more scarce. Furthermore, increased acreage has not provided a solution to the food problem. In part this is due to the orientation of that production toward a world market; in part also it is because land reclamation is often more costly than increasing production on existing land. The expectation that the Amazon Basin, for example, would become a breadbasket for all of South America has not been realized. More often than not, such great efforts have ended in equally spectacular failures. Other land areas are precluded from coming under production because of water-borne diseases; in still others the insecticides used to control flies and disease have had unacceptable environmental effects. In some Caribbean countries such as Haiti, with its denuded hillsides and the topsoil washed away, it is probably no longer possible to reclaim the land; El Salvador and some other parts of Central America have also reached their limits. Overall, there is now widespread agreement that agrarian reform—if that means the division of larger landholdings—results in less production rather than more, thus compounding the problem. Agrarian reform may still be desirable for other reasons, but the case for its economic rationality seems weak.

There is, derived from the U.S. experience, an argument for higher population density, which presumably would also assist agriculture.[18] By permitting economies of scale in the provision of infrastructure and services, it is argued, population increases may also help induce improvements in agriculture. In the United States, rising population in the nineteenth century stimulated the development of transportation, which in turn aided agriculture in bringing its products to markets more cheaply and raised the prices of agricultural products. These potential benefits to be gained from higher population density are not likely to be realized in the Latin American countries because (1) the landholding system is entirely different, with few medium-sized family farms manned by risk-taking yeoman farmers; (2) the topography is entirely different, ruling out either mechanization or a nationwide grid of farm-to-market transportation; (3) Latin America's attitudes toward agriculture are different (as much feudal as capitalist); and (4) several governments of the area (especially Brazil and Mexico) have decided to concentrate production (soybean and other crops) for world markets rather than domestic use. Hence, even though Brazil is a thriving food producer and exporter, its people are literally starving to death. Governments of the area pay little attention to "poor people's food" because only by concentrating on export products will these countries be able to cope with their international debts. It is one more problem on top of many others.

Thus in countries like Brazil, even if it were possible to keep food production ahead of population growth, there would be no guarantee that people could have a healthier diet. Where incomes are low, and particularly where the already-meager per-capita income is unevenly distributed, *most* of the population may not be able to afford the food they need. Although the amount of labor used in agriculture has risen in most Latin American countries, most families have experienced little or no increase in real wages or nutritional levels. Hence most *campesino* families may actually be regressing, as shown in the rising figures for infant mortality throughout the region.

These complex pressures on the land and on agriculture are making living conditions for the rural poor more difficult rather than better, even in areas where productivity and exports are increasing. And at the base of these pressures is the problem of still-spiraling population, unplanned, unchecked, and no longer rational in terms of the wishes of people for smaller families, the capacities of economic or agricultural systems to absorb them or the families' ability to feed and take care of them. And if the problems are intensifying now, we need to remember that the next generation of still greater problems has already been born.

Urbanization and Migration. In the past thirty years there has been a massive and unprecedented move toward the cities in all the Latin American countries. Salaries may be low in the cities by U.S. standards, but for the marginal and landless peasant the lure of a job and a better education for his children overrides all other considerations. In Latin America, which is the most highly urbanized region in the third world, over 65 percent of the population now lives in cities, most of these in the capital cities (see table 7-5).

Mexico City is a case in point. Sometimes called "the capital of underdevelopment," it adds at least 350,000 immigrants from small towns and the countryside per year—this in addition to its natural annual increase by births of 2.5 percent, another 425,000. Estimates place the population of Mexico City by the year 2000 at 26 million. Even now the city does not have the governmental infrastructure, economy, or social services to handle its population—let alone that to come. It has one of the world's worst pollution problems, people spend about one-third of their day commuting to and from slums and jobs, and the traffic problems are legendary. The city is sinking several inches per year as ground-water is progressively drawn from its swampy base. Conservative estimates put infant deaths at 30,000 a year from the effects of air pollution and poor or no sewerage.[19] The severe earthquake that hit Mexico in September 1985 not only killed thousands and devastated the central city but also exacerbated the longer-term problems.

Mexico City is not unique in Latin America. Urban life requires a large and complex set of services—water, sewerage, electricity, to say

TABLE 7–5
LATIN AMERICAN POPULATION GROWTH RATES AND URBAN
POPULATION, 1980–1985

	Growth Rates per Thousand 1980–85	Percent Urban 1985
Latin America	23.9	66.05
Andean region	25.6	68.31
Bolivia	26.8	50.54
Colombia	21.4	69.50
Chile	16.7	80.31
Ecuador	31.2	47.49
Peru	27.9	65.88
Venezuela	32.5	78.04
Atlantic Region	20.9	68.66
Argentina	11.9	82.96
Brazil	23.0	66.09
Paraguay	30.0	40.04
Uruguay	6.5	84.63
Central American region	29.2	45.59
Costa Rica	23.1	49.20
El Salvador	29.2	46.66
Guatemala	29.1	37.78
Honduras	33.8	42.17
Nicaragua	32.6	57.24
Panama	22.0	58.89
Mexico and Caribbean region	25.8	64.81
Cuba	6.2	70.39
Haiti	25.0	25.03
Mexico	28.6	68.54
Dominican Republic	24.3	50.83

SOURCE: Centro Latinoamericano de Demografia, *Boletin Demografico*, vol. XIV, no. 28, Santiago, Chile, July 1981.

nothing of schools and housing—that cannot easily or quickly be scaled up as population and migration accelerate. Cities are proverbially short of money, especially in Latin America where they have little or no taxing power, and in most cases also lack the administrative and technical capacity to cope with a doubling of size in a single decade. The results are familiar: unemployment, underemployment, woefully inadequate housing (*millions* of persons, including abandoned children, are living in the streets), deteriorating public service, higher mortality and morbidity, congestion, pollution, crime, burning of buses, protests, and riots.

There are, of course, benefits to urbanization. These include economies of scale, more differentiated labor markets, and concentration of suppliers and consumers. Most people move to towns and cities for higher incomes and greater opportunities. Once in the cities, three out of four migrants make economic gains. A move from the parched Northeast of Brazil to Rio de Janeiro or São Paulo, or from the bleak Peruvian sierra to Lima, can easily triple the income of even unskilled workers. The higher costs of urban living may narrow rural-urban differences in real terms, but urban dwellers have better access to the limited services that do exist, and therefore their family income and prospects are likely to be considerably higher. Women can also more easily find employment as factory workers, maids, or vendors in the cities than in the rural areas.[20] While urbanization and migration may be beneficial in these ways, the sheer size and the uncontrolled nature of the cityward migration threaten to produce such paralysis and chaos in Latin America as to rule out the potential for gains.

Even though there has been extraordinarily rapid urbanization in Latin America, that has not so far had much effect on slowing population growth. It is usually assumed, based on the European and North American experiences, that urbanization helps stimulate the so-called demographic transition—that is, that as people become more urban, educated, and sophisticated, and as the argument for more hands in the field becomes thus less rational, the population growth rate tends to drop. In some Latin American countries a form of this demographic transition seems already under way. But the evidence is also strong that as the *campesinos* stream to the cities they carry with them traditional attitudes and behavior regarding reproduction. That is, they tend still to desire large families, *machismo* remains strong, and few avail themselves of family planning services even where those are available. Hence the migrants move to the city but still contribute to population growth at the higher, more traditional rural rate.[21]

Urbanization and internal migration are thus adding to the burdens of societies already woefully ill-equipped to cope with present-day problems, let alone the more severe ones of the future. Urbanization and cityward migration are further ingredients in the trends toward fragmentation, paralysis, and breakdown that we have repeatedly seen as the disturbing prospects in Latin America's future. And at the root of these interlocking crises lies the population problem, the problem of unplanned, unchecked, uncontrolled growth and all the destabilizing potential associated with it. The security and foreign policy implications of these trends are immense; yet as we shall see in a later section it is doubtful if very much will or can be done about it.

Emigration and Refugee Problems. For several Latin American countries—Mexico, El Salvador, the Dominican Republic, Haiti, Colombia, Cuba, and others in Central America and the Caribbean—the pattern of migration is not just from countryside to capital. For many migrants cityward movement in their own countries is only a first step; their ultimate destination is the United States. In some cases the flow from rural to urban areas and then to the United States is direct and rapid; in other cases it may take years or even two or three generations.[22] Whether direct or drawn out, the result is that the United States has itself become a Caribbean/Central American nation: New York City has the second largest Puerto Rican, the second largest Dominican, the second largest Haitian, and the second largest Colombian populations in the world; and Miami, Atlanta, Dallas, Houston, and Los Angeles—to name only the largest—have also become main centers of Latin American populations.

The motivation for most international migration is the same as for internal migration: higher wages and better opportunities. International migration can also be spurred by repressive and unsettled political situations, as is the case in Haiti, Guatemala, El Salvador, Nicaragua, and Cuba.

Emigration by the unskilled and politically disaffected does not necessarily mean a loss of production in the countries of origin. In fact, the emigrants may be encouraged to leave by their own governments. Because these countries have surplus populations, emigration to the United States serves as a way for hard-pressed governments to relieve internal population pressures. Presidents of Colombia have openly told Colombians in New York that they should stay where they were—but should continue sending their remittances back home! In other Central American/Caribbean capitals governments extensively assist their "surplus populations" to leave (though neither they nor the local U.S. embassies can say so publicly).

The problem of extensive and virtually uncontrolled emigration to the United States will eventually have to be faced. The problem, even spectacle, of a porous border, and of American inability to control its own entryways—and the rising social, economic, and political problems to which it has given rise—must be dealt with. The situation is complicated by the fact that immigration is now a major U.S. domestic issue: employers want to continue having available a large pool of cheap, nonunionized laborers, and organized labor argues that American jobs are being lost to illegal aliens. The burden on U.S. gateway cities of educating migrant children, providing housing and services, and dealing with the other problems of recent migrants has also produced strains.[23]

The United States needs to address the problem of illegal immigration and needs to be able to control its own borders. In this light the new immigration law, which sought to give immigration officials greater enforcement authority is, even with all its defects, probably better than no action at all. But it must be remembered that if we are successful in reducing illegal immigration, we thereby add to the explosive potential of Latin American countries. For nations such as Mexico the "safety valve" of allowing, even encouraging, emigration to the United States has eased internal tensions; should that outlet for surplus population be closed off, the possibilities for greater future instability in Latin America increase.

Economic Frustrations. The economic dilemmas facing Latin America are familiar and need not be analyzed in detail here.[24] These include poverty, the world's highest per-capita debt, unemployment and underemployment that may affect 40–50 percent of the work force, negative growth rates over the past five years, immense income inequalities, declining terms of trade, immense capital flight, very little new investment, little U.S. foreign assistance, increased protectionism on the part of those countries with whom Latin America must trade, rising prices for the goods Latin America must import, and (in some countries) devastation of their economic infrastructure by guerrilla forces. The vicious circles of Latin American underdevelopment are such that it seems doubtful, even without being unduly pessimistic, they will *ever* be resolved.

Governments of the area are caught in what might be called the "population treadmill effect." High-fertility countries that face a doubling or even tripling of the school-age population by the end of the century will require major increases in spending for education even if the objective is just to maintain the present, rather low educational levels. The same population treadmill affects electric power, transportation, jobs, housing, health care, and other basic services. Given present and projected population growth, the Latin American economies must move ahead at unprecedented rates just to stay even. Nowhere, under present economic projections, is that likely to happen.

The population-treadmill effect means hard choices in a period of retrenchment. When the economic pie in Latin America was growing, along with the population, it was easier to maintain at least the existing, albeit inadequate, level of services. Now, however, in a period of economic contraction, tough decisions must be made.

Should scarce resources go to open farm-to-market roads so food crops do not spoil before they reach the cities, or should these limited resources provide schools, health services, or labor training programs for the new urban dwellers? These are difficult decisions; the case can reasonably be argued either way. As long as economic growth was going forward faster than population growth in the 1950s, 1960s, and until the mid-to-late 1970s, Latin America had the luxury of time in making some of these decisions and could probably afford to do all or most of these things at once. But now, in conditions of economic downturn where population growth has not slowed apace, all decisions become zero-sum decisions: for every gain in one area there must be losses in others.

It must also be recognized that current deprivations will certainly have important effects later on. Lack of or insufficient spending on education, for example, will mean a less- or nonskilled labor force in years to come. This lack comes at a time when the Latin American countries require a better and more technically trained population to diversify their economies, which is a key to economic growth. In addition, there is mounting evidence that a poorly nourished infant population means, to put it bluntly, less brainpower in years to come. Unchecked population growth also means the income inequalities that are already severe in Latin America will surely become worse, as will the poverty, the unemployment, the bitterness, and the frustration.

What concerns us as well, however, are the implications for U.S. foreign policy and security in the area. Aid programs such as the Caribbean Basin Initiative and the Kissinger Commission recommendations, drafted and passed into law with such difficulty, will have little or no effect in the face of unchecked population growth. Neither principal nor interest on the foreign debt will ever be paid if population growth continues unabated, and that spells trouble for U.S. banks as well as for the international financial community. Social tension is sure to rise and so will the likelihood of political breakdown. Precisely at the time when the United States is enormously preoccupied with internal stability, democracy, and the creation of viable economic and political systems in the nations on our southern border, unchecked and uncontrolled population growth threatens to wipe out all the gains made. The present rate of population growth not only is a root cause of the current endemic instability in the region but also threatens to have even more devastating and destabilizing effects in the future.

Rising Social Tensions. Unchecked population growth rates, in a time of economic downturn, have undoubtedly contributed to rising social tension in Latin America. In almost all countries of the region petty and general crime rates are up, there is more wife- and child-beating, violence and violent behavior are increasing, the incidence of abandoned children (10 million in Brazil alone) has reached epidemic proportions. Tension, frustration, and violence at the societal level is certain also to have an impact politically.[25]

Here we focus chiefly on unemployment and underemployment. Unemployment in most Latin American countries (depending in part on how one counts it) may reach 20–25 percent of the work force. Underemployment, often referred to as invisible unemployment, may add 20–25 percent more. Underemployment refers to the vendors who may sell a few single cigarettes and matches per day, the shoe-shine boys who may have only two or three customers per day, the book and magazine salesmen who go all day without customers—the vendors who deal in what Sol Tax long ago called penny capitalism.[26] Together, underemployment and unemployment may total 40–50 percent of the work force.

This "lumpenproletariat," the residents of the urban slums surrounding all the Latin American capital cities, is a powder keg waiting to explode. Few if any social or city services ever reach their neighborhoods. The slums in which they live are wretched, filthy, unhealthful, increasingly victimized by crime, disease, and violence. Yet these are no longer isolated, diffused "sleepy" peasants, among whom we know from history revolution is unlikely to start. These are people who have been uprooted, who have ambition and raised expectations, and hence among whom revolutionary and demagogic appeals are likely to find receptivity. We know that revolution does not occur among the most traditional and backward of people but among those who have been uprooted, whose expectations once raised have been dashed again.[27]

It takes relatively little—a change in bus fares, an increased tax on gasoline, rising prices for basic foodstuffs—to set off violent or anomic protests in the cities' teeming slums. In the spring of 1984, for example, increases in the cost of rice and beans as a result of a government- and International Monetary Fund–imposed austerity program sparked food riots in the Dominican Republic. Thousands of Dominicans spilled into the streets in protest, and several score were killed by the police. Fortunately, the democratic Dominican government was able to survive.[28]

Similar protests and food riots, though little noticed by the media, have recently occurred in Brazil, Colombia, Peru, Nicaragua, and Mexico. These are generally unorganized, what social scientists call anomic movements—without leadership or clear political goals. The

144

danger to U.S. interests and policy is that a more or less spontaneous movement of this sort may be captured by a disciplined Marxist-Leninist political movement with the potential to undermine, topple, and capture a government. The literature on these more organized, usually carefully orchestrated protest movements in Latin America, with their potential for great violence both physically and to the political fabric, is extensive.[29] Such movements, if they occur when other circumstances are propitious (the middle class is also feeling austerity's bite, the armed forces are divided, the government is weak or illegitimate), can produce revolutionary consequences.

The prime recruiting grounds for such movements are of course the slums of the big capital cities, the legions of unemployed or underemployed concentrated in the downtown streets, the surplus population with nothing to do, the abandoned street children looking for adventure and diversion. It is usually but a short march from there to the national palace where greater violence may be provoked or a minister or a government may be forced from office. These kinds of movements, arising from social tension and problems but carrying clear political overtones, derive directly from unchecked population growth; and we are likely to see more of them in the future.

The Unraveling of Political Systems. It sometimes surprises North Americans (and Latin Americans as well) to learn that there is a pattern, a system, of Latin American politics. We assume, condescendingly and ethnocentrically, that a region as unstable as Latin America must have no form of systematic politics whatsoever.

Actually, Latin American politics has a rhythm and system of its own; the problem is not that there is no system but that outside observers are unacquainted with the system and how it works.[30] Historically, the system of Latin American politics incorporates military as well as civilian regimes, and the route to power often involves direct action of the kind outlined in the previous section (street movements, general strikes, marches on the national palace, carefully orchestrated political violence, coups, and revolutions) as well as elections. The Latin American political process is more informal than formal: cliques, class, family, and patronage groups, as well as formal political parties, interest associations, and governmental institutions, compete for power. The mandate of any political leader is tentative and indefinite and does not necessarily correspond to any given electoral timetable. As long as a political leader who comes to power by whatever means can legitimize his rule, and as long as he enjoys popular and corporate group support, he may stay in office; but should he at any time lose legitimacy and support he can quickly fall.

145

The politics is hurly-burly and often unstable but with well-understood rules and persistent regularities.

Latin American politics has been not only more systematic than we usually think, but quite accommodative—again contrary to much popular lore. The traditional systems of Latin American politics have been far more flexible and far less rigid (closed or oligarchic) than we ordinarily think. Two conditions must be met by a group seeking admission to the system: it must demonstrate its power to disrupt or take over the system, and it must not become excessively greedy or revolutionary by seeking to destroy other more traditional groups so as to monopolize power and privileges for itself.

In the 1930s, 1940s, 1950s, and 1960s this process and system worked not entirely intolerably, inefficiently, or even undemocratically—though the meaning of the last term in Latin America often differed from that in the United States. First the rising business and commercial groups, then a sizable portion of the middle class, and then some more accommodative labor groups were assimilated into the system. In most countries pluralism increased, power changed hands, and progress occurred. The system worked, more or less.

But the system depended on an ever-expanding economic pie to continue functioning democratically and well. As long as there were more pieces to hand out, no group needed to be deprived. But with the negative growth rates of the past several years the rivalry for the fewer pieces became more intense, violence and full-scale revolutionary challenges increased, and the existing political systems began to unravel—as in El Salvador, Nicaragua, Bolivia, Peru, and elsewhere. In addition, it proved far more difficult to adapt the prevailing political systems to the new challenges of the 1970s and 1980s than it had been to the more traditional business and middle-class groups of the earlier era.

There is no doubt that the mass discontent and challenges to established ways and institutions that we now see in Latin America have been fueled by the population and urbanization explosion. Once more, the relationship is indirect rather than direct but no less important for being so. The youthfulness of the Latin American populations, the absence of jobs and opportunities, the growing impatience, the economic downturn, and the rising social tensions have combined to make traditional accommodative politics in Latin America difficult at best and almost impossible in some countries.

It is not just regimes-of-the-moment that are being challenged in Latin America but an entire system (more or less accommodative and more or less democratic) of politics. That fact is not sufficiently understood in the U.S. government. The political unraveling and the undermining and destruction of a whole system of Latin American politics have immense destabilizing implications not only for the Latin American countries but for U.S. policy as well. The transition to democracy that we have recently seen in Latin America will likely be halted or reversed. Not only can democracy not flourish in this context, but *any* kind of moderate, middle-of-the-road government will be hard-pressed to survive.

War. Although Latin America has been remarkably free of the international wars that have periodically ravaged Western Europe over the past five hundred years, the area is not without its flashpoints, its irredentism, and its *Realpolitik*.[31] There is potential for violence in Mexico's longstanding bitterness toward the United States for depriving it of half its former territory, tension on the Mexico-Guatemala border over streams of Guatemalan refugees flowing into Mexico, territorial disputes between Guatemala and Belize, civil war in El Salvador, barely submerged conflict between El Salvador and Honduras, and border problems between Honduras and Nicaragua as well as between Costa Rica and Nicaragua. Haiti and the Dominican Republic are rarely at peace on Hispaniola, the Caribbean (Cuba, Jamaica, Grenada) is torn by domestic and international conflicts, Nicaragua claims islands under Colombian control and is embroiled in conflicts on both its Honduran and Costa Rican borders, Panama wants complete control of the Panama Canal before the year 2000 specified in the treaty, and Venezuela claims more than half the territory of Guyana. Farther south, Ecuador claims a large share of the Peruvian Amazon, landlocked Bolivia wants an outlet to the sea, Peru still resents Chile for depriving it a hundred years ago of its two richest southern provinces, Paraguay and Bolivia fought a war fifty years ago and are still not amicable neighbors, Brazil has imperial designs on all its surrounding neighbors, and Chile and Argentina (to say nothing of Brazil and Argentina) will probably never get along well. There are also disputes over the Falklands/Malvinas Islands and over Antarctica. The potential for territorial and other forms of conflict is strong and increasing.

Not all of these conflicts are directly population related, but many of them are. At the root of the Haitian-Dominican conflict, for example, is the fact that historically Haiti has had twice the population of the Dominican Republic on half of the national territory. Although Mexico and El Salvador are similarly overpopulated, Honduras and Nicaragua have lower population densities and considerable open space for settlement. Brazil wants *lebensraum*—breathing space for her great power designs, and everyone who borders on it wants access to the near-empty Amazon basin for population resettlement, mineral resources, and other purposes.

The war that could be most directly attributed to population pressures was the El Salvador–Honduran conflict of 1969, the so-called Soccer War.[32] The war had a long history; at its root was overpopulation in El Salvador (with the densest population in mainland Latin America) and the beckoning open spaces of Honduras. Over the years thousands of Salvadorans settled, often "informally" and without papers, across the border in Honduras. They developed the land, built houses, had children, and settled in. The tension between the more enterprising Salvadorans and the more easygoing Hondurans was always palpable, and eventually the Honduran government forced the Salvadoran settlers out. The forced exodus was sometimes bloody and traumatic. At a soccer game between the two countries the violence spilled over into a conflict between the two sets of fans, insults were traded, the armies of the two countries mobilized, and a short conflict ensued. More Salvadorans were forced out, leaving a legacy of bitterness and tension between the two countries.

It is unlikely that the geopolitics of Latin America will result in widespread war or that population will always be at the root of the conflict. Nevertheless as Latin America runs out of frontiers and open spaces, as population pressures mount inexorably, and as internal tension and conflict result, the need for external outlets will also increase. Some of these will produce conflict with neighboring countries who may not see the issue in quite the same way. The mass exodus of Guatemalans from their country and the nervousness of the Mexicans about this, including stepped-up border controls and real tension and conflict in Mexico's southernmost provinces, provides a case in point.[33] Similar population pressures with the potential for international conflict continue to be felt in Haiti, El Salvador, the Dominican Republic, and Mexico itself. When it reaches the level of war and international conflict, we then are able to see clearly the effect of unchecked population increase—albeit too late. It is likely we will begin to see more such population-induced conflicts in Latin America in the years ahead.[34]

Population and U.S. Security

This chapter has attempted to link population growth in Latin America to internal unrest—economic, social, political, even military—and to draw the implications of these trends for U.S. security policy. The evidence is overwhelming, we think, of both indirect and direct causal relations between unchecked population growth and the possibilities for rising social tension, violence, political upheaval, and breakdowns of entire national social and political systems. As yet, however, almost no one in the U.S. government—and certainly not at decision-making levels—is paying attention to these issues. Nor, we predict, is anyone likely to in the near future. But if the problem is so severe, and the relationships so clear, why, one might ask, is nothing being done or likely to be done? The answer calls for some knowledge of Washington policy making and the place of population policy making within that context.

U.S. Preoccupations in Latin America. U.S. policy in Latin America has consistently been preoccupied with preserving stability and preventing another outside power (Britain, France, Spain, Germany, now the Soviet Union) from securing a beachhead there that might threaten U.S. security. That was the preoccupation of President James Monroe when he promulgated his famous doctrine, and it has consistently, albeit with sometimes differing emphases, been the policy of all U.S. administrations since the United States first became a major power approximately one hundred years ago. Economic investment by private U.S. firms was viewed both as a good in its own right and as a means to help preserve the stability and independence of Latin America from other outside powers. The same goes for democracy, development, and human rights: the United States values these as ends in themselves and also as a means to help maintain friendly and stable governments. More recently other concerns—drug traffic and debt, for example—have come to the fore, but these are also viewed chiefly in terms of their potential for destabilizing the area and paving the way for Soviet and Cuban advances.[35]

Only rarely have population issues been considered part of this equation. When Lyndon Johnson spoke on the population issue, he did so largely because he had been convinced of the security dimensions of the problem; and his views were strongly lauded by the community of population policy activists. Johnson had been persuaded that unchecked population growth would have profoundly destabilizing effects and would undermine U.S.-sponsored development projects, which are aimed primarily at preventing such destabilization. But since the 1960s there has been less preoccupation with population issues in official Washington; indeed the trend has been to separate population issues from security issues—or to stay away from population policy altogether.

That trend helps explain the sudden popularity of the theories of economist Julian Simon. Simon holds that population increase can be strongly correlated with economic development, providing larger markets, economies of scale, and so forth. That is a nice model theoretically, but in my view it has little relevance for the chaotic, unchecked population growth of Latin America. Nor does it pay sufficient attention to the noneconomic arguments, such as the social, political, and security dimensions presented here or to the Latin Americans' desire to limit family size. Simon's arguments do not hold up under close scrutiny or in the light of Latin American realities. But in political Washington they have been seized upon as providing rationalizations for decisions already made. They provide a convenient set of arguments that politicians or governments can use to justify positions arrived at on other grounds.[36]

The question is: If the real facts are so obvious, if unchecked population growth is as potentially calamitous a problem as it has been presented here, why are American policy makers so strongly opposed to doing anything about it? Or are they really that reluctant?

The Politics of Population Policy in Washington, D.C. Several reasons may be adduced for the declining attention to population policy in the nation's capital. These reasons also make it clear why, despite the severity of the problem, we can expect little in the way of new policy initiatives in this area in the near future.

First, the climate of the country has changed. Since Vietnam, U.S. policy makers are less inclined to get deeply involved in the internal affairs of other nations; and population policy is no longer considered a cure-all. The country is also more conservative and less inclined to legislate in this most intimate of private and family affairs: regulating births.

Second, Catholic, Protestant evangelical, and pro-life lobbies are far stronger than before. No congressman or presidential candidate is going to risk political suicide by bucking these groups. If the primary concern of politicians is reelection, as the political science literature strongly suggests,[37] in the current climate they would have to be downright irrational to support population policy.

Third, population issues tend to be long-term and based on demographic projections rather than immediate and obvious. When demographers tell us that by the year 2025 Latin America's population will be "umpteen" million, the eyes of politicians, whose chief concern is the 1986 or 1988 election, glaze over. If population issues become dramatic and immediate, in the form of food riots and collapsing governments, then politicians will become concerned; but not before.

Fourth, population policy has no constituency in this country. In this regard it is like foreign aid. Moreover, if the politician believes support of population policy or of foreign aid will cost him votes at home, he will avoid it like the plague. Unchecked immigration into Miami and the Southwest may cause this perception to change in some voting districts; but it is not yet perceived as a national problem requiring national attention. Population policy has a considerable number of dedicated and activist supporters, but they are insufficient to force legislation or administrative action when so many other, seemingly more pressing issues demand attention.

Fifth, U.S. foreign aid generally is down since the late 1960s. The decline has affected programs that are believed to have an effect on population, such as education, health, income generation, and agrarian reform. As Congress and the executive branch continue to dispute the dollar amounts to be included in the foreign aid bill, how much of that would go to population versus other programs, and what kind of population policy to have, the U.S. Agency for International Development (AID) lacks direction as well as finances for dealing with population issues or for supporting stronger family planning efforts abroad.

Sixth, some of the U.S., UN, and private organizations responsible for carrying out population policy have a spotty record. Some are losing U.S. financial support because of their activities in support of abortion. Quite a number have been accused of overbureaucratization and of granting sinecures, of supporting bogus programs, of doctoring statistics, of providing misleading information about their programs, of failing to provide adequate medical follow-up, and of a host of other sins of omission and commission. Some ostensibly private groups have become fronts for the U.S. government and have engaged in various deceptive practices. Others have turned to "safe" projects like demographic studies while ignoring action programs. In some cases these actions can be justified, but overall the activities of the population agencies leave a lot to be desired. Their overzealous and ill-advised actions in far too many instances have helped poison the climate for the very programs they are charged with carrying out.

Seventh, neither President Carter nor President Reagan has been convinced of the efficacy of population policy, or of its morality. Nor is it likely that the present administration will change its mind on this issue. This is an issue on which the president feels deeply, and it is unlikely that lobbying or the commissioning of polls showing most Americans to be pro-choice or indifferent will make much dent. Those groups that are lobbying to change Mr. Reagan's mind are probably wasting their time.

Eighth, when the president and the politicians feel strongly on an issue, the bureaucracy tends to be cautious. AID, for example, which administers population programs abroad, is likely to be very circumspect at least for the duration of Mr. Reagan's second term. Its administrators do not wish to be put out to pasture if they espouse a policy contrary to the administration's, as occurred in the 1984 debate over the U.S. position to be presented at the world population conference held in Mexico City; nor do they wish to be targeted by conservative or pro-life groups for being out of line. It seems likely that officially sponsored and sanctioned activities in the population field, short of any new directives from the executive, will be very carefully brought forward in the next several years.

Yet, population policy continues to be implemented, and the programs continue to grow. The rhetoric against some aspects of population policy (such as abortion programs) has sometimes been strong, but in practice not much has changed or is likely to. Congress continues to provide and even augment the funding, AID's population programs continue to expand, and the White House has generally, though quietly, gone along.[38] Except for occasional blips (such as the headlines generated over the Mexico City conference) the trend line in U.S. government support of population policy has gone steadily upward since at least the 1960s. The lessons for population policy advocates seem to be: (1) support population policy quietly rather than loudly; (2) do it in a way that does not antagonize key domestic interest groups; (3) do it in a way that avoids embarrassing the White House or congressmen; and (4) do not expect to be able to criticize some aspects of administration policy and still get funding for population programs. With these lessons in mind, much can be done in the population policy area—not necessarily dramatically but quietly, incrementally, and with quite impressive results.

Conclusions and Implications

There are strong arguments for a sound and serious population policy as part of overall U.S. foreign policy in Latin America. Such a policy should be modest and restrained; unrealistic expectations should not be raised. Limits should be recognized on what population policy can produce, what can be expected. Population policy can be a useful component of a larger, overall development policy; it cannot be viewed as a panacea, a cure-all, or a substitute for a more broadly-conceived developmental strategy. But today, most Latin Americans, including key decision-making elites, now support one or another form of family planning—a marked turnabout from the situation twenty years ago. That Latin America's unchecked population growth is beginning to have, in the form of massive migration to the U.S. South and Southwest, an effect on the United States and on its politicians and their constituencies provides an added reason to pay serious attention to the issue.

If population policy is to receive serious attention in the United States, however, these concerns will have to be combined with national security concerns. That is how Robert McNamara "sold" population policy to Lyndon Johnson; national security was also the principal grounds for launching such notable programs as the Alliance for Progress and the Caribbean Basin Initiative.[39] "That is where the money is," as the notorious Willie Sutton said when asked why he robbed banks; national security is also "where the money is" in mobilizing the American public and, eventually, its politicians to support population policy.

This chapter has explored and analyzed the national security implications of unchecked population growth in Latin America. We have examined the interrelations between population growth, crowding, and tension; the implications of a disproportionately young and dependent population and of this younger generation's coming soon to power; the rising pressures on the land and on agriculture caused by the population explosion throughout the hemisphere; the effects of too-rapid urbanization and migration in producing ungovernability; the strong effects of emigration and refugee problems; the worsening economic conditions of the area; the rising social tensions and potential for explosion; the unraveling of the region's political systems and the dimming of the prospects for democracy; and finally the potential for war and international conflict. These facts and trends add up to a compelling case for population policy on U.S. national security grounds. They also suggest a strategy for advocating a stronger U.S. role in the population area.

And yet, at least in the near to intermediate term, for all the reasons already given, nothing dramatic is likely to happen. The climate is not propitious. Too many strong interests are opposed. Politicians do not wish to touch it for fear of being burned. The population agencies have not always acted responsibly, and there are a lot of old skeletons and scandals to be dredged up. For these reasons and others, it will likely require a real crisis for population policy to progress further and for the United States to begin implementing an effective program. That is, after all, how U.S. foreign policy in Latin America most often is initiated: in response to crisis. That would have to take the form of really massive (if El Salvador or Guatemala, for example, begin to disintegrate or if Mexico is destabilized) emigration from Latin America to the United States and an equally massive clamoring that the U.S. government do something about it. Or perhaps policy action would be precipitated by the collapse and takeover

153

by the revolutionary left of one or more Central American governments in ways that pointed dramatically to unchecked population growth as a major contributing factor. Neither of these two things is likely to happen soon or in the manner described, which also helps explain why any new, let alone dramatic, initiatives in the population policy area are also unlikely to be forthcoming. Meanwhile, at lower and less dramatic levels, and keeping in mind the lessons suggested, quite a bit continues quietly to be accomplished.

Notes

1. Paul Ehrlich, *The Population Bomb* (New York: Ballantine, 1968).

2. John V.D. Saunders, *Population Growth in Latin America and U.S. National Security* (Boston: Allen and Unwin, 1986), Preface. See also U.S. Department of Commerce, Bureau of the Census, *Illustrative Projections of World Populations to the 21st Century* (Washington, D.C.: U.S. Bureau of the Census, 1979).
It should be noted that in the so-called middle-income countries of Latin America, birth rates have fallen more than death rates, which has slowed the rate of population growth somewhat. In Brazil, Mexico, Colombia, and Cuba the declines have been noticeable (from more than 2.5 percent to around or below 2 percent growth rate per year). Venezuela, probably the richest country per capita, has gone from a 5.8 percent growth rate between 1975–1980 to an estimated 3.3 percent growth rate for 1980–1981. The poorer countries such as El Salvador, Guatemala, Honduras, and Nicaragua still show growth rates of close to or greater than 3 percent per year. In Bolivia and Peru the growth rate is still 2.5 percent. Overall the growth rate for Latin America is still above 2.5 percent and shows no sign of changing greatly in the short term—although there are considerable variations between countries. U.S. Department of Commerce, Bureau of the Census, *Demographic Estimates for Countries with a Population of 10 Million or More: 1981* (Washington, D.C.: U.S. Bureau of the Census, 1981).

3. One of the best sources for the early history of U.S. involvement remains Phyllis T. Piotrow, *World Population Crisis: The United States Response* (New York: Praeger, 1973).

4. Julian L. Simon, *The Ultimate Resource* (Princeton, N.J.: Princeton University Press, 1981); Simon, *The Economics of Population Growth* (Princeton, N.J.: Princeton University Press, 1977).

5. J. Mayone Stycos, *Human Fertility in Latin America: Sociological Perspectives* (Ithaca, N.Y.: Cornell University Press, 1968).

6. Ibid.; see also the essays on these groups in Terry McCoy, ed., *The Dynamics of Population Policy in Latin America* (Cambridge, Mass.: Ballinger Publishing Co., 1974).

7. David K. Willis, "World Population," series in the *Christian Science Monitor*, August 6–13, 1984; Bart McDowell and S. Maze, "Mexico City: An Alarming Giant," and Robert Fox, "The Urban Explosion," *National Geographic* (August 1984), pp. 138–86.

8. The best sources on these changes for many years were the annual Factbooks written by Dorothy Nortman for the Population Council. The earlier positions of Latin American governments (up to 1970) are summarized by Vivian X. Epstein, "The Politics of Population in Latin America," chapter 7 in David Chaplin, ed., *Population Policies and Growth in Latin America* (Lexington, Mass.: Lexington Books, 1971).

9. Howard J. Wiarda, "The Politics of Population Policy in the Dominican Republic: Public Policy and the Political Process," chapter 13 in McCoy, ed., *Dynamics*. See also Pranay Gapte, *The Crowded Earth* (New York: W. W. Norton, 1984).

10. Iêda Siqueira Wiarda and Judith F. Helzner, *Women, Population and International Development in Latin America* (Amherst, Mass.: International Studies Program, University of Massachusetts, 1981).

11. Iêda Siqueira Wiarda, "Approaches and Strategies of Population Policy-Making in a Democratic Context: The Case of Venezuela," chapter 14 in McCoy, ed., *Dynamics*; Benjamin Viel, *The Demographic Explosion: The Latin American Experience* (New York: Irvington Publishers, 1976); Aaron L. Segal, ed., *Population Policy in the Caribbean* (Lexington, Mass.: Lexington Books, 1975).

12. Good reviews of the literature on this subject may be found in Nazli Choucri, ed., *Multidisciplinary Perspectives on Population and Conflict* (Syracuse, N.Y.: Syracuse University Press, 1984).

13. Alistair Hennessey, *The Frontier in Latin America* (Albuquerque, N.M.: University of New Mexico Press, 1978). Jane M. Loy, *The Llanos in Colombian History: Some Implications of a Static Frontier* (Amherst, Mass.: Program in Latin American Studies, University of Massachusetts, 1976).

14. For a perceptive account of deteriorating conditions in Lima, Peru, see *New York Times* (December 28, 1984).

15. S. M. Lipset, ed., *Rebellion in the University* (Chicago: University of Chicago Press, 1976).

16. Thomas Walker, ed., *Nicaragua in Revolution* (N.Y.: Praeger, 1982).

17. John Womack, *Zapata and the Mexican Revolution* (New York: Knopf, 1968).

18. World Bank, *World Development Report 1984*. p. 93.

19. "Mexico City: The Population Curse," lead article in *Time* (August 6, 1984).

20. World Bank, *World Development Report 1984*, p. 97.

21. For good reviews of these matters, see Lorene Y. L. Yep, "The Attraction of Cities: A Review of Migration Literature," *Journal of Development Economies*, vol. 4 (1971), pp. 239–64.

22. Glenn Hendricks, *Dominican Diaspora: From the Dominican Republic to New York City, Villagers in Transition* (New York: Teachers College Press of Columbia University, 1974).

23. Michael S. Teitelbaum, "Migration and United States-Latin American Relations in the 1980s" (Washington: The Wilson Center Latin America Program, Working Papers No. 151, 1984).

24. Recent analyses include Joseph Grunwald, "Perspectives on the Latin

155

American Economic Crisis" in Howard J. Wiarda, ed., *The Crisis in Latin America: Strategic, Economic and Political Dimensions* (Washington, D.C.: American Enterprise Institute for Public Policy Research, 1984); and William Glade, "Latin America: Options and Non-Options in Contemporary Development Strategy," in Howard J. Wiarda, ed., *The Alternative Futures of Latin America: AEI Foreign Policy and Defense Review,* vol. 5, no. 3 (Washington, D.C.: American Enterprise Institute, 1985). See also Howard J. Wiarda, *Latin America at the Crossroads: Debt, Development and the Future* (Boulder, Colo.: Westview Press, 1987).

25. "Recession Exposes Fragility of Latin American Social Progress" (Geneva: International Labor Organization, December 1984).

26. Sol Tax, *Penny Capitalism: A Guatemalan Indian Economy* (Chicago: University of Chicago Press, 1963).

27. Crane Brinton, *The Anatomy of Revolution* (New York: Random House, 1965); and Ted Robert Gurr, *Why Men Rebel* (Princeton: Princeton Unviersity Press, 1970).

28. Michael J. Kryzanek, "Dominican Republic" in Jack Hopkins, ed., *Latin America and Caribbean Contemporary Record* (New York: Holmes and Meier).

29. See especially James Payne, "The Politics of Structured Violence," *Journal of Politics* 27 (May 1965), pp. 362–74; Payne, *Labor and Politics in Peru: The System of Political Bargaining* (New Haven, Conn.: Yale University Press, 1965).

30. For a more complete description of that system, see *The Conflict Society: Reaction and Revolution in Latin America* (New York: American Universities Field Staff, 1966); Charles W. Anderson, *Politics and Economic Change in Latin America: The Governing of Restless Nations* (Princeton, N.J.: D. Van Nostrand, 1967); and Howard J. Wiarda and Harvey F. Kline, eds., *Latin American Politics and Development* (Boulder, Colo.: Westview Press, 1985), part one.

31. A useful overview is Mark Falcoff, "Arms and Politics Revisited: Latin America as a Military and Strategic Theater," in Wiarda, ed., *Crisis.*

32. Thomas P. Anderson, *The War of the Dispossessed* (Lincoln, Neb.: University of Nebraska Press, 1981).

33. Edward J. Williams, "Mexico's Central American Policy: National Security Implications," in Howard J. Wiarda, ed., *Rift and Revolution: The Central American Imbroglio* (Washington, D.C.: American Enterprise Institute, 1984), pp. 303–28.

34. An astute observer of Latin America, Victor Alba, has predicted increased international conflict in the future between and among the Latin American countries; see his *The Latin Americans* (New York: Praeger, 1969).

35. For further background see Howard J. Wiarda, *In Search of Policy: The United States and Latin America* (Washington, D.C.: American Enterprise Institute, 1984).

36. A scholarly and balanced review of Simon's work appears in "Review Symposium on *The Ultimate Resource," Population and Development Review,* vol. 8 (March 1982), 163–78. For a perspective at odds with the one presented here see Ben Wattenberg and Karl Zinsmeister, ed., *Are World Population Trends a Problem?* (Washington, D.C.: American Enterprise Institute, 1985).

37. David Mayhew, *Congress: The Electoral Connection* (New Haven: Yale University Press, 1974).

38. "Analysis and Commentary I and II: 1984 Developments, 1985 Implications," *Washington Memo*, Jan. 9 and 11, 1985.

39. For McNamara's most recent arguments, see his "Time Bomb or Myth: The Population Problem," *Foreign Affairs*, vol. 62 (Summer 1984), pp. 1107–31.

8
Updating U.S. Strategic Policy: Containment in the Caribbean Basin

Latin America has long been of peripheral interest in terms of a global U.S. foreign policy. Historically U.S. concerns have chiefly centered on the European countries, on the European military and strategic theater, and since World War II particularly on the Soviet Union. In the ordering of our foreign policy concerns the area ranks behind the Soviet Union, Western Europe and NATO, the Middle East, Japan, China, and the broader Pacific Basin. Because of the crisis in Central America, and in the broader area of the Caribbean Basin, however—regions that are close to the United States geographically—our historic lack of interest has begun to change. Latin America and our Latin America policy are now being taken seriously for the first time; the area is coming under increased scrutiny from scholars, research institutes, strategic analysts, and policy makers.[1]

The question is not just whether we have devoted sufficient attention to Latin America, however, but also whether the fundamental assumptions of the policy we have followed are adequate and still relevant and appropriate in the altered circumstances of today. For Latin America has changed greatly in the past twenty years, and so has the United States, as well as the nature of the relations between us; these changes prompt us to ask whether policy must correspondingly be adjusted.[2]

Historic U.S. Policy in Latin America

U.S. policy in Latin America and the strategic thinking and assumptions undergirding it have not changed greatly since Admiral Alfred

Published in Terry L. Deibel and John Lewis Gaddis, eds., *Containment: Concept and Policy* (Washington, D.C.: National Defense University Press, 1986).

Thayer Mahan (and with him Teddy Roosevelt) first articulated a coherent and integrated policy for the region almost exactly one hundred years ago.[3] In fact, strategic policy has not changed greatly since the days of the famous Monroe doctrine. Moreover the fundamentals of the policy have been remarkably consistent and continuous over this long history, regardless of the party or administration in power. Only the means used to achieve these agreed-upon goals have varied.[4]

The bedrocks of U.S. policy in the Caribbean Basin include the following:[5]

- Protect the "soft underbelly" of the United States. Since we have thousands of miles of oceans on our east and west coasts, and a friendly nation to our north, our primary strategic concern in this hemisphere has been with the small, unstable nations to our south. Indeed it is their smallness, weakness, and chronic instability that gives rise to the fear in the U.S. that a hostile foreign power will take advantage of their debility and establish a base in the Caribbean region from which to launch offensives against the United States itself. The U.S. has therefore maintained—particularly since the building of the Panama Canal—a string of bases, radar tracking stations, and the like throughout the Caribbean.
- Maintain access to the area's raw materials, primary products, markets, and labor supply. This implies supporting a policy of free trade, open markets, and easy and direct U.S. investments. U.S. economic activity in the area is also viewed as a way to maintain stability and to discourage potential competitors.
- Keep hostile foreign powers, or maybe *any* foreign powers, away from an area thought of as lying within our sphere of influence. This policy in the past has meant directing action against Russia, Spain, France, Britain, and Germany; since World War II it has meant excluding the Soviet Union from the area.
- Maintain stability in ways that are supportive of the basic interests listed above. In general, this means supporting whatever government friendly to our interests happens to be in power, while also keeping lines of communications open to the moderate opposition. Maintaining stability means not necessarily defending the status quo but includes supporting change and reform to head off the possibility of instability arising from popular dissatisfaction.

From these basic principles of U.S. policy in Latin America, which is in fact a long-term and historic strategy of exclusion and containment, several corollaries follow:

159

• U.S. policy has consistently been more concerned with the countries in Central America and the Caribbean that are close geographically than with those more distant in South America.

• U.S. policy in the area has historically been oriented toward crisis.
Because ours is essentially a defensive policy in an area we have not
thought of as very important, we have responded to crises after
they occur rather than developing a more positive, mature, long-
term, and anticipatory policy.

• Democracy and human rights have been accorded secondary importance. We have supported democracy and a strong human
rights policy to the degree that they have helped secure stability
and protect our other interests, but not usually for their own sake or
as a fundamental aspect of U.S. policy.

• The same is true of economic and social development. We tend to
emphasize these programs as a means to preserve stability when
the nations of the area are threatened by Castro-like revolutions. In
noncrisis times, however, our attitude is generally one of benign
neglect.

Our basic policy in Latin America, therefore, has been one of
hegemony, containment, and balance of power. The question is
whether these historic bases of policy, which still undergird a great
deal of policy thinking today, continue to be useful and relevant
under the changed conditions in which we and the Latin Americans
now find ourselves.

New Realities in U.S.–Latin American Relations

Changes in the United States, in Latin America, and in the inter-
American system strongly affect the continuity, relevance, and utility
of U.S. containment policy vis-à-vis Latin America. They are the "new
realities" that need to be examined.[6]

The United States. Among many basic changes in the United States in
the past twenty years, the following may be of special importance:

• The United States since Vietnam is considerably chastened and
wary of foreign entanglements. We do not wish to be involved
deeply in Central America, and we certainly do not want to commit
U.S. ground forces.

• Because the public and Congress will not countenance large new
foreign aid programs for Latin America, the United States has fewer
levers of influence in Latin America.

• The Department of Defense is also wary of new interventions in countries where the goals are not clear, public opinion is divided, a prolonged war may result, and discredit is likely to be reflected on the military. We want no more "Vietnams."

• The U.S. foreign policy–making process is more fragmented, chaotic, and paralyzed than before. It is now far more difficult for us to carry out a long-term, coherent, bipartisan foreign policy.[7]

• Isolationist sentiment is strong. We want no more "Cubas" in the Caribbean, but we are unwilling to provide the funds or programs to ensure that does not happen.

• The United States is a weaker presence in Latin America than it has been. Our political, military, diplomatic, cultural, and economic leverage has been significantly lessened. Our capacity to act in the region has thereby been reduced.

Latin America. In Latin America the following changes have occurred.

• Latin America is more developed, modern, and sophisticated than before. We can no longer treat its nations as "banana republics" amenable to quick fixes.

• Latin America is more assertive and nationalistic; it now listens to the United States reluctantly if at all. We can no longer easily impose our will.

• Latin America is now more socially and politically differentiated and pluralistic. We must deal with these new complexities.

• The Latin American nations are now pursuing more independent foreign policies than before. They wish to distance themselves from the United States while not losing our assistance programs in the process.

• Latin America's priorities are now quite different from those of the United States. Our concerns are overwhelmingly strategic, theirs are primarily economic.

• Latin America is going through both a period of crisis and a period of experimentation with new forms. They plead for patience, and we frequently confuse the two tendencies.

Inter-American Relations. The following changes have taken place in the realm of the inter-American system.

• The structure of the inter-American relationship has been badly damaged through neglect, inattention, and failure to live up to its obligations—in Central America and in the 1982 Falklands/Malvinas war, for example.

• Although the United States seems more chastened and weaker

than it was twenty years ago, the larger and more militarily powerful Latin American states (Argentina, Brazil, Mexico, Venezuela,
Cuba) are far stronger, have become middle-ranking powers, and
are pursuing more independent foreign policies.
• Several new outside powers—West Germany, France, Spain,
Japan, the Soviet Union, and others—have begun to play a larger
role in the area. The United States no longer has the monopoly it
once had.
• New issues—drugs, debt, human rights, democracy, protectionism, trade, migration—have begun to replace the historic strategic ones. Latin American priorities in these matters are often quite
different from U.S. priorities.
• The United States has become more dependent on Latin America
for manufactured and primary goods, rendering our relationship
one of far more complex interdependence than in the past.
• Latin America has greatly diversified its international ties in recent
years, opening new relations with Eastern Europe, China, and the
Soviet Union, among others; the United States is no longer the only
country with which it has important relations.

These trends must be factored into the new equations of inter-
American relations and into our assessment of the adequacy of traditional U.S. containment policy. To these must now be added the rising
presence of the Soviet Union and of its proxy Cuba throughout the
area.

The Soviet Presence in Latin America

Containment policy was aimed at excluding the Soviet Union from the
Western Hemisphere, and until the late 1950s the policy worked quite
well. There were small Communist parties in most countries of the
hemisphere, but they lacked popular support or a strong organizational base, and the notion of Stalinist troops disembarking on Latin
America's shores was—as it deserved to be—dismissed as ludicrous.
In 1954 the United States intervened in Guatemala to help oust a
populist-leftist government in which some Communists held key
posts, but until Cuba the walls that excluded the Soviets from Latin
America remained unbreachable.[8]

The Cuban revolution of 1959, Fidel Castro's declaration of Marxism-Leninism, and the incorporation of Cuba into the Soviet camp
changed all that. From that point on, the Soviets had a base in the
Western hemisphere for political and military operations. During the
1960s the Cubans tried, with Soviet assistance, to export their revolution to other Latin American countries. The United States responded

with what came to be called the "no-second-Cuba doctrine," taking vigorous steps to prevent what happened in Cuba from happening in other countries.

In 1962, with the installation of offensive Soviet missiles in Cuba pointed at the United States, a new element was added to the equation. In a tense confrontation, the United States forced the Soviet Union to remove the missiles from Cuba while itself agreeing tacitly not to continue seeking the overthrow of the Castro regime. With this showdown the no-second-Cuba doctrine acquired a double meaning for the United States: the prevention of Castro-like revolutions throughout the hemisphere and the insistence that no Latin American country be used as a base for the implantation of sophisticated Soviet military hardware with an offensive capability that might threaten the United States. It remained unclear precisely where the lines would be drawn, but certainly the United States was unwilling to accept the presence of MIG fighter planes in Nicaragua.

The response of the United States to the Cuban revolution was massive. For the first time we began paying serious attention to Latin America. We quarantined Cuba, broke relations, and imposed a trade embargo on the island. We launched the Peace Corps and the Alliance for Progress (see chapter 9), as well as a host of other development-related programs, as a way of heading off the growth of revolutionary sentiment. We initiated training programs in civic action and counterinsurgency for the Latin American militaries, and we assisted several countries in defeating their Cuba-inspired and -assisted guerrilla movements. When these other measures failed, the United States intervened militarily in the Dominican Republic in 1965 to prevent what it thought was a Cuba-like revolution from succeeding.

These efforts were remarkably successful in medium-range terms. The embargo of Cuba kept that country isolated and economically unsuccessful, which meant Cuba never became an attractive model for the other Latin American countries. By the late 1960s, especially with the death of Che Guevara in Bolivia, the Cuba-like guerrilla movements had been all but eliminated in most countries. Even though many of its assumptions were erroneous concerning the political role of the Latin American middle class and the capacity of the United States to bring democracy to Latin America, the Alliance for Progress stimulated some badly needed development in Latin America and helped enable the United States to avoid more Cubas. By the end of the 1960s the threat to Latin America seemed sufficiently minimal that the United States could revert to its traditional policy of "benign neglect."

The inattention devoted to Latin American in the early to

mid-1970s was understandable but ultimately mistaken in long-range terms. Preoccupied by Vietnam and Watergate, we virtually ignored Latin America for most of the decade. We thus missed the opportunities in the early 1970s to influence the course of events in El Salvador, Guatemala, and Nicaragua that would have prevented those countries from becoming such problem cases later on. Our foreign assistance decreased significantly. The number of U.S. personnel and programs in Latin America was greatly reduced. In not paying attention to the area we sacrificed most of the levers of influence that we had once had. Meanwhile new realities discussed earlier rendered obsolete many of our traditional security doctrines. Hence when Latin America (Nicaragua, Grenada, El Salvador) blew up again in the late 1970s we were quite unprepared.[9]

In the meantime some additional new realities had been added, the primary one being the rising Soviet presence in Latin America. During the 1970s its normal state-to-state relations with almost all the countries of the area had increased enormously. Using Cuba as its agent, the Soviet Union has become a significant military presence in the Caribbean. Soviet trade and commercial relations have grown enormously—the Soviet Union is, for example, Argentina's largest export customer. In Peru the Soviets have military equipment and military training programs. Soviet cultural and diplomatic activities have increased, as have Soviet political and subversion efforts. The Soviet Union is by no means an equal of the United States in Latin America, but its influence and presence are clearly increasing.[10]

The Soviet Union is practicing far more sophisticated tactics and strategies. It is less heavy-handed and more subtle, playing for the long term while not ignoring possibilities for the short term. It ingratiates itself with the democratic regimes while simultaneously seeking to push them toward nonalignment (and in some cases continues to aid their opposition forces). It deftly uses aid, scholarships, military programs, and trade to advance its interests. It has a different strategy for different countries, following a flexible course rather than a rigid ideological formula. In the meantime it has imposed order, coherence, and unity of direction on otherwise disparate guerrilla groups. It cleverly uses Cuba and Nicaragua as its proxies while also directing and overseeing a sophisticated division of labor among its fellow Communist bloc countries. The Soviets have also become far more clever at manipulating opinion in Western Europe and the United States.[11]

Finite limits also exist, however, on the Soviet role in Latin America. The Soviets still do not function especially well in that context, and Latin America is not particularly sympathetic to a Communist system. What the Soviets have been able to do cleverly and quite successfully, however, is to attach themselves to popular revolutionary movements ostensibly designed to promote national independence and social justice throughout Latin America, and to play upon and take advantage of Latin America's rising nationalism and anti-Americanism. The Soviets do not wish to challenge the United States unnecessarily in a part of the world that allows the United States an overwhelming local advantage and that is of only peripheral importance to the Soviet Union. Within these limits, nonetheless, the Soviet gains in the past fifteen years have been impressive.[12]

The U.S. response to the new Soviet initiatives has been a resurrection of the older containment policy. We suppressed the revolution in Grenada through military intervention, and we have put immense pressures—military, political, economic, and diplomatic—on the Sandinista regime in Nicaragua, though the exact goals there remain ambiguous. We threatened to "go to the source" by, presumably, eliminating Cuba as a root cause of the troubles in Latin America. We proclaimed, at least in the early months of the administration, that the conflict in El Salvador was an East-West struggle; and there were some hints, almost certainly exaggerated, that the cold war might be decided or turned around there. Our military/strategic buildup in the region has been immense.[13]

A strong case can be made that this military buildup was necessary, and it is certainly to be preferred to the hand-wringing and inaction of the Carter administration. Again we need to ask, however, whether the traditional containment policy we have followed is any longer adequate in the changed circumstances. The answer is that it is not; that it badly needs updating and greater sophistication; that we need to go, as in the title of one of the better books on the subject, beyond containment;[14] and that the current administration recognizes this and has begun to move in the directions that are absolutely necessary if our policies in Latin America are to be successful.

"Economy of Force": Containment Policy in Latin America

An important part of American strategic policy in Latin America is based on the notion of what strategic planners call economy of force. The strategy assumes that the Soviet Union is the country with which the United States is most likely to engage in any future conflict. It goes on to assume that such a conflict, were it to break out, would most likely occur in Central Europe or perhaps the Middle East. In such an eventuality the United States would want to rush all its resources to the locus of the conflict as soon as possible. It would not want to have its forces tied down or preoccupied with some local skirmish or by a local adversary when the more vital strategic needs lie elsewhere. Hence if the region of the Caribbean Basin can be kept free of Communist regimes and revolutions, if only an economy of force can be used to pacify that area, then U.S. resources can be concentrated where the real conflict is likely to be—on the plains of Central Europe.[15]

The economy-of-force strategy has in the past been fairly successful. We managed to isolate Cuba and kept it from meddling in the internal affairs of other nations. We limited Cuba's capacity to export its revolution to other countries. On a small island, Grenada, our intervention got rid of the local Marxist-Leninist regime and replaced it with one that would not sow revolution in the other small islands. In Nicaragua we have, through our support of and assistance to the resistance forces (the so-called contras), tied down the Nicaraguan armed forces, which had been enormously built up since the revolution, kept Nicaragua from spreading its revolution to its neighbors, and employed a mercenary army as a way of avoiding any commitment of U.S. ground forces.

But the economy-of-force strategy has several problems and conceptual flaws. First, it continues to treat Latin America as a sideshow, peripheral to the main action. Many analysts, however, are convinced that continuing to ignore Latin America or treating it as if it were of only peripheral importance is precisely what foments revolutions and anti-Americanism in the area and that this attitude is at the root of our policy difficulties there. Second, it underestimates the difficulties domestically of sustaining a long-term proxy war in Central America, of carrying out a coherent policy over time given the play of domestic interest groups and opposition forces, and it overestimates the capacity of the United States to intervene with military force where necessary.[16]

Third, it assumes that Europe will be the main theater and that the war will be fought like the last one, involving tank and ground forces and perhaps some limited tactical nuclear weapons, in the heartland of the Continent. A strong argument can be made, however, that such a high-technology but conventional war in the European center is the *least* likely kind of war we will be called on to fight. Far more likely are murky guerrilla struggles of the kind we are now witnessing in Central America or that we had previously seen in Cuba, Vietnam, and Angola. Unfortunately it is these more irregular wars that the United States, even with all its verbal commitments to counterinsurgency training and preparation over the past twenty years, is the least equipped and trained to deal with.[17]

The Evolution of Administration Policy

The administration of President Reagan got off to a rather uncertain start in dealing with Latin America. In part that stemmed from its efforts to resurrect the rather unrefined containment policy of the past rather than the more nuanced policy that later evolved and that is absolutely essential if policy is to be successful. That is, the administration saw Cuba and the Soviet Union as the prime causes of the insurrection in Central America, it pictured the conflict in exclusively East-West terms, and it tended to view the problem and its solution in a purely military way. One recalls not only the early and sometimes unfortunate statements of administration spokesmen to this effect but also their denigrating other related aspects of the problem—agrarian reform, human rights, and foreign aid.

Since then the administration has developed a much more sophisticated and multifaceted approach. In part the changes are due to opposition to the administration's policies from the Congress, the media, our allies, and the public, which have forced the administration to compromise and to temper its policies. In part the changes are due to bureaucratic politics and rivalries within the government and to the reassertion of State Department and foreign policy professionals of their expertise and more moderate views. And in part it is due to a learning process that has occurred within the administration, stimulated by the polls as well as by the more middle-of-the-road views and expertise found in the research institutes and other advisory organizations. These and other influences have forced the administration back to a more mainstream foreign policy position.

The administration now sees Central America as both an East-West and a North-South issue. It understands the indigenous roots of revolution in the area as well as the capacity of the Cubans and Soviets to fan the flames of revolution, to exacerbate a crisis that already exists, and to take maximum advantage of the situation to embarrass the United States in its own backyard as well as to score gains for themselves. U.S. policies are now multifaceted rather than unidimensional. These new tacks are both more moderate and more refined than the older, sometimes heavy-handed orientation, which occasionally led to policy gaffes and thereby often defeated the purposes it sought to accomplish.

The administration's response has been increasingly pragmatic as well. It now understands the need to balance its military and strategic emphasis with a concern for democracy and human rights. It sees the necessity for social and economic assistance as well as military aid. It supports agrarian reform and other programs of change as a way of securing long-term stability in the area and diminishing the appeals of communism. It has learned to work indirectly, behind the scenes, and through third parties rather than by means of the either-or confrontational strategies of the past. It has built up the U.S. military presence in the area but also recognizes the dire need of these countries for economic recovery. It has put enormous political, economic, and military pressures on the Sandinista regime, but it has also kept open the possibilities for diplomatic negotiations.

The concrete manifestation of these more sophisticated strategies may be found in the Caribbean Basin Initiative and in the Kissinger Commission recommendations. The CBI is a forward-looking assistance program combining public foreign aid with the encouragement of private investment that is not much different from Kennedy's Alliance for Progress. The Kissinger Commission Report contains similar recommendations for a judicious blend of public and private assistance, economic and military aid, strategic and democratic/human rights concerns. It is a complex, multifaceted package that reflects the new, more moderate and sophisticated stance of the administration, and the commission itself was an instrument in forging a more tempered and balanced strategy. The commission's recommendations are in fact now administration policy in Central America, although not all of them have been formally enacted into law by the Congress.[18]

Conclusion: Toward an Updated Containment Strategy

The containment strategy and the companion economy-of-force doctrine would seem in the present, more complex circumstances to be woefully outdated—at least as these strategies were practiced in their traditional forms.[19] The containment strategy was based on an earlier conception of the global conflict as exclusively bipolar, grounded on mutual understanding of spheres of influence, derived from the idea that both superpowers could and would police their own backyards, organized exclusively around an East-West axis, and based on the principle that whatever disruptions occurred in the first power's backyard must be due to the machinations of the other power. There were considerable elements of truth in all of these assertions, but they are inadequate as a complete and sufficient explanation for the recent upheavals in Central America.

In Central America the problems are far more complex, deeprooted, and intractable than the administration first thought. Many of them cannot be resolved as easily, quickly, or cheaply as originally envisaged. The fundamental problem, however, in dealing with Central America is, I believe, conceptual.[20] We are still relying on policies and strategies having to do with great power tactics, containment, geopolitical position, spheres of influence, and balance of power that in Latin America need badly to be rethought and updated. Some of these strategies are anachronistic, others need to be reconceived. The fact is they were designed for an earlier and simpler era, and they no longer have the same relevance in today's Latin America. For Latin America's new realities—a changed and generally weaker U.S. role, a new assertiveness and independence on the part of the Latin American nations, a desperate desire on the part of their peoples for development and social justice, the presence of other outside actors in the area, the changed inter-American system—all imply the need for a fundamental reevaluation of policy.

We cannot here provide a complete analysis of the policies that ought to be pursued, but we can at least provide some guidelines.[21] We need to be *engaged* in Latin America with empathy and understanding and not just view it as a sideshow. We need to normalize and regularize our relations with the area and not pay attention to Latin America only in times of crisis. We need a sophisticated and multifaceted program for the area as proposed by the Kissinger Commission but so far only partially implemented. We need a policy that incorporates expanded cultural and student exchanges, economic and debt aid, a vigorous human rights program, investment and trade programs, assistance for social modernization, support for democratization, and greater contacts between U.S. and Latin American groups, as well as attention to the strategic and military considerations. We need to provide training for responding to guerrilla war, and we require a reassessment of strategic thinking and tactics. On this basis a prudent, realistic, and more sophisticated policy can be developed for the area.

Specifically, we need to do the following: we need far more training in limited and irregular war capacity and counter-insurgency, in both rural and urban settings. We need to increase our foreign assistance and our leverage. We need to examine and understand thoroughly the several changed conditions of Latin America outlined here and their concrete implications for foreign policy. We need a program to develop our capacities to understand Latin America in its own terms and context rather than through our own biased and often ethnocentric lenses.[22] We certainly need better language and area studies programs in our foreign policy–making agencies, not just in Spanish and Portuguese but also in such native Indian languages as

Quechua and Aymará. We need to understand and respond realistically to the rising Soviet and Cuban presence in the area and their new, more sophisticated tactics. And we need to develop programs, such as the Army's medical-vaccination teams, or in AID, to deal with Latin America's problems on the ground, close to the people, in terms the Latin Americans will both know and appreciate. In these ways we can also update and modernize our containment strategy, which is still a viable policy for the United States in Latin America but which is badly in need of a new formulation.

Notes

1. These themes are elaborated in Howard J. Wiarda, *In Search of Policy: The United States and Latin America* (Washington, D.C.: The American Enterprise Institute for Public Policy Research, 1984).

2. A series of research projects and reports of the American Enterprise Institute reexamines the bases of U.S. policy toward Latin America in the political, economic, and foreign assistance areas. See Howard Wiarda, ed., *Rift and Revolution: The Central American Imbroglio* (1984), *The Crisis in Latin America: Strategic, Economic and Political Dimensions* (1984), *The Alternative Futures of Latin America: AEI Foreign Policy and Defense Review,* vol. 5, no. 3 (1985), *Human Rights and U.S. Human Rights Policy* (1982), and *The Crisis in Central America* (1982), all published in Washington, D.C. by the American Enterprise Institute. See also Wiarda, "At the Root of the Problem: Conceptual Failures in U.S.-Central American Relations," in Robert Leiken, ed., *Central America: Anatomy of Conflict* (New York: Pergamon Press, 1984), pp. 259–78.

3. See especially Alfred Thayer Mahan, *The Interest of American Sea Power, Present and Future* (Boston: Little, Brown, 1898).

4. J. Lloyd Mechan, *A Survey of United States-Latin American Relations* (Boston: Houghton-Mifflin, 1965).

5. From Howard J. Wiarda, "The United States and Latin America: Change and Continuity," in Alan Adelman and Reid Reading, eds., *Confrontation in the Caribbean Basin* (Pittsburgh, Pa.: Center for International Studies of the University of Pittsburgh, 1984), pp. 211–26.

6. A more complete discussion is found in Howard J. Wiarda, *Latin America at the Crossroads: Debt, Development and the Future* (Boulder, Colo.: Westview Press, 1987), chapter 5.

7. The author has treated this subject in more detail in "The Paralysis of Policy: Current Dilemmas of U.S. Foreign-Policy Making" (chapter 11 in this book).

8. Cole Blasier, *The Giant's Rival: The USSR and Latin America* (Pittsburgh, Pa.: University of Pittsburgh Press, 1983).

9. See the discussion in *Rift and Revolution,* esp. the Introduction.

10. Jiri Valenta and Virginia Valenta, "Soviet Policies and Strategies in the Caribbean Basin" in *Rift and Revolution.* An updated version is forthcoming in Mark Falcoff and Howard J. Wiarda, *The Communist Challenge in the Caribbean*

and Central America (Washington, D.C.: American Enterprise Institute, forthcoming).

11. Ernest Evans, "Revolutionary Movements in Central America: The Development of a New Strategy" in *Rift and Revolution* and, in revised form, in *The Communist Challenge in the Caribbean and Central America.*

12. Howard J. Wiarda, "Soviet Policy in the Caribbean and Central America: Opportunities and Constraints," in *The Communist Challenge in the Caribbean and Central America.*

13. For an assessment, see Howard J. Wiarda, "Aftermath of Grenada: The Impact of the U.S. Action on Revolutionary Prospects in Central America," in Herbert Ellison and Jiri Valenta, eds., *Grenada and Soviet/Cuban Policy, Internal Crisis and U.S. Intervention* (Boulder, Colo.: Westview Press, 1985).

14. Aaron Wildavsky, ed., *Beyond Containment: Alternative American Policies Toward the Soviet Union* (San Francisco: Institute for Contemporary Studies, 1983).

15. Robert Kennedy and Gabriel Marcella, "U.S. Security on the Southern Flank: Interests, Challenges, Responses," in James R. Greene and Brent Scowcroft, eds., *Western Interests and U.S. Policy Options in the Caribbean Basin* (Boston: Oelgeschlager, Gunn and Hain, for the Atlantic Council, 1984), pp. 187–242.

16. For a full discussion see chapter 11, "The Paralysis of Policy."

17. See the discussion of the former American commander in El Salvador, Col. John Waghelstein, in "Post Vietnam Counterinsurgency Doctrine," *Ft. Leavenworth Military Review,* May 1985.

18. See the *Report of the President's National Bipartisan Commission on Central America* (New York: MacMillan, 1984), as well as Howard J. Wiarda, ed., "U.S. Policy in Central America: Consultant Papers for the Kissinger Commission," special issue of the *AEI Foreign Policy and Defense Review,* vol. V, no. 1 (1984)—see chapter 10 of this volume.

19. For discussion see George F. Kennan ("X"), "The Sources of Soviet Conduct" *Foreign Affairs* 25 (July 1947); John Lewis Gaddis, "Containment: A Reassessment" 56 *Foreign Affairs* 55 (July 1977), pp. 873–87; Edúard Mark, "The Question of Containment: A Reply to John Lewis Gaddis," *Foreign Affairs* 56 (January 1978), pp. 430–40; Charles R. Wolf, Jr., "Beyond Containment: Redesigning American Policies," *Washington Quarterly* 5 (Winter 1982), pp. 107–17; Louisa S. Hulett, "Containment Revisited: U.S.-Soviet Relations in the 1980s," *Parameters* 14 (Autumn 1984), pp. 51–63: Barry R. Poser and Stephen Van Evera, "Defense Policy and the Reagan Administration; Departure from Containment," *International Security* 8 (Summer 1983), pp. 3–45; Robert W. Tucker, "In Defense of Containment," *Journal of Contemporary Studies* 6 (Spring 1983), pp. 29–49; and K. N. Lewis "Reorganizing U.S. Defense Planning to Deal with New Contingencies: U.S.-Soviet Conflict in the Third World," (Santa Monica, Calif.: Rand Corporation, 1982).

20. The analysis in this paragraph follows closely the similar conclusion of G. Pope Atkins, "U.S. Policy in Central America: International Conditions and Conceptual Limitations," paper presented at the Annual Convention of the International Studies Association, Washington, D.C., March 8, 1985.

21. Further details on what I have termed a "prudence model" of U.S. policy in Latin America are presented in *In Search of Policy*, chapter 8. For an analytic discussion that places this strategy in the context of other alternative views see Harold Molineu, "Latin American Politics and the U.S. Connection," *Polity* XVIII (Fall 1985), pp. 167–75.

22. For a full discussion see Howard J. Wiarda, *Ethnocentrism in Foreign Policy: Can We Understand the Third World?* (Washington, D.C.: American Enterprise Institute, 1985).

9

Did the Alliance for Progress "Lose Its Way"?

Or Were Its Assumptions All Wrong from the Beginning? And Are Those Assumptions Still with Us?

The title of this chapter is taken from the title of the well-known book by Jerome Levinson and Juan de Onis, *The Alliance that Lost Its Way: A Critical Report on the Alliance for Progress*.[1] That title, in turn, derives from a well-known essay on the Alliance by former Chilean president Eduardo Frei that appeared in *Foreign Affairs* in 1967.[2] The implication of both these titles is that while the Alliance for Progress began satisfactorily—maybe even nobly by some accounts—it somehow went astray, was perverted, and lost its direction.

The responsibility for the Alliance "losing its way" is variously assigned.[3] Some place heavy emphasis on the transition from Presidents Kennedy to Johnson to Nixon and thus on the dying interest in, or commitment to, the Alliance. Others assign blame to the Latin American oligarchies, or the Latin American militaries, or both together. Some place responsibility for failure on the internal mechanisms of the Alliance, on the lack of coordination between the various institutions, both in North and in Latin America, charged with carrying out Alliance goals. Some blame the Latin American governments and others the U.S. government. But in all these interpretations, the original goals and presumptions of the Alliance are assumed to be correct.

Presented at the conference "The Alliance for Progress: 25 Years Later," Center for Advanced Studies of the Americas, Washington, D.C., March 12–14, 1986; published in revised form in *Foreign Policy* (Winter 1986–87), under the title "Misreading Latin America—Again."

My own interpretation takes another direction. I believe the Alliance was well-intentioned but that its assumptions, from the beginning, were erroneous. It is not just that subsequent implementation was faulty, in my view. Rather, I argue that the fundamental presuppositions of the Alliance were misconceived from the start. Moreover, I fear that those mistaken assumptions of a quarter-century ago are often still with us, in the Kissinger Commission recommendations, the Caribbean Basin Initiative, and the Democracy Agenda. This paper proceeds to examine the original assumptions of the Alliance, the degree to which we are still prisoners of those early assumptions, and whether anything can be done to change them or whether we should just accept them as fundamental assumptions of American policy destined to remain with us forever.

The Alliance: Context and Origins

The Alliance for Progress was a ten-year multibillion dollar assistance program launched in 1961 and designed, at least ostensibly, to aid the social, economic, cultural, and political development of Latin America. Though its institutional machinery was put in place by the Kennedy administration, its roots lay in the preceding Eisenhower administration, particularly in the report on Latin America prepared by Milton Eisenhower for his brother,[4] and in the revised thinking about Latin America in the Eisenhower administration during its last three years. Just as the Good Neighbor Policy of Franklin D. Roosevelt and its origins in the preceding Hoover administration, so did the Alliance for Progress build upon and greatly expand a policy reorientation that preceded the inauguration of John F. Kennedy.

A powerful and earlier impetus to the Alliance had also come from Latin America. As early as 1955 President Juscelino Kubitschek of Brazil had begun to call for a vast program of assistance to and self-help for Latin America, which he called Operation Pan America, that incorporated most of the main ingredients of the Alliance. He was later joined by President Alberto Lleras Camargo of Colombia in pushing for such a program. Other Latin American presidents advocated similar measures. The founding in 1959 of the Inter-American Development Bank, a regional multilateral but largely U.S.-funded assistance bank, was an integral part of this same campaign.[5] Indeed one of the unique aspects of the Alliance as an assistance program was the degree to which it initially grew out of, and partially incorporated, ideas emanating from Latin America. One is tempted to suggest at this early point in the discussion that had the Alliance continued seriously to reflect Latin American input, it would likely not have gone in all the wrong directions that it did.

The election of John F. Kennedy in 1960 was a key turning point. It was Kennedy who proposed, spoke passionately for, shepherded through the Congress, and put in place the Alliance for Progress. President Kennedy had been prodded into taking this bold new initiative by the reports he had received on Latin America by such foreign policy advisers as Adolph A. Berle and General William Draper. Such White House intellectuals and policy advisers as John Dreier, John Kenneth Galbraith, Lincoln Gordon, DeLesseps Morrison, Walt W. Rostow, and Arthur F. Schlesinger, Jr., similarly played a strong role in the design and formulation of the Alliance.[6]

The Alliance for Progress was formally inaugurated on August 17, 1961, when the so-called Charter of Punta del Este was signed by all the member states of the Organization of American States (OAS), with the exception of Cuba. The Alliance was a comprehensive program of social, economic, and political assistance sponsored by the United States and designed to improve the life and welfare of the people of the Latin American republics. The Alliance aimed to stimulate economic growth in Latin America at the rate of at least 2.5 percent per year, and to provide for a vast array of social and political programs: agrarian reform, tax reform, improved water supplies, electrification, literacy programs, housing, health care, development banks, plans and planning agencies, technical assistance, educational reform, legal reform, family planning, military reform, labor reform, democratization, and a host of other activities.[7] It was a vast and ambitious program which now, with hindsight, we know was too vast and too ambitious. Its aim was to promote change, under U.S. auspices, and presumably in the right direction. The program was launched with great enthusiasm and fanfare; the rhetoric indicated that the United States was to assist and itself help initiate, with the recipient countries' cooperation, a democratic social and political revolution in Latin America.

It is important to sort out what was new and what remained the same in U.S. policy toward Latin America under the Alliance. Quite a number of the programs under the Alliance were clearly new. The sheer size and ambitiousness of the effort was surely new. So was the enthusiasm, at least initially. Within the State Department bureaucracy, President Kennedy had brought in some new faces and shifted others around; these personnel changes signaled a considerable shift of emphasis under the new program.[8] There were also structural changes within the administrative machinery, most notably

175

the considerable infrastructure created for the Alliance itself and the greater coordination now expected between the Department of State's Bureau of Inter-American Affairs and the Agency for International Development (AID). The Alliance also tapped the enthusiasms and commitments of key career persons within the foreign policy-making agencies. Finally, it is important to emphasize that the Alliance for Progress was a White House initiative and enjoyed the full backing of President Kennedy, which gave it added pizzazz and authority. As Arthur F. Schlesinger remarked, it would have been impossible, because of bureaucratic inertia, to expect such a large and ambitious program to emanate from the State Department.[9]

Lest one be carried away with enthusiasm for the democratic reformism incorporated in the Alliance, however, one must also bear in mind its fundamental strategic purpose. That purpose was the prevention of any additional Castro-like Communist regimes in the hemisphere inimical to U.S. interests. At its root the Alliance for Progress was an anti-Communist and cold war strategy designed to serve U.S. strategic interests. What was new and ingenious about the Alliance was that humanitarian and social and political reformist goals could be served simultaneously, apparently, with the advancement of U.S. security interests. An economically developing, more socially just, and politically democratic Latin America was now seen as best protecting U.S. strategic interests there.

This program was a considerable shift, at least in tactics, from the early Eisenhower Administration. Under Eisenhower the orientation had been to prop up even right-wing dictators as best preserving stability, protecting U.S. interests, and keeping out Communism. But the revolution in Cuba changed all that. The Cuban experience demonstrated that rather than thwarting Communism, dictatorships such as Batista's might instead make the conditions ripe under which Communism can thrive. Batista's regime had, after all, just been replaced by the Marxist-Leninist regime of Fidel Castro, a fact that weighed heavily on strategic thinkers and policy makers and forced them to reassess past policies. Henceforth under the Alliance, the United States would be opposed to dictators of both the left and the right and would work to advance development and democratization as the best means to achieve our primary goal of preventing Communism. But note that the goal of pursuing a strong anti-Communist strategy in Latin America, and of providing for its handmaidens—stability, moderation, and a middle-of-the-road course—had remained the same. Only the means or tactics had now changed.[10]

The point has been indirectly referred to before but it deserves direct mention here: the Alliance for Progress was a direct response to and outgrowth of the Cuban Revolution. This was not just some starry-eyed, altruistic, humanitarian, give-away program, as it was sometimes portrayed at the cartoon level. It was that and a whole lot more: a program designed to serve basic U.S. strategic purposes in Latin America. Or it could be said that the Alliance would enable the United States to serve *both* humanitarian and self-interest goals at the same time. That combination of serving both U.S. moral concerns and fundamental strategic interests is of course typically American; it is also what enables programs like the Alliance to be "sold" to diverse constituencies and to get through the Congress. But it also implies the possibility for future conflict when these diverse goals later prove contradictory—as they in fact later did prove under the Alliance. The conflict between long-term developmentalist goals and shorter-term U.S. strategic interests was in fact one of the key reasons the Alliance ultimately proved unsuccessful.[11]

Having hinted at one of the key contradictions that would plague the Alliance from the beginning, I must also say that the Alliance was not designed by naive or incompetent persons. After rereading all the early literature on the Alliance, I can attest that the Alliance architects were experienced, sophisticated experts in their respective fields. It is necessary to say this because the history of the Alliance was marred by so many failures and mistakes that one could easily conclude the persons who conceived it must also have been incompetent. In fact the Alliance's architects were among the most able people in the U.S. government. Where they failed was not in their experience, competence, or technical expertise in their respective fields, but in their woeful ignorance of Latin America. The designers of the Alliance knew history (or at least U.S. and European history), knew economics, knew about planning and taxes, knew the theoretical literature on development, knew their technical fields well, and knew agrarian reform and family planning from the Japanese and Taiwanese experiences. What they lacked was understanding of how all these programs that sounded wonderful on paper and in the general theoretical literature would actually be received or "play" in Latin America.[12] Therein, I believe, lay *the* fundamental flaw in the Alliance. It is also the gap between general theory and Latin American reality that lies at the heart of the analysis in this paper.

The Assumptions of the Alliance:
Ten Fatal Flaws in Search of a Theory[13]

The fatal flaws in the Alliance, we argue here, were not in its implementation—although implementation often did leave a great deal to be desired. It is therefore not so much a problem of the Alliance "losing its way." Rather, the fatal flaws were conceptual. That is, the problems of the Alliance stemmed principally from the wrong assumptions on which the program was based. To the person inexperienced in, or totally ignorant of, Latin America, and who relied on the Western European or United States experiences for models and examples, the Alliance assumptions looked quite coherent and rational. To the experienced Latin Americanist, however, or at least to those who could see beyond wishful thinking about the area in favor of hard-headed reality, the assumptions of the program appeared hopelessly naive and wrong-headed. The Alliance in fact reveals an appalling lack of knowledge and understanding about Latin America. One suspects that the reason for this is that the policy was designed by persons who had little knowledge of Latin America.[14] In fact, the program *was* designed by economists and foreign policy generalists most of whom were located in the White House; very few of what we might call "experienced Latin America hands," either governmental or academic, were involved in the initial planning and program design.

Hence the Alliance was based not so much on Latin American realities but on an abstract theoretical scheme derived from other areas and superimposed ill-fittingly on the Latin American region. The model used was based on the developmental experiences of Western Europe (actually, Northwest Europe) and the United States, with some reference to Japan, Taiwan, or the countries of the British Commonwealth. It assumed that Latin America would follow the same developmental course as had these earlier modernizers. Or else, the formula derived from the general development literature then rising in currency, most of which was tied to the experiences of the "new nations" or the "non-Western areas"—models and concepts which had little to do with Latin American realities either. None of these models, or the corresponding assumptions of the Alliance, was based on actual Latin American realities, social structure, political dynamics, or culturally conditioned ways of doing things.[15] That is (or was) the fundamental problem with the Alliance: it had little to do with actual operating Latin American realities. As the Alliance was implemented, these flaws in the assumptions on which the program was based became more and more apparent. It is not therefore so much that the program went off track during the course of the 1960s (although that happened too). Rather it was never on track to begin with, a fact that became entirely obvious only as the program went forward.

Let us review some of the major flawed assumptions on which the Alliance was grounded. I list ten such fatal flaws, but that, we shall see, will not exhaust the list; and some of these flawed major assumptions need to be further subdivided into numerous flawed sub-assumptions. Actually, each of these assumptions requires discussion in more detail than is possible here; my intention in this paper is to be both provocative and brief, raising the main issues but not presuming by any means to have exhausted the subject.

Assumption 1. The "One-Minute-to-Midnight" Thesis. In the late 1950s and early 1960s, reflecting the fear that the Cuban revolution would be repeated throughout the length and breadth of the hemisphere, the Latin America issue was always posed in stark, immediate, and crisis terms. It was "one-minute-to-midnight in Latin America," as the title of one widely read study of the time put it,[16] and the clock was about to toll.

Posing the issue in such a dramatic way, and using "scare" tactics, is of course useful for galvanizing the bureaucracy, gaining public attention and support for the new program, and prying greater funds from an otherwise reluctant Congress. But it had little to do with Latin American realities. Throughout the hemisphere in those years, the local Communist parties were weak and disorganized, there were no guerrilla movements in other countries that constituted much of a threat, and the possibility that all of Latin America would soon explode in Cuba-like revolution—if examined more than superficially—was preposterous.[17] The organizational base and groundwork for launching such revolutions were simply not there. Even the Cuban revolution, if looked at closely, could be seen as a fluke, the product of such unusual circumstances on that island that they were unlikely to be repeated elsewhere. And of course Latin Americans are not themselves above—and in fact are quite good at—exaggerating their problems so as to secure greater attention and funds from the United States. Old-time Latin America hands know that in this sense Latin America is perpetually in "crisis," and therefore that we should not become unduly alarmed. That is a normal Latin American condition.

It is probably accurate to say that in 1961–1962 not a single country in Latin America had even a slight possibility of going the way of Castro's Cuba. Even the Dominican Republic, to which the administration in Washington devoted so much attention because conditions superficially resembled those in pre-Castro Cuba (a poor nation, wide social gaps, one-crop economy, bloody dictator, neighboring island), was in fact quite different from Cuba and had no possibilities whatsoever, at that time, of "going Communist."[18] The bell was not about to toll anywhere in Latin America—or if it was, it was unlikely that it would anywhere lead to a Marxist-Leninist re-

179

gime. The Alliance was in this sense vastly oversold, a product of bloated rhetoric and verbal overkill. And of course as this was increasingly realized during the course of the 1960s, the program lost its appeal and was more and more ignored by everyone from the president on down. It became just another economic give-away program and was finally (though unofficially) abrogated—in favor of a policy of "benign neglect" which did in fact eventually contribute to the conditions in Latin America that made revolution again, in the late-1970s, flourish.

Why was the "one-minute-to-midnight" thesis so widely accepted in the United States, even by persons whose education and experience should have led them to know better? One suspects that it had to do in strong measure with the historic disparagement of Latin American institutions and ways of doing things that is so strong in this country, the myth of Latin America's incapacity to solve any of its own problems by itself. Actually Latin America has a considerable history of coping with its problems in its own ways, sliding through from crisis to crisis, and fashioning ad hoc, often crazy-quilt solutions to seemingly intractable difficulties. But if these processes and institutional arrangements, which are in fact highly "developed," are not recognized or are dismissed with disparagement, then it is easy to see why the "one-minute-to-midnight" thesis would have some credibility. We will return to this issue later.

Assumption 2. The "Economic Development Produces Political Development" Thesis. The Alliance for Progress was essentially a U.S. strategic design that was largely based on economic determinist assumptions. It was designed and largely run by economists and economic historians. Initially, and sporadically thereafter, some limited attention was paid to political development,[19] which was almost universally (though much too simply and perhaps mistakenly) defined as meaning democratization along U.S. lines. But over time the political development efforts—by their nature much more complex and difficult to carry out—were shunted aside in favor of an agenda devoted almost exclusively to economic development.

Put in bold and only slightly oversimplified terms, the economic determinist argument, dominant in the development literature of the time (and still present, as we shall see, in many U.S. programs today), is as follows: if only we can pour in enough capital, prime the pumps, and start the engines for take-off, meanwhile providing *our* advice and technical assistance, then not only will the Latin American economies develop but, even more important, certain social, political, and strategic concomitants will inevitably and universally follow.[20] A business elite will grow up alongside the old landed elite presumably with a sense of social responsibility that the latter lack; the middle class will grow and become a bastion of stability, moderation, and democracy; the lower classes will also become more affluent and therefore less attracted by the appeals of Communism; trade unions will be oriented toward U.S.-style collective bargaining and will eschew more radical and divisive political action; and so on. Economic development would thus have its ramifications in various social areas as well, producing a more literate and therefore a more participatory-democratic citizenry, expanding mass media and therefore producing freer and more pluralistic societies, enabling governments to expand social services and therefore also cutting down the appeals of communism that way.[21]

The trouble with all these theories, which in fact sound quite plausible and even reasonable, is that they are all based on the previous developmental experiences of northwest Europe and the United States and have almost no, or only limited, relevance to Latin America. The new business elites in Latin America have, for the most part, precious little social responsibility; the middle class, as we shall see in more detail below, have not become bastions of stability; and the lower classes have not become less radical or eschewed political action. Expanded literacy and other social mobilization programs produced not more participatory and pluralist regimes in the 1960s but in fact prompted a series of military takeovers destructive of all these features.[22]

In short, the social, political, and strategic concomitants that were supposed to follow automatically from economic development did not in fact follow. This form of economic determinism did not result in happier, more stable, more democratic societies; in fact it produced quite the reverse. The maxims therefore follow that economic development is far too important to be left to economists and that we ignore social, cultural, and political determinants of behavior at great peril.

Assumption 3. The "Latin America Couldn't or Wouldn't Do Anything on Its Own" Thesis. North American prejudices and biases about Latin America are strong and deeply ingrained. We tend to think of the area as unstable, backward, "less-developed," incompetent, and "unsuccessful" historically. Our material progress in the United States has been so great and our democracy so stable that, assuming Latin America wants the same things and in the same ways, we label our history a "success" and theirs a "failure." It follows that we would tend to assume we could solve Latin America's problems for them. And that in doing so, we would feel we could ignore—or not bother to learn—Latin American history.

We tend to think of Latin American leadership in much the same way: not very competent, unstable, quasi-infantile, children whom *we* must guide and lead.[23] True, in the Alliance's case, there was some Latin American input which was seldom taken too seriously in the U.S. government, and, through the so-called Committee of Nine Wise Men, Latin American advice was sporadically sought on assistance matters. But the assumptions, overall plan, and program of the Alliance remained exclusively an American operation. It was we who knew best and who would presumably bring the benefits of our civilization to Latin America.

This disparagement of Latin America and its leadership and the belief that Latin America couldn't or wouldn't do anything on its own had deep roots in the United States. In part it stemmed from historic prejudice by Protestant, Anglo-Saxon civilization toward the fundamental assumptions of a Catholic, Thomistic, Latin, scholastic, maybe even inquisitorial civilization. In part it stemmed from long-held assumptions in the social sciences, both Marxian and non-Marxian, about Latin America. Marx thought of Latin America, with its lack of industrialization or well-formed classes, as rather like "Asiatic societies," a label Marx used not just as a neutral scientific term but with scorn and derision. Hegel said that Latin America had "no history," a judgment that in the Hegelian metaphysic consigned the area to the most primitive of categories. Social Darwinism condemned Latin America, with its racially mixed populations, to an inferior place on the evolutionary ladder; in the positivist hierarchy Latin America among the continents, because of its presumed lack of accomplishments and progress, also ranked low. More recently one thinks of Henry Kissinger's famous quip that the axis of the world flows through Moscow, Berlin/Bonn, Paris, London, Washington, and Tokyo—thus excluding Latin America entirely!

Building upon these earlier traditions and prejudices was the development literature which loomed so large in the early 1960s and from which many policy makers took their categories if not their cues.[24] In this influential body of writings Latin America and its institutions were consigned to the realm of the "traditional" which either had to be destroyed or to be altered "fundamentally" if the region was ever to modernize. Seldom in this literature or in the policy initiatives (such as the Alliance, which was fashioned almost wholly out of this influential body of work) emanating from it were the notions advanced that traditional institutions such as those of

Latin America might in fact be quite flexible and accommodative, that they could bend to change rather than be overwhelmed by it, that they were themselves capable of a great deal of modernization, and that sweeping them away or shunting them aside might well leave Latin America with the worst possible legacy: with neither "modern" institutions (that we presumably would implant) sufficiently well-rooted and institutionalized, nor with traditional institutions (even with their admitted problems) capable of providing coherence and holding political society together during the trauma of transition. I have written on these themes in more detail elsewhere;[25] here let me simply say that if there is one primary cause of the Alliance's failures, it is these wrong assumptions of the literature on development that so strongly undergirded our policy initiatives, maybe now as well as then. By ignoring the realities of Latin American history and experience, we not only made manifest our ignorance about the region but also condemned worthwhile initiatives like the Alliance to failure.

Assumption 4. The "Salvation through the Middle Class" Thesis. Not all of the Alliance's assumptions were explicit in the actual language of the program. Nor were AID and other technicians and managers of the Alliance always fully aware of the theoretical literature on which the program was based. Nevertheless that literature was enormously important in shaping the assumptions of the Alliance and the kinds of programs supported. Such was surely the case with the thesis of "salvation through the middle class."

The assumption, once again based on the Northwest European and North American experiences, was that a large and prosperous middle class was closely correlated with a stable, democratic, middle-of-the-road polity—precisely what the United States wanted to help evolve in Latin America.[26] The main arguments for this assumption were based on economic history as well as the emerging field of political sociology. There was even some writing, fatally flawed by errors of logic, reasoning, and history, from a prominent Latin Americanist that supported this thesis.[27] The argument was that if only we could create in Latin America more middle class societies, then more stable, more just, more democratic, and more anti-Communist attitudes would surely prevail. To that end we created programs in both rural and urban areas that would lead to a larger middle class: agrarian reform in the countryside that would presumably produce a class of medium-sized family farmers who would then be able to resist the appeals of Communism to the "peasants" (presumably what happened in Cuba; actually Cuba's was by no means a peasant revolution); *and* a variety of economic development and social service programs in the cities designed to swell the middle class there. The model was Western Europe or the New Deal in the United States.

It should be understood that the problem here is not agrarian reform per se or any of these other programs. Rather the problem is the assumption that by pursuing such programs we could create a moderate, middle-of-the-road, happy, bourgeois society that looked just like ourselves. For while the middle class has in fact grown in size in Latin America, it has taken on few of the presumed middle class virtues that the literature based on Western Europe or the United States would lead us to expect. Rather, the literature from Latin America suggests that the middle class tends to ape upper class ways and attitudes, it lives way beyond its means, it holds aristocratic attitudes even more strongly than the real aristocrats, it is non-egalitarian and perhaps antidemocratic, it disparages manual labor, it disdains the peasant and working classes even more than the elites do, it holds very conservative attitudes, and it is not above staging coups and supporting military regimes that freeze society in place and are repressive of progressive social forces.[28] That is not a set of attitudes designed to institutionalize a stable, moderate, pluralist, democratic, middle-of-the-road polity.

It may be that in the present circumstances when the Latin American militaries have themselves been thoroughly discredited and when democracy is on the rebound, the middle class *may*, at least for the time being, be supportive of democratic rule—if for no other reason than that representative government is temporarily viewed as protecting their interests and providing stability better than military rule. But such expediency is not a very sturdy rock to build one's hopes on for the future, and certainly in the wave of coups and repression that swept Latin America in the 1960s it was—contrary to all the Alliance's hopes and assumptions—the middle class that urged and in some cases brought the military into power and supported the severe measures, both economic and political, that the armed forces then used on the lower classes.

Assumption 5. The "Integration-as-Critical" Thesis. One of the key aspects of the Alliance—a part of its ten-point program—was its effort to achieve economic integration in Latin America. To this end the Latin American Free Trade Association (LAFTA) was organized; the Central American countries formed the Central American Free Trade Association; Venezuela, Colombia, Ecuador, and Peru (Chile's position was usually uncertain) organized the Andean Pact; and the small islands of the Caribbean joined in the Caribbean Community (CARICOM). The theory and logic for such organizations seemed sound enough: larger markets for more products would thereby be created than presently existed, industrialization could hence be expanded, the lowering of tariffs and increased trade would have a multiplier effect on the participating economies, affluence would spread thereby diminishing the *Fidelista* threat, and presumably, again using Western Europe and the Marshall Plan as examples, economic integration might well lead to political integration or at least greater unity, which would help produce political stability that would serve U.S. interests. On this topic a great body of romantic and rather wishful literature was produced in the 1960s.

Latin American economic integration is another one of those grandiose schemes produced by abstract planners, economists, and technicians who knew nothing of, or preferred to ignore, the realities and politics of the area. Actually, the integration movement has produced some rather notable results, if one focuses only on the economic statistics; but its more fundamental political goals were never realized. It would be difficult to argue, for example, that Latin America is any more unified now, as an anti-Soviet or any other kind of bloc, than it was in the early 1960s. One would be equally hard-pressed, looking at all the coups, military takeovers, and full-scale revolutions that have occurred in the last twenty-five years, to argue that the area is now, or in the foreseeable future will be, more stable. The political rivalries, petty jealousies, and nationalistic hatreds between the Latin American states are just as intense now—and there is a great deal of evidence they have become even more bitter, that Latin America may become the next area of international conflict and irredentism.[29]

Hence the movement toward integration, by ignoring the political realities and simply hoping they could be superseded, foundered. Costa Rica could never get along with Nicaragua and still cannot; El Salvador and Honduras went to war; Brazil did not fit anywhere; Chile and Argentina are rivals and sometimes enemies as are Chile, Bolivia, and Peru. Peru and Ecuador have long-time border problems and a history of conflict in the Amazon basin; Venezuela was distrustful of Colombia and could not compete with Colombia's labor costs. The largest island in the Caribbean, Cuba, was excluded from CARICOM countries on political grounds; nor did the English-speaking Caribbean want to join forces with the Spanish-speaking Caribbean. And so it went.

The integration movement is a sad illustration among many that could be cited under the Alliance's auspices of what happens when economists and technicians design programs that ignore political variables or assume that these can be overcome by brave acts of political will. Political scientists tend not to talk much about "political will," and many doubt that there is such a thing; rather they talk about the balance of political interest groups, the role of power and influence, and the importance of national interest in shaping if not determining international outcomes. All this is not to praise political scientists and disparage economists, but to say that those who designed the Alliance, while they had political and strategic goals in mind as the ultimate purpose of the Alliance, nonetheless ignored fundamental political realities in carrying out the program. They focused almost exclusively on the economic goals while ignoring the political factors or assuming that the economic accomplishments would render the political rivalries irrelevant. But that did not happen; that is also why the high-priority political and strategic goals of economic integration were never realized and why the several regional integration efforts, though not completely dead, continue today to limp along with only modest accomplishments to show for all the efforts.[30]

Assumption 6. The "Democracy versus Dictatorship" Dichotomy. In the early 1960s the United States saw but three possibilities in Latin America. The first was a Castro-like regime, "another Cuba in the Caribbean," which had to be avoided at all costs. The second was a dictatorial or authoritarian regime. The third was a democratic regime which was our first preference. But as John F. Kennedy reminded us, the United States could not renounce authoritarian regimes in favor of democracy unless first assured that a Castro-like regime could be avoided.[31] In effect that gave the United States only two choices in Latin America: dictatorship or democracy.

I wish to submit here that this choice, as artfully and articulately put forth in numerous books on Latin America at the time, was and is a false choice, a misleading choice, a choice that even wreaks harm on Latin America as well as our policy interests there. In fact there are many choices that lie between dictatorship and democracy: for example, a combined civil-military junta, gentlemanly understood alternations between civil and military rule, civilian rule where the military is the power behind the throne, military rule where civilians man many cabinet and other posts, parallel and coexistent power structures as in present-day Honduras, Guatemala, and Panama where civilian and military elements live uneasily together side by side and where their precise relations with each other is a matter of almost everyday renegotiation. Not only is this image of numerous "halfway houses" between dictatorship and democracy a more realistic portrayal of Latin American politics than the dichotomous either-or scheme, but the ongoing genius of Latin American politics is to continue fashioning such in-between solutions to avoid an often unrealistic choice between the one or the other.[32]

I am of the view that by posing the issue in such dichotomous terms, American policy did a disservice to the creative genius of Latin American politics and politicians. By making the issue appear to be *either* dictatorship *or* democracy, we forced Latin American politics into a straitjacket and denied its creative capacity for ad hoc and combined solutions. The point is controversial but it needs to be made: by pressing so hard for democracy in the early 1960s, a democracy which I am not sure Latin America really wanted or wanted all that much or wanted in the pure U.S. form that it came or for which many Latin American countries lacked the institutional capacity to support at the time, we and the Alliance undoubtedly also prepared the way for the wave of repressive military coups that followed in the mid- to late 1960s. Had we not pressed so hard and so precipitously, had we allowed more room for mixed or halfway solutions, or— heaven forbid—had we allowed the Latin Americans with our assistance to work out their own murky solutions to their own muddy problems, I do not think we would have had the same kind of bloody, repressive regimes that we did in fact have in the late 1960s and 1970s. Thus the Alliance not only misread Latin America and its *multiple* developmental possibilities, but by its misinterpretations of the area, indirectly brought downright harm, both to Latin America and to the Alliance for Progress.

Assumption 7. The "Reform or Revolution" Thesis. Just as the choice of regime for Latin America—dictatorship or democracy—was posed in dichotomous terms, so was the ultimate goal or purpose of government and of public policy: *either* reform *or* revolution. That is the language and message used in so many books, articles, and speeches of public officials to describe the options open for Latin America: either reform from within in quite radical ways or face the almost certain prospect of being overthrown by revolution, as in Cuba.[33]

The problems with this approach and the assumptions undergirding it were similar to those posed by the "one-minute-to-midnight" and "dictatorship-versus-democracy" approaches. Two comments especially need to be made. First, the United States was exceedingly arrogant, and downright unrealistic, to prescribe such a detailed agenda of reform proposals as we did for Latin America under the Alliance for Progress. The agenda included vast agrarian reform proposals, sweeping educational reform, an overhauling of the tax structure, new norms of bureaucratic and political behavior, vast

187

changes affecting the family, legal reform, social policy reform, military reform, labor reform, economic reform, and much, much else. In short, in preferring and pursuing the "evolutionary" path over the revolutionary one, we were advocating a *complete* restructuring of all Latin America's basic institutions. To put it in an unkind light, Latin America was to be used as a laboratory for a vast range of social programs and experimentation, quite a number of which would not willingly have been carried out in the United States or have passed muster in the U.S. Congress. The agenda was far too broad and all-encompassing to be accepted in Latin America—and certainly not all at once. In addition, Latin America often resented the paternalism involved and the implied conclusion that *all* its institutions were misguided, unworkable, and therefore required a thorough restructuring.

Quite apart from these important considerations, the either-or approach was also wrong and unhelpful. Latin America had not only a variety of regime types from which to choose but also a great variety of possible policy responses. Moreover, as should have been recognized by Alliance planners had they known more about the area, the Latin American polities are like most other polities: they have problems, they cope, they seek to muddle through. Only *gringos* really believe that problems are ever really finally *solved* or that political choices represent either-or propositions. The rest of the world faces problems by coping and muddling through, which in fact is what the United States in reality also does. Moreover a good case can be made that such muddling through, and the need for consultation and trial-and-error, lies at the heart of the democratic process. By forcing on Latin America too much and too soon we not only ran roughshod over the region's own, gradual, accommodative political processes,[34] but overloaded the system and contributed to the wave of military coups that swept the region from 1962.

Assumption 8. The "We Know Best for Latin America" Thesis. There was a lot of arrogance and presumptuousness in the Alliance for Progress. The presumption was that we knew best for Latin America, that we could solve Latin America's problems for it. In part this attitude stemmed from the myth of Latin America's own incapacity to solve its own problems; in part it derived from the missionary, proselytizing tradition of the United States, the belief that we are a "city on a hill," a "new Jerusalem," the "last best hope of mankind"; and in part from the certainties imparted by the new literature on development, which seemed to provide universal social science legitimacy to the reformist impulses of American academics and policy makers.[35]

Surely the Alliance for Progress is a case *par excellence* of inappropriate U.S. meddling, usually with the best of intentions, into matters that we actually knew little about. It was a modern-day expression of that larger missionary, Wilsonian, peculiarly American inclination to bring the benefits of democracy and social progress to our poor, benighted brethren in Latin America. The United States was certainly sincere in wanting to bring democracy and development to Latin America, while also serving our strategic interests there; but we sought to do so without really understanding the societies with which we were dealing, or their dynamics or political processes. We used simplistic labels to describe the changes desired ("development," "modernization," the "revolution of rising expectations"). Without really knowing how to work *within* the Latin American system to accomplish our purposes, we frequently rode roughshod over them (in the name of superseding "traditional" society) when they stood in the way or proved inconvenient. Only rarely did an occasional voice suggest that "They know how,"[36] that Latin America itself knew its own problems best and was probably better than we were at resolving them. The dominant orientation was that *we* knew best, and our development literature suggested that our model was both universal and inevitable. That was a deadly combination: the arrogance attached to the idea that we knew best, and the certainty that what we were doing was part of an inevitable march of historical processes.

Assumption 9. The "American Model of Development." While presuming that we knew best for Latin America and that Latin America was incapable of solving its own problems, we used models of development in Latin America that were all derived from the U.S. experience.

These models grew out of what Louis Hartz called the liberal-Lockean principles of American democracy.[37] The question is whether these principles apply also in Latin America, or apply in the same way, and what happens when a fundamentally liberal polity in the Hartzian sense runs up against a society and political culture whose values and experience were so much at odds with our own.

As applied to foreign policy and development issues, the liberal principles upon which the United States was founded and which undergirded our historical experience imply the following mistaken assumptions which we now sought to apply in Latin America:[38]

1. Change and development are easy, as they were in the United States, with our vast frontiers and natural resources. But in Latin America with its meager resources, change and development have never been easy.

2. All good things (social, economic, and political development)

189

go together. But in Latin America they have not always gone together; frequently economic and social development has been disruptive of political development rather than contributing to it.

3. Stability must be maintained; instability is to be avoided at all costs. But in Latin America stability has often entrenched bloody dictators in power, and instability and even revolution have often been the means to achieve democracy and development.[39]

4. Distributing power is more important than concentrating it. But in Latin America the problem is not necessarily to achieve checks and balances; rather the problem is to gather up sufficient central power to get something done.

It is easy to see why these fundamental principles of the U.S. polity and historical experience would often lead us astray in attempting to promote development in Latin America. But the problem went deeper than the grounding of the Alliance on the vague and sometimes fuzzy principles of American democracy. It also involved the use of very specific and concrete U.S. models and ways of doing things which had little relevance in the realities of Latin America. Since the author has written on these themes before,[40] only a brief summary will be provided here.

For example, the model of agrarian reform which we attempted to export to Latin America was based on a model of the American family farm—middle-sized, capitalistic, self-sufficient, using the most advanced technology, peopled by yeoman farmers with a high degree of civic consciousness who were participatory democrats. None of this applied in Latin America.[41] The model of labor relations we sought to impart was based on nonpolitical collective bargaining, when the tradition of Latin American labor had always been political bargaining.[42] The model of local government was of a self-governing town meeting, when the entire experience of Latin America was of a centralized, top-down, Napoleonic tradition.[43] We sought to professionalize the Latin American military in our mold, which frequently had the effect of promoting more military interventions, not less.[44] The educational reform we brought was derived from the pragmatic educational system of the United States inspired by John Dewey; it had no firm grounding in Latin America. And so on. In virtually every area (and, recall, the Alliance sought reform in almost all areas of Latin American life), the model used derived from the United States and lacked foundations in Latin American experience. That fitted our notion that Latin American institutions were wholly "traditional," incapable of reform, and therefore deserving to be swept away; but that of course was not an accurate reading, and it led us to press our institutions and programs onto societies where they could not possibly work.

Assumption 10. Internal Contradictions. This final criticism focuses not on any further wrong or mistaken assumptions of the Alliance about Latin America but on its internal contradictions. These were also numerous:

1. The Alliance sought to strengthen both democracy in Latin America and anti-Communism. But the Latin American armed forces, the agency we chose to ensure anti-Communism, were also the agency that destroyed a whole gamut of democratic governments in the region.[45]

2. We sought to build up the Latin American middle class as a bastion of stability and democracy, but we also tried to mobilize peasants and workers to stave off *Fidelista* appeals and to increase societal pluralism. The mobilization of the lower classes frightened the middle classes, who turned to the military. They then repressed the lower classes, destroyed democracy, and snuffed out pluralism.[46]

3. We tried to create a trade unionism that was both nonpolitical and anti-Communist, a strategy that was inherently contradictory and in a number of countries helped to divide and fragment the labor movement.[47]

4. The United States often sought to stimulate Latin American local government and grass roots participation, but used a national organization as the agency to achieve that goal and thereby centralized power still further.[48]

5. The United States sought to promote independence and self-sufficiency in Latin America, but the practical result of the Alliance was to increase vastly Latin America's dependence on the United States.

6. The Alliance had clear long-term development goals but numerous short-term political and strategic expediencies kept getting in the way. Eventually the short-term expediencies all but overwhelmed the long-term goals, and the Alliance ended in disarray and with a sense of failure.

Conclusions

The Alliance for Progress was formulated, designed, and administered by some of the country's ablest scholars and public officials. The Alliance brought together some of the nation's foremost economists, planners, lawyers, sociologists, economic historians, statesmen, and specialists in development. It truly incorporated the "best and the brightest."[49] Unfortunately almost no one in this group had the detailed background or expertise in Latin America necessary to understand fully why the fundamental assumptions of the Alliance would not work there.

The failures of the Alliance are legendary. There were endless snafus and missteps. Enormous amounts of money and effort were wasted on a large number of misguided and misdirected programs. The policy measures we sought to implement produced a host of backfires, unanticipated consequences, and sheer disasters. The false assumptions on which the Alliance was based led us in numerous wrong directions. Moreover a strong case can be made that the Alliance helped bring about the repressive military regimes that swept Latin America in the 1960s, wiping out earlier democratic gains and making way for some of the bloodiest practices ever seen in Latin America. Because the internal contradictions of the Alliance were never resolved, the strategic considerations (in the form of Latin American military regimes) ultimately prevailed over the democratizing and developmentalist ones. Indeed one could say that it was the Alliance's very reforms (mass mobilization and the like) that helped trigger the armed forces to intervene. Further, under the Alliance we may have left the hemisphere with the worst of all possible worlds: a complete vacuum, caused by the undermining of Latin America's traditional institutions—institutions that were not necessarily progressive but did have some viability and legitimacy in the Latin American context—before anything new or "modern" had been created and sufficiently institutionalized to replace them.[50]

But the Alliance also produced major successes. New roads, highways, housing projects, water systems, electrical grids, hospitals, and schools were built under Alliance for Progress auspices and with Alliance funds. The health and educational levels of millions of Latin Americans were improved. The infrastructure—bureaucratic and administrative as well as in more concrete form—was put in place for future development. Alliance capital provided a great deal of economic pump-priming (and even some "trickle down"), which helped the Latin American countries to develop. Latin American living standards and per capita income went up impressively. Most important in the strategic sense, the Alliance helped prevent for over two decades any other countries from following the route of Castro's Cuba—which, after all, was the chief purpose of the Alliance to begin with. Between 1959 and 1979 not a single Latin American country went Communist or became an ally of the Soviet Union. In short, even though its assumptions were all wrong, the Alliance could be considered successful in its primary purpose. In this sense the Alliance *worked*, but for almost all the wrong reasons. Therein may lie some lessons for the present.

The first lesson has to do with the Caribbean Basin Initiative and the Kissinger Commission recommendations for Latin America, both of which bear a striking resemblance to the Alliance for Progress.[51] The CBI and the Kissinger Commission recommendations can in fact be seen in a sense as a "warmed over" version of the Alliance—and are based on many of the same assumptions as that earlier program. Now, while the outside scholar in me suggests that these new programs and initiatives are likely to repeat the mistakes of the past, the Washington person in me suggests that the Alliance, the CBI, or the Kissinger Commission recommendations with all their faults are—given our frequent and widespread lack of understanding of Latin America, our historical lack of attention to the area, our condescension, and our still powerful belief that *we* know best for the hemisphere—about as good as we can devise. One comes to accept the Alliance and these other recent programs not as "pure" or "ideal" policy and not without their many flaws and problems—not the least of which is that we seem to have learned relatively little about Latin America since the 1960s. We accept such programs prudently as a second-best solution and certainly better than no program at all or than several far more wild-eyed alternatives. We probably cannot reasonably or realistically expect more than the Alliance, the CBI, or the Kissinger Commission recommendations. That is the first lesson.

The second lesson involves assessing which of the Alliance programs worked and which did not. The analysis here and elsewhere makes clear that the best and most successful programs were those aimed at building social infrastructure (roads, housing, schools, health) as well as economic development. The narrower and more technocratic the programs, the better they worked. What did not work well—indeed were dismal failures—were all the grandiose social and political engineering programs of the Alliance: all the efforts to refurbish Latin American society and politics and recast it in our own image. Virtually all of these programs were failures.[52] The moral for current policy, therefore, is, Don't get so deeply involved in Latin American social and political life; for the most part let the Latin Americans handle their own political problems and processes in their own murky way; concentrate on simple and straightforward social and economic aid; and largely forget about "reforming" and "restructuring" Latin America from top to bottom. We would, I have reluctantly concluded (and only half in jest), generally be better off simply dropping the assistance money randomly from helicopters than getting as deeply involved in all the everyday issues of Latin American life as we did before.

The third lesson has to do with understanding what the Alliance actually did. Essentially, it bought us some time—twenty years to be exact. Few of the grandiose designs worked well or as expected, we have seen, and the assumptions were all wrong, but in its fundamental strategic purpose the Alliance succeeded: it bought us time, and it kept any additional Marxist-Leninist regimes from coming to power. Only after the Alliance was abandoned and we returned in the 1970s to our traditional policy of benign neglect did any new revolutionary regimes in Latin America come to power. Now, buying time is not a great and glorious dream—as the Alliance was—but as former Secretary of State George Marshall once noted, in an offhand response to an interview question, it is not a bad basis for American foreign policy. That lesson, and its broader implications for U.S. assistance programs, is as true now as it was when Marshall articulated it.

Notes

1. Jerome Levinson and Juan de Onis, *The Alliance that Lost Its Way: A Critical Report on the Alliance for Progress* (Chicago: Quadrangle Books for the Twentieth Century Fund, 1970).

2. Eduardo Frei Montalva, "The Alliance that Lost Its Way," *Foreign Affairs*, 45 (April 1967), pp. 437–48.

3. The better full-length critiques, in addition to Levinson-Onis, include Victor Alba, *Alliance Without Allies* (New York: Praeger, 1965); William Manger, ed., *The Alliance for Progress: A Critical Appraisal* (Washington, D.C.: Public Affairs Press, 1963); and Harvey S. Perloff, *Alliance for Progress: A Social Invention in the Making* (Baltimore: Johns Hopkins University Press, 1969).

4. Milton S. Eisenhower, *The Wine Is Bitter: The United States and Latin America* (New York: Doubleday, 1963).

5. See the discussion in Howard J. Wiarda, *Latin America at the Crossroads: Debt, Development and the Future* (Boulder, Colo.: Westview Press, 1987).

6. Adolf A. Berle, *Latin America: Diplomacy and Reality* (New York: Harper and Row for the Council on Foreign Relations, 1962); DeLesseps S. Morrison, *Latin American Mission: An Adventure in Hemisphere Diplomacy* (New York: Simon and Schuster, 1965).

7. The main literature on the founding and assumptions of the Alliance include William Benton, "Latin Americans Must Do Their Part," *Challenge*, 10 (January 1962), pp. 9–13; Chester Bowles, "The Alliance for Progress: A Continuing Revolution," *Department of State Bulletin*, 45 (November 6, 1961), pp. 239–45; Joseph Grunwald, "The Alliance for Progress," *Proceedings of the Academy of Political Science*, 27 (May 1964), pp. 78–93; John C. Dreier, *The Alliance for Progress: Problems and Perspectives* (Baltimore: Johns Hopkins University Press, 1962); Lincoln Gordon, *A New Deal for Latin America: The Alliance*

for Progress (Cambridge, Mass.: Harvard University Press, 1963); Nathan A. Haverstock, "The Alliance for Progress," *Americas,* 15 (August 1963), pp. 3–9; Albert O. Hirschman, "Second Thoughts on the Alliance for Progress," *The Reporter,* 24 (May 25, 1961), pp. 20–23; John F. Kennedy, "Fulfilling the Pledges of the Alliance for Progress," *Department of State Bulletin,* 46 (April 2, 1962), pp. 539–42; Jerome I. Levinson, "After the Alliance for Progress: Implications for Inter-American Relations," *Proceedings of the Academy of Political Science,* 3 (1972), pp. 177–90; Alberto Lleras Camargo, "The Alliance for Progress: Aims, Distortions, Obstacles," *Foreign Affairs,* 42 (October 1963), pp. 25–37; Abraham F. Lowenthal, "Alliance Rhetoric versus Latin American Reality," *Foreign Affairs,* 48 (April 1970), pp. 494–508; Thomas C Mann, "The Alliance for Progress," *Department of State Bulletin,* 50 (June 1, 1964), pp. 857–63; Ernest R. May, "The Alliance for Progress in Historical Perspective," *Foreign Affairs,* 41 (July 1963), pp. 757–74; J. Warren Nystrom and Nathan A. Haverstock, *The Alliance for Progress: Key to Latin America's Development* (New York: Van Nostrand, 1966); John N. Plank, "The Alliance for Progress: Problems and Prospects," *Daedalus,* 91 (Fall 1962), pp. 800–11; Brandon Robinson, "The Alliance and a Divided Heritage," *Foreign Service Journal,* 40 (January 1963), pp. 38–41; W. W. Rostow, "The Alliance for Progress," *Department of State Bulletin,* 50 (March 30, 1964), pp. 496–500; Dean Rusk, "The Alliance for Progress in the Context of World Affairs," *Department of State Bulletin,* 46 (May 14, 1962), pp. 787–94; Arthur F. Schlesinger, Jr., "The Lowering Hemisphere," *The Atlantic,* 225 (January 1970), pp. 79–88; Robert M. Smetherman and Bobbie B. Smetherman, "The Alliance for Progress: Promises Unfulfilled," *American Journal of Economics and Sociology,* 31 (January 1972), pp. 79–85; Adlai E. Stevenson, "Problems Facing the Alliance for Progress in the Americas," *Department of State Bulletin,* 45 (July 24, 1961), pp. 139–44; Tad Szulc, "The First Year of the Alliance for Progress," *The World Today,* 18 (October 1962), pp. 407–15; "The U.S. and the Alliance for Progress," *Congressional Digest,* 42 (March 1963), pp. 67–96; United States Senate, Committee on Foreign Relations, *Survey of the Alliance for Progress* (Washington, D.C.: Government Printing Office, 1969).

8. Based on interviews by the author with a number of the State Department persons involved in these changes.

9. Schlesinger, "Lowering Hemisphere."

10. For a full discussion see Howard J. Wiarda, "The Context of United States Policy Toward the Dominican Republic: Background to the Revolution of 1965," paper presented at the Center for International Affairs, Harvard University, December 8, 1966.

11. Pat M. Holt, *Survey of the Alliance for Progress: The Political Aspects* (Washington, D.C.: Government Printing Office for the Committee on Foreign Relations, United States Senate, 1967).

12. For earlier, more extended treatments by the author see *Politics and Social Change in Latin America: The Distinct Tradition* (Amherst: University of Massachusetts Press, 1982); *Corporatism and National Development in Latin America* (Boulder, Colo.: Westview Press, 1981); and *Ethnocentrism in Foreign Policy: Can We Understand the Third World?* (Washington, D.C.: American Enterprise Institute for Public Policy Research, 1985).

13. The subtitle derives from Daniel Bell's essay on how to interpret the Soviet Union: "Ten Theories in Search of Reality: The Prediction of Soviet Behavior in the Social Sciences," *World Politics*, 10 (April 1958), pp. 327–65.

14. See especially Schlesinger's comments in "Lowering Hemisphere," p. 81; for a more general treatment of our lack of knowledge about Latin America see James W. Symington, "Learn Latin America's Culture," *New York Times* (September 23, 1983); and Howard J. Wiarda, *In Search of Policy: The United States and Latin America* (Washington, D.C.: American Enterprise Institute for Public Policy Research, 1984).

15. For a more detailed critique see Chapter 5 of *Corporatism and National Development.*

16. *One Minute to Midnight in Latin America* (Washington, D.C.: League of Women Voters, April 1963).

17. Luis Mercier Vega, *Roads to Power in Latin America* (New York: Praeger, 1969), chapter 4.

18. Howard J. Wiarda, *Dictatorship, Development, and Disintegration: Politics and Social Change in the Dominican Republic* (Ann Arbor: University Microfilms Monograph Series, 1975).

19. See the discussion in Holt, *Survey.*

20. The main literature includes C. E. Black, *The Dynamics of Modernization* (New York: Harper and Row, 1966); Robert L. Heilbroner, *The Great Assent: The Struggle for Economic Development in Our Time* (New York: Harper and Row, 1963); and W. W. Rostow, *The Stages of Economic Growth* (Cambridge: Cambridge University Press, 1960).

21. Seymour M. Lipset, *Political Man: The Social Bases of Politics* (New York: Doubleday, 1960).

22. See the two volumes edited by Claudio Véliz, *The Politics of Conformity in Latin America* (London: Oxford University Press, 1967); and *Obstacles to Change in Latin America* (London: Oxford University Press, 1965).

23. See, for example, John Bartlow Martin, *Overtaken by Events* (New York: Doubleday, 1966).

24. Especially, Gabriel A. Almond and James S. Coleman, eds., *The Politics of the Developing Nations* (Princeton, N.J.: Princeton University Press, 1960).

25. Particularly in *Ethnocentrism in Foreign Policy.*

26. Lipset, *Political Man;* and Rostow, *Stages.*

27. John J. Johnson, *Political Change in Latin America: The Emergence of the Middle Sectors* (Stanford, Calif.: Stanford University Press, 1958).

28. See, among others, Richard N. Adams et al., *Social Change in Latin America Today* (New York: Vintage, 1960); and Charles Wagley, *The Latin American Tradition* (New York: Columbia University Press, 1968).

29. Mark Falcoff, "Arms and Politics Revisited: Latin America as a Military and Strategic Theater," in Howard J. Wiarda, ed., *The Crisis in Latin America* (Washington, D.C.: American Enterprise Institute for Public Policy Research, 1984), pp. 1–9.

30. Some balanced assessments include Miguel S. Wionczek, "The Rise and Decline of Latin American Economic Integration," *Journal of Common Market Studies*, 6 (September 1970), pp. 49–67; and Hermann Sautter, "LAFTA's Successes and Failures," *Inter-Economics*, 5 (May 1972), pp. 149–52.

31. Arthur F. Schlesinger, Jr., *A Thousand Days: John F. Kennedy in the White House* (Boston: Houghton Mifflin, 1965), pp. 769–70.

32. Howard J. Wiarda, ed., *The Continuing Struggle for Democracy in Latin America* (Boulder, Colo.: Westview Press, 1980); also Wiarda and Kline, *Latin American Politics and Development* (Boulder, Colo.: Westview Press, 1985).

33. Among this genre, Karl M. Schmitt and David D. Burks, *Evolution or Chaos: Dynamics of Latin American Government and Politics* (New York: Praeger, 1963); Mildred Adams, ed., *Latin America: Evolution or Explosion?* (New York: Dodd, Mead, 1963).

34. Charles W. Anderson, "Toward a Theory of Latin American Politics," Occasional Paper No. 2, Graduate Center for Latin American Studies, Vanderbilt University, Nashville, Tennessee.

35. *Ethnocentrism in Foreign Policy.*

36. After the title of the volume prepared by the Inter-American Foundation, *They Know How* (Washington, D.C.: Government Printing Office, 1977).

37. Louis Hartz, *The Liberal Tradition in America* (New York: Harcourt, Brace and World, 1955).

38. For a full elaboration see Robert Packenham, *Liberal America and the Third World: Political Development Ideas in Foreign Aid and Social Science* (Princeton, N.J.: Princeton University Press, 1973).

39. Anderson, "Toward a Theory"; also Kalman H. Silvert, *The Conflict Society: Reaction and Revolution in Latin America* (New York: American Universities Field Staff, 1966).

40. Howard J. Wiarda, "The Problem of Ethnocentrism in the Study of Political Development: Implications for U.S. Foreign Assistance Programs," Paper presented at the XIII World Congress of the International Political Science Association, Paris, July 15–20, 1985 (chapter 6 in this book).

41. Especially, T. Lynn Smith, *Agrarian Reform in Latin America* (New York: Knopf, 1965).

42. James L. Payne, *Labor and Politics in Peru: The System of Political Bargaining* (New Haven, Conn.: Yale University Press, 1965).

43. Carlos Mouchet, "Municipal Government" in Harold E. Davis, ed., *Government and Politics in Latin America* (New York: Ronald Press, 1958), pp. 368–92; also Arpad von Lazar and John C. Hammock, *The Agony of Existence: Studies of Community Development in the Dominican Republic* (Medford, Mass.: Fletcher School of Law and Diplomacy, 1970).

44. Alfred E. Stepan, *The Military in Politics: Changing Patterns in Brazil* (Princeton, N.J.: Princeton University Press, 1971).

45. Edwin Lieuwen, *Generals versus Presidents: Neo-Militarism in Latin America* (New York: Praeger, 1964).

46. José Nun "The Middle Class Military Coup," in Véliz, ed., *Politics of Conformity*, pp. 66–118.

47. Wiarda, *Dictatorship, Development, and Disintegration*, chapter 7.

48. See the exchange between the author and a U.S. community development official in *The Nation*, 206 (February 19, 1968) and (May 6, 1968).

49. After the title of the book by David Halberstam, *The Best and the Brightest* (New York: Random House, 1972).

50. *Ethnocentrism in Foreign Policy.*

51. Compare *The Report of the President's National Bipartisan Commission on Central America* (New York: Macmillan, 1984). The author served as a lead consultant to the commission.

52. See, by the author, *Ethnocentrism in Foreign Policy;* "The Problem of Ethnocentrism"; and "At the Root of the Problem: Conceptual Failures in U.S.-Central American Relations," in Robert S. Leiken, ed., *Central America: Anatomy of Conflict* (New York: Pergamon Press for the Carnegie Endowment, 1984), pp. 259–78.

PART THREE

Understanding Policy Processes

10

The Kissinger Commission Report on Central America

The Report of the National Bipartisan (Kissinger) Commission on Central America is important for a number of reasons: it helped raise the level and seriousness of the debate on Central America; its findings and the legislation introduced as a result of the commission's work have dominated the policy discussion and the legislative agenda on Central America since 1984; and the report proved initially to be quite controversial. But it has more recently become both the basis for administration policy and an instrument for building policy consensus in dealing with Latin America.

The work of the commission and its findings have frequently been misrepresented in the media and in academic writings where only some of the report's more controversial aspects have received attention. Actually, it is a quite remarkable document: elegantly written in many passages (thanks in part to the editorial magic lavished on it by former presidential speechwriter Ray Price), containing a sophisticated analysis of the complex *multi-causality* of the Central American upheaval, and offering a range of balanced policy prescriptions that bear a striking resemblance to John F. Kennedy's Alliance for Progress. Far from being the conservative and radical right-wing statement some reviewers have sought to label it (the radical right has in fact denounced the commission's findings and recommendations, as has the radical Left), the report is in fact a centrist and middle-of-the-road statement—at least as measured in terms of the center of American national public opinion if not always that of professional Latin Americanists.

The moderate and pragmatic nature of the report becomes clear if one looks at the document itself rather than relying on often superficial secondary accounts. The character of the report also comes out

An earlier version of this chapter was published in the *AEI Foreign Policy and Defense Review*, vol. 5, no. 1 (1984).

clearly in the several expert background papers prepared as part of the commission's work. For in addition to issuing the actual report, the commission also commissioned a series of papers both by Central America specialists and by general foreign policy experts. In the attention given the report, these background papers have been almost completely ignored. They are crucial, however, not only in demonstrating the essentially moderate and centrist nature of the report but also in showing the bases on which a politically diverse commission achieved a remarkable degree of consensus and the logic and analysis on which their recommendations were based.[1]

The Background

In this brief chapter we cannot do full justice to the background and dynamics of the commission, and we await an assessment of the report based on the memoirs of the commissioners and on a full understanding of the processes and decision making involved. Only a few of the main events and currents that would go into such an analysis are offered here.

Briefly, the idea for a presidential commission grew out of Ambassador Jeane J. Kirkpatrick's report to the president delivered in the spring of 1983 that the situation in El Salvador and all of Central America was deteriorating rapidly and was, if anything, worse than had been reported in the press; it grew out of a rising sense of desperation in the White House that existing policy was not working well and may have reached a crisis point; it emerged from the growing conflict over Central American policy between Congress and the White House and the strong feeling than an effort of bipartisanship was necessary; it was a response to rising criticism of the president's policies by the public and major interest groups; and it emerged from fear and reelection calculations in some circles that, as Lyndon Johnson once put it, no American president could be reelected who permitted a "second Cuba" in the Caribbean. The actual idea for a presidential commission on Central America is widely said to have come from the late Senator Henry Jackson, Democrat from Washington state.

That is the other element of background that should be recalled: the Kissinger Commission was created in the context of two recent, successful, and widely praised presidential commissions—the so-called Greenspan Commission on social security and the so-called Scowcroft Commission on the MX missile. Two things should be remembered: the first involves the politics of presidential-level commissions. Such commissions are frequently seen as useful because they enable a president to play for time on difficult and divisive issues, they allow a president to put off a potentially damaging decision while still appearing to be doing something, they help to defuse the criticism a president is receiving at least for a time, they deflect the criticism from the president personally, they give a president needed room to maneuver, and, in the best of circumstances (the Greenspan and Scowcroft commissions), they actually do help give the president an opportunity to make his case to the American public and maybe even help achieve a measure of national and bipartisan consensus. That is what presidential commissions do, and we need to be realistic about their political purposes and limits.[2]

But it is also important to state that presidential commissions differ and that the Kissinger Commission was quite different from either the Greenspan or the Scowcroft Commission. In those two cases there was already widespread and bipartisan agreement on what had to be done: the Scowcroft Commission had to find an appropriate and practical locus and mechanism for a land-based strategic missile system that everyone agreed was necessary but which no one wanted nearby; the Greenspan Commission had to reduce benefits to bail out the social security program in a way that would not place political blame on either party. With an existing consensus about what needed to be done, the architects of these commissions could concentrate on the politics of ensuring bipartisan unity in the Congress to guarantee overwhelming approval for their recommendations.

But the Kissinger Commission was different from the other two: it was both a fact-finding body and an agency of hoped-for consensus. In the considerable emphasis on the former, something in the latter was bound to be sacrificed. The commission took its charge of investigating and issuing a fresh and original report seriously but in the process lost some of its political purpose of forging a consensus. The comparative neglect of the preeminently political or consensus-building purposes of the commission also helps explain the considerable early criticism its final report received, compared with those of the other two commissions.

Makeup of the Commission

The bipartisan commission consisted of twelve members, six Democrats and six Republicans.[3] Most were centrists politically, although quite a number of the commissioners were strong-willed and independent, and their positions on individual issues or on the report as a whole could not be assumed in advance. As would be expected, a number of the commissioners had private agendas (prestige, future jobs, political ambitions) as well as the publicly stated one. The commission members were, in the main, moderate and pragmatic; there were few ideologues of whatever stripe.

In addition to the commissioners, counselors to the commission included high-ranking congressmen as well as some senior State Department officials: Ambassador Jeane J. Kirkpatrick, U.S. Permanent Representative to the United Nations; Winston Lord, president, Council on Foreign Relations; William D. Rogers, attorney at law; Sen. Daniel K. Inouye (D-Hawaii); Sen. Pete V. Domenici (R-N. Mex.); Sen. Lloyd Bentsen (D-Tex.); Sen. Charles McC. Mathias (R-Md.); Rep. William S. Broomfield (R-Mich.); Rep. Jack F. Kemp (R-N.Y.); Rep. James C. Wright (D-Tex.); and Rep. Michael D. Barnes (D-Md.). There was obviously considerable room for partisanship here and some ideological posturing. But the main thrust among the counselors was moderation and centrism.

The staff consisted of State and Defense Department career personnel, with few, if any, ideologues. The dominant orientation was professional and apolitical. The staff was chosen for its efficiency and knowledge, not to satisfy any preordained political criteria.

The commission also brought on a number of what were called lead consultants. Their role, a critical one that has received almost no attention, was to help select witnesses for the Commission, to solicit expert testimony, and to prepare background papers for the commissioners and, in some cases, early drafts of the report's several chapters. The lead consultants included: Ambassador William H. Luers, Department of State; Carl S. Gershman, U.S. Mission to the United Nations; Alan Stoga, First National Bank of Chicago; Sidney Weintraub, Lyndon B. Johnson School of Public Affairs, University of Texas; William C. Doherty, Jr., American Institute for Free Labor Development; Edward Marasciulo, Pan American Development Foundation; Howard J. Wiarda, University of Massachusetts and American Enterprise Institute for Public Policy Research; Ambassador Viron P. Vaky, Georgetown University; Margaret Daly Hayes, Senate Foreign Relations Committee; Gen. Gordon Sumner; Gregory Treverton, Harvard University; Mark Falcoff, American Enterprise Institute for Public Policy Research; and Robert Hunter, Center for Strategic and International Studies.

There was to be, as on the commission itself, a bipartisan lineup to the lead consultants. That is, for each section of the report (such as political development, social and economic development, military and security assistance, and diplomatic initiatives) one Republican appointment and one Democratic appointment were to be made. In fact, no one ever checked closely the partisan affiliations of the lead consultants. Rather, like the professional staff and the commission itself, they were for the most part pragmatists and centrists rather than ideologues. The position papers and initial drafts of chapters that they wrote were generally middle-of-the-road—so much so that some of them supposedly representing conflicting partisan backgrounds wrote joint reports rather than two separate ones. In other cases the teams of lead consultants and their papers were so close that they were complementary and not conflictive. The consensus achieved in the lead consultant papers was also important in shaping the consensus eventually achieved by the commission.

Work of the Commission

The commission labored all through the fall of 1983. It heard over 300 witnesses and briefers and received reports from over 230 individuals and groups. It put in long days. It digested mountains of materials and heard many points of view. The commission did its homework.

Initially, given the partisan alignments and the diverse backgrounds, the commission was quite deeply divided. And, as would be expected from any group of strong-minded persons with divergent agendas, there was considerable posturing. But eventually a consensus began to emerge. This was a remarkable process and helps explain the unanimity of the report and the presence of only a few quite minor dissents from it.

The elements contributing to the building of a consensus may be identified as follows: first, there was simply the matter of time and the fact of living and working together over several months. Eventually the commissioners learned respect for each others' views. The early posturing gave way to serious discussion.

Second, the commission was impressed by the remarkable agreement and consensus among the senior professional staff and the lead consultants. Virtually everyone among the senior staff and the consultants agreed that the roots of the crisis in Central America were complex and multidimensional and that the issue of the socioeconomic versus Soviet/Cuban causes of the upheaval was, since both of these as well as other causes were involved, a false and misleading one. They were also agreed on the need for a bipartisan and a long-term solution; they further agreed, for political reasons as well as sound policy considerations, that a solution was required that spoke to the multiple causes of the Central American problem and that therefore required major economic and social assistance, some mili-

205

tary aid, political development and democratization, expanded cultural exchanges, and the like. The issues came to be seen more as pragmatic ones rather than as necessarily partisan or ideological.

Third, the commission's trip to Central America in October 1983 was critical. The commissioners were strongly impressed by several different things. Liberals on the commission, who might have been persuaded otherwise, were strongly impressed by the growing Marxism-Leninism of the Nicaraguan revolution and its leaders and especially by the threat perceived by all its neighbors concerning Nicaragua's extensive military buildup. Conservatives were strongly impressed by the extent and horror of El Salvadoran death squads. The result, again, was a strong trend by both groups toward a center position, toward condemnation of both right- and left-wing extremism, and toward a pragmatic and broadly based middle way.

Politics of the Report

The Kissinger Commission Report, viewed simply as an intellectual exercise, is well written, balanced, careful, more or less internally consistent. But it is also, and preeminently—necessarily so as the product of a presidential commission—a political document. It is not and cannot be a pristine academic treatise, but is and must be a report serving diverse political purposes and constituencies. Critics have not usually recognized that fact, but it is essential for a proper understanding of the document and of the diversity and the range of its recommendations.

First, the report is the product of a *presidential* commission. That means that the first reader of the report is the president himself, or a delegated aide in the White House. If the commission had produced a report satisfactory to the Latin American Studies Association but not to the White House, the report would never have seen the light of day. Hence the first criterion had to be a report that the White House could accept and support rather than repudiate. Edwin Meese, then a presidential adviser, was actually the first White House reader of the report.

Second, the report had to be bipartisan. It was, after all, a bipartisan commission. And the report it produced had to be acceptable to both sides of the political aisle. If it were not bipartisan, the congressmen who served as counselors to the commission and the Congress itself would not have approved it.

Third, the report had to be centrist. The reviews it has received indicate it is not acceptable to the American left, but it is important to note that in its emphasis on socioeconomic aid, family planning, agrarian reform, and the like, it has been repudiated by the far right as well. The report hence sought to occupy the broad middle of the American political spectrum, to forge a centrist consensus.

Fourth, the report had to satisfy diverse constituencies, bureaucratic as well as political. That is why, in part, it contains sections on military aid as well as social and economic assistance, human rights as well as security doctrine, public assistance as well as private investment, political development and democratization, cultural exchanges, and aid to labor movements. Not only had the commission agreed on such an intellectual balance, but as politicians they also saw the need to speak to diverse interests. Any report of this sort must necessarily represent such a smorgasbord approach. That makes it not entirely acceptable to any particular group, but it does provide a little something to virtually everyone. Although the approach may not be acceptable from the point of view of purists, it is certainly how things work in Washington, D.C.

Conclusion

The Kissinger Commission Report's recommendations are familiar and need not be reviewed in detail here. Briefly, the report called for a major program of socioeconomic aid, stepped-up military and security assistance, a vastly expanded program of cultural and scholarly exchange, aid for political development and democratization, a vigorous human rights policy, as well as a new agency—the Central American Development Organization (CADO)—to administer the program. The report emphasizes the "seamless web" of Central America's development and security-related dilemmas and suggests that there can be neither security without reform nor reform without security. The report suggests the United States can live with indigenous socialist revolutions but not those that meddle in the internal affairs of their neighbors or ally themselves with the Soviet Union. The report suggests support for the Contadora negotiating process but indicates that U.S. interests are also affected in Central America and that any settlement in the region must, obviously, involve and be satisfactory to the United States as well.

The report—and a package of legislative recommendations prepared concurrently by the staff—were sent in 1984 to the Congress. Since 1984 was an election year and some congressmen felt they could get political mileage out of Central America, the Congress quibbled, amended, stalled, and sat on the report for a time. But the report and its policy prescriptions commanded the center, they dominated the legislative agenda, and no one in the Congress was able to come up with a better plan. Eventually, parts of the plan were enacted by the Congress, principally those recommendations having to do with scholarships, cultural exchange, and socioeconomic assistance—but other key aspects were stalled in the bureaucratic labyrinth of Capitol Hill.

While all of the commission's recommendations were not immediately enacted, the report did serve as an agency of consensus building and as a basis for future administration policy. It not only helped defuse a dangerous and divisive issue at the time (1983), but it also served as the basis for the consensus on most aspects of policy forged by the fall of 1985. Almost no one in political Washington at this stage disagrees much about how we should be aiding El Salvador or about the nature and policies of the Sandinista regime. Nor do any disagree about the need to balance socioeconomic and military assistance, security doctrine with a vigorous democracy and human rights campaign, and son on. Hence, although not all of the Kissinger Commission's suggestions have been formally adopted into law, the report does serve as the foundation now for both a more enlightened and prudent administration policy in Latin America and a far higher level of national consensus on policy than had existed before.

Notes

1. The report is available in the following editions: *Report of the National Bipartisan Commission on Central America* (Washington, D.C.: U.S. Government Printing Office, 1984) Order no. 040-000-00477-7; *Appendix to the Report of the National Bipartisan Commission on Central America* (Washington, D.C.: U.S. Government Printing Office, 1984) Order no. 040-000-00478-5, (a collection of consultant papers and testimony); *The Report of the President's National Bipartisan Commission on Central America* (New York: Macmillan Publishing Company, 1984), ISBN 0-02-074610-5 (English-language edition), ISBN 0-02-074620-2 (Spanish-language edition). See also the special issue of the *AEI Foreign Policy and Defense Review,* "U.S. Policy in Central America: Consultant Papers for the Kissinger Commission," vol. 5, no. 1 (1984), Howard J. Wiarda, guest editor.

2. See George T. Sulzner, "The Policy Process and the Uses of National Governmental Study Commissions," *Western Political Quarterly* XXIV (September 1971), 438–48.

3. Henry A. Kissinger, chairman; Nicholas F. Brady, managing director, Dillon, Read & Co.; Henry G. Cisneros, mayor, San Antonio; William P. Clements, Jr., former governor of Texas; Carlos F. Díaz-Alejandro, professor of economics, Yale University; Wilson S. Johnson, president, National Federation of Independent Business; Lane Kirkland, president, AFL-CIO; Richard M. Scammon, political scientist; John Silber, president, Boston University; Justice Potter Stewart; Ambassador Robert S. Strauss, attorney at law; and William B. Walsh, president, Project Hope.

11
The Paralysis of Policy: Current Dilemmas of U.S. Foreign Policy Making

This chapter, originally written in the spring of 1985 at the time of the wrenching, divisive, congressional vote on U.S. aid to the Nicaraguan *Contras*, discusses the creeping paralysis, fragmentation, and immobilism that then seemed to be the prevailing—and highly disturbing—characteristics of American foreign policy.

But after that the situation was turned around considerably, especially in Central America, which is the focus of this chapter. Although the spring 1986 vote on the same *Contra* aid issue was similarly divisive, other events—U.S. action in the Philippines, Haiti, and the Mediterranean—gave a stronger, more decisive aspect to American foreign policy. There even seemed to be at that time an emerging and hopeful consensus concerning the main lines of an overall Central America policy.

To reflect these changes and the newer, more positive developments of that time, the author added a brief postscript that was considerably more optimistic and upbeat than the pessimistic view expressed in the body of the paper. Now, however, in the wake of the disarray in the administration following the revelations concerning the Iran-Contra transfers of arms and money, it seems that the original pessimism is again justified.

Neither the original chapter nor the postscript should be read alone or by itself. Rather, they should be read in sequence as a measure of the changing context and conditions of foreign policy as well as of the author's reassessment over time.

The Current Context

President Reagan's overwhelming electoral victories in 1980 and 1984; his image as a strong, forceful charismatic president, "standing tall"

A briefer version of this chapter was published in *World Affairs* (1987).

and leading the country out of economic recession and a decade-long political funk; and occasionally decisive military actions, as in Grenada, have helped obscure the increasing paralysis that has come to characterize our foreign-policy-making apparatus. Instead of a strong, coherent, and forceful foreign policy, the United States now has a foreign-policy-making system increasingly marked by incoherence, fragmentation, the too-frequent preeminence of domestic political considerations over foreign-policy priorities, and stalemate. These changes, which are related to profound structural transformations in the American society and polity over the past twenty years, add up to a situation from which we can expect little in the way of a more harmonious, consensual, long-term, and rational policy, regardless of the issue or area involved and independent of the person occupying the White House. We have reached a stage of advanced policy sclerosis and *immobilisme*, a term the French used to describe the fragmented and ineffective Fourth Republic.

A generation ago Harvard scholar Graham Allison suggested that the "rational actor model" of foreign-policy decision making was inadequate to explain how in fact decisions get made.[1] The rational actor model posits a well-oiled decision-making machinery in which various options are presented, the pros and cons of each are weighed, and a presumably rational or best decision is made from these choices. Allison and various foreign-policy specialists since then, however, have shown that most foreign-policy decisions involved not just the rational weighing of alternatives and choosing among the options. Rather, decision making also was affected by intense rivalries among competing foreign-policy bureaucracies (such as State, Defense, NSC, CIA—what Allison called the "bureaucratic model"), as well as organizational and regular administrative procedures inherent in the workings of government (what Allison called the "organizational model").

Today we would have to add some other "models" to Allison's list. These would doubtless include a "domestic politics model," a "media model," a "rival-interest-group model," a "candidate reelection model," a "competitive–think tanks model," and a "self-interest/self-aggrandizement model." These new perceptions of policy-making are related to the more fragmented, more self-centered, less consensual society and polity that we have become in the past two decades. Major interest groups now compete, in the foreign policy as well as domestic arenas, to see that their point of view prevails. The fact is that big money and status, as well as opportunities for career advancement, can result from seeing one's own solution become official policy. In addition, individual and narrowly partisan views now routinely take precedence over the broader national interest.

Doubtless readers can envision other such explanatory "models" (the term is here used neutrally to designate a particular approach or conceptual frame of reference, rather than implying approval or disapproval) to add to the list. None of these other models, however, implies or is likely to lead to a logical, bipartisan, and coherent foreign-policy-making process that better serves the public interest or the nation as a whole. Instead, private interests frequently come before and often literally overwhelm considerations of the national interest, which is then served only as a byproduct of these other considerations.

To the question "Hasn't the system always worked this way?" the answer would have to be that private, partisan, and particularistic considerations *have always* been part of the U.S. foreign policy-making process; so have checks and balances. The difference now is that the divisions are deeper, the stakes higher, the rivalries more intense, the polarization and fragmentation more pronounced, the private interests involved more blatant, and the sheer numbers of actors and interests involved greater than ever before—all causing the paralysis of policy to be more pronounced than in the past. Only in extraordinary circumstances, it now seems, when the president is willing to put the full force of his office and prestige behind a policy that is not particularly crucial to the national interest (let us say military aid to Guatemala), can the system be made to function rationally and well. On larger issues and those on which the White House is not willing to commit itself, the system barely functions. Paralysis and immobility have now become the *norm*, not the exception. The result is an often directionless foreign policy that is frequently ineffective and sometimes unmanageable.

Let us review some of the major cultural, societal, and political areas where the domestic changes of the past twenty years have rendered our foreign policy so inoperative. We will treat briefly the changing role of public opinion; the influence of domestic political considerations; the role of new one-issue interest groups; the position of the proliferating Washington think tanks; the changing role of Congress and of a system of divided government; the effect of bureaucratic rivalries and infighting; and the vastly increased role of the media, particularly television. We will conclude by discussing whether a Democratic president would likely face the same drumbeat of opposition to his policies as the present Republican has, and what if anything can be done to overcome our present immobility and restore us to a greater measure of foreign policy coherence and rationality.

Public Opinion. In the United States isolationist sentiment is still strong. Even now, some forty-five years after the United States en-

211

tered World War II, which supposedly sounded the death knell for isolationism, we are still very much an isolationist nation. Surveys indicate that of the American population, about one-third may be dubbed liberal internationalist in terms of how they see the U.S. role in the world, one-third are conservative internationalist, and the remaining third isolationist.[2] For a person involved in Washington foreign-policy making, that last figure is truly astounding—particularly given all we have seen and heard in the past four decades about American economic interdependence with the rest of the world, our obligations as the leader of the free world, our defense requirements, our needs for OPEC oil, our raw materials shortages, our dependence on imported manufactured goods, and so on. Isolationism is too blind, too weak, and too divorced from the real world in which we exist to constitute still a viable basis for foreign policy. The United States is too interdependent with the rest of the world in major political, military, diplomatic, economic and strategic ways to countenance a strategy of isolationism.

One-third of the American public apparently still believes, however, that we can essentially "go it alone" in the world, throw up protectionist walls, ignore our allies and clients, neglect them, withdraw, and follow a purely defensive strategy in foreign affairs—even in the age of missiles, spy satellites, and Soviet-inspired revolutions now occurring uncomfortably close to home. The isolationist sentiment helps explain why our foreign-language and area-studies training in this country are woefully inadequate; it also explains our frequently superior and condescending attitudes toward other cultures, our sometimes insistent belief that we know best for the rest of the world. This pervasive isolationism further helps explain why it is so difficult to get foreign-aid bills, the Caribbean Basin Initiative (CBI), and a "Marshall Plan" for Latin America through Congress.

The Vietnam War added to our cynicism, self-doubt, and wariness of foreign entanglements and also forced a split between the liberal and conservative wings of the internationalists. The liberal internationalist demands that America's role in the world be "moral," that it stand for democracy and human rights. If these elements are lacking, if the morality of the case is murky as in El Salvador, if only the national interest is at stake and not some presumably higher purpose, then the liberal internationalist is prepared to sit on his hands, join the isolationists, and do nothing. Or, as in Central America, the liberal internationalists may go into active opposition to U.S. policy.

Conservative internationalists are sometimes similarly prepared to sit on their hands unless their agenda of a strong defense, vigorous anticommunism, and support for American ways is met. From the beginning, therefore, an internationalist president of whatever political stripe faces the strong possibility that two-thirds of the electorate will oppose his actions, that his program will be defeated if his opposition joins with the element that is automatically isolationist. That is a major shift from the era of an essentially bipartisan policy in the 1950s and early 1960s, when a president could count more or less automatically on two-thirds of the electorate to support his policy. Now the proportions have been reversed, meaning that a president must walk a very fine line between a liberal and a conservative foreign policy or he will quickly lose his working majority.

The American public, we know, is strongly opposed to foreign aid. Roughly 85–90 percent of the public is opposed to foreign assistance *in any form,* a percentage that makes it easy for demagogic congressmen to rail against it. At the same time, at least 75 percent of the population does not want the United States to commit troops or get involved in a ground war in Lebanon or Central America, where the objectives are sometimes unclear, where American soldiers may get killed, and where U.S. forces may be bogged down in another Vietnam-like imbroglio. Almost the same percentage, two-thirds, is opposed to U.S. covert support to those seeking to overthrow the Sandinista regime in Nicaragua.[3] Of course, it is also easier to decry foreign aid when in so many instances it is misused, squandered, and used to feed corruption by the recipients. Because we often receive meager thanks for our generosity, congressmen understandably feel compelled to give aid only with many strings attached and on the condition that those on the receiving end provide some, however modest, support—or at least stay neutral and silent—when controversial measures about which the United States feels strongly are on the docket at the United Nations and in other forums. Many Americans are justifiably tired of being criticized by the very people who get our aid and stay in power thanks to it.

Ironically, the proportion of the public that does not want the United States to become involved overseas also wants no second Cubas in the Caribbean. Roughly two-thirds to three-quarters of the population will countenance no more Marxist-Leninist states allied with the Soviet Union in the area often referred to as "our lake." Therein lies the foreign policy dilemma for any U.S. administration: how to prevent second Cubas in the Caribbean without any of the tools necessary to do so: no foreign aid, no military interventions, no covert operations. How an administration can carry out a foreign policy objective effectively when American public opinion will grant it none of the instruments by which to do so is among the great unanswered questions of our time. It requires great skill and finesse to manage even a modicum of policy under such conditions when the natural tendency of the system is toward do-nothingness and immobility.

It is hard enough for an administration to manage these contradictory aspects of mass public opinion, but the task is even harder with informed or elite opinion. Elite opinion in this case means the views and predispositions of the elite media, the publishing world, television and the movies, and the universities.[4] Within the media, for example, Democrats outnumber Republicans by ratios of about four to one; the book industry seems to have moved significantly to the left; and in the universities the "Berkeley generation" of anti-Vietnam protesters not only has come to power but also has tenure. Inevitably these biases and predispositions are reflected in the news coverage we receive, the books and movies produced, and the content of the courses taught in our colleges and universities.

Elite opinion in this country, because of Vietnam, Watergate, and doubtless other factors, has become overwhelmingly negative. This change is dangerous for foreign policy and has made a positive foreign policy all but impossible. Elite opinion has largely accepted the third-world critique that most of the poverty, the oppression, the military dictatorships, and the racism and imperialism in the world are the fault of the United States. Hence there is an enormous amount of liberal-radical angst and guilt about the fate of the world and our role in causing it. All the evil in the world, some of the spokespersons seem to be saying, can be blamed on the United States, on capitalism, and on U.S. "hegemony." It is never the fault of the Soviets or venal local elites. These negative attitudes have helped sow a sense of profound distrust of all U.S. actions and policies and have added a new dimension to our foreign policy paralysis. The United States is viewed not as a source of possible good in the world but of threat, danger, and even sin, *all* of whose initiatives must therefore be vigorously opposed. In this context the opposition to everything the United States does or stands for becomes reflexive and total.

This overwhelming preponderance of power among elite opinion molders on the radical-liberal and negative side (while in office, Jimmy Carter was as much despised by this element as Ronald Reagan is) makes it difficult for any president to carry out an effective policy—and doubly difficult for a conservative Republican. During the past five years virtually every action by the president in the foreign affairs area has brought down the full wrath of the liberal-radical establishment. The drumbeat of opposition was intense, the verbal abuse extreme, the mobilization of bias extensive—so much so that pro-administration spokesmen on campus, in the media, and in publishing have been largely cowed into silence. In some cases of course, the administration's policy deserves the criticism it receives, but in others—for example, the CBI, the election of a democratic government in El Salvador, the Kissinger Commission recommendations, the assistance to and triumphs of democratic forces throughout the hemisphere—it deserves some credit and support. Indeed a case could be made that if the critics really supported democracy, then they logically would be at the forefront in supporting elections, the newly formed Democracy Endowment, and the Kissinger Commission recommendations.

The critics refused to give any credit even to the administration's better initiatives, however, because they had a hidden political agenda. Their goal was often to undermine and destroy the administration's very legitimacy. There were times when the administration could not find a single credible and willing spokesman in the academic community to defend even its best initiatives because vocal opinion on the other side was so strong. No one wanted to be a part of an unpopular minority, and the intimidation practiced against those like Jeane Kirkpatrick who forcefully articulated an alternative viewpoint was often severe. The result not only inhibited serious foreign policy discussion but also produced such a loud chorus of opposition among elite opinion makers as to all but hamstring American foreign policy. And all this was in direct contradiction to the overwhelming popular mandates that Ronald Reagan received in both 1980 and 1984, mandates that encompassed support for both his domestic and his foreign policies. Something is clearly amiss if in a democracy majority sentiment can be stymied and virtually silenced by a loud, vocal, articulate, well-entrenched, and strategically located minority.

Domestic Political Considerations

In observing American foreign–policy making from a Washington perspective, one concludes that seldom if ever is anything done solely for its foreign-policy merits; rather the overwhelmingly important consideration is U.S. domestic politics. One is tempted to conclude that good foreign policy is most often an accidental byproduct of domestic considerations; more charitably, one could say that nothing is done unless it serves both foreign-policy considerations *and* the private ambitions and self-interests of the politicians proposing it. To the three models of foreign-policy decision making described by Graham Allison—rational-actor, bureaucratic, and organizational—we propose here the addition of two closely interrelated models: a "political model" and a "self-interest model."

215

The problem is particularly acute as regards Latin America. Unlike Africa and the Middle East, for example, Latin America has little in the way of an articulate and organized constituency in the United States. The number of Hispanics in the United States is increasing rapidly, but the influence of the Hispanic community is still fragmented, diffused, and not very effective. Hence politicians can afford to be reckless, condescending, ethnocentric, and downright wrong about Latin America to a degree they cannot afford to be concerning other geographic areas. The primary reason is that few of them will have to pay politically for the mistakes of omission and commission that frequently characterize our policy toward Latin America. That situation may change as more Hispanics are involved in the political process and as the Central American crisis comes closer to home, but now a politician can still get away with statements on Latin America that would cost him dearly if used about other areas.

The problem is multidimensional and cuts across party lines. At the White House, at least during Mr. Reagan's first term, it meant that little was done vis-à-vis Latin America without first weighing the possible effect on the president's reelection possibilities. During Mr. Reagan's first year in office, the White House relegated foreign-policy issues to the background as much as possible, while the president and his advisers—in part for domestic political reasons—concentrated on reviving the U.S. economy. Later, when the Central American situation worsened and threatened to jeopardize the president's 1984 reelection, decision making was more and more concentrated in the hands of White House political operatives so as to minimize the potential damage. For a time after the departure of Assistant Secretary Thomas Enders from the State Department's Bureau of Inter-American Affairs, it appeared that White House election campaign strategists, few of whom were foreign-policy experts, were really making Latin American policy. Throughout Mr. Reagan's first term, the White House paid close attention to Richard Wirthlin's poll results, which showed clearly the wishes of the American public for no second Cubas and also for keeping U.S. ground forces out of Central America. These same polls showed when the president should begin paying close attention to Latin America—and when he could safely ignore it.

The Congress and its members have many of the same domestic political preoccupations. Indeed, given their obligations to their constituencies and their two-year terms, it could be argued that congressmen feel these pressures even more acutely. One of the major contributions of American political science is to show that when all other factors—race, religion, party, region, seniority, and the like—

are held constant, the one factor that explains congressional voting more than any other is: the desire to be reelected.[5] For congressmen as well as the president, reelection considerations loom paramount.

Hence the mastering by congressmen of the thirty second one-liner, guaranteed to get them on the television news in the home district and, for skillful practitioners, maybe even on the national evening news. Hence the virtually nonstop hearings covered constantly by the Cable News Network and C-Span if not always by ABC, CBS, and NBC; hence also the requirements of certification of human rights progress in countries like El Salvador, designed as much to embarrass the administration and get the congressmen in the headlines as to shed light on the situation in El Salvador. Congressmen must run for reelection every other year, and because the preparations and positioning begin so far in advance there is virtually no between-elections respite for a reasoned discussion of the real issues.

Even the debate itself is structured to achieve maximum domestic political impact and television exposure rather than serious consideration of policy alternatives. President Reagan's famous speech on Central America to a joint session of the Congress in the spring of 1983 was scheduled for prime-time national television and designed to deliver a strong message to the public and especially to the congressmen. The president's message to congressmen was, in effect: If you vote against my aid package and El Salvador falls to communism, we in the White House will remember and in your next reelection campaign will not hesitate to brand you as the ones who "lost" El Salvador. That sort of message has a profound influence on congressmen thinking of reelection. In return, the Congress voted Mr. Reagan just enough aid to put him in up to his chin and in effect told him, OK, now it's your war to sink in or survive. This is hard-ball politics, but with domestic politics as the underlying motivation, not El Salvador.

The domestic political considerations are so overwhelming that one arrives at the conclusion it is chiefly a U.S. political agenda that is acted on when we decide Central American or other foreign policy issues, rarely that of the countries affected. U.S. efforts to promote democracy, human rights, agrarian reform, professionalization of the Salvadoran military—these are all issues primarily in the U.S. domestic political debate; only tangentially and partially do they relate to the realities of Central America. Central America has become a stage on which we act out our domestic political dramas, and almost never do we bother to look at the issues in Central America's own terms or context.[6]

The debate over Central America has often been an internal U.S.

debate, over whether we have overcome our Vietnam complexes or whether Central America is a "second Vietnam," whether we can act decisively in the world, whether we can still export our model to the less-developed countries, and so on. And it is not just the president and Congress who are playing for the benefit of domestic political audiences; one gets the impression that the major American interest groups and lobbies are similarly pursuing their *private* domestic priorities independently of the realities of Central America. How a coherent, rational, enlightened foreign policy can be carried out when policy makers are primarily influenced by domestic considerations and their own reelection possibilities is worrisome and does not inspire great confidence in the kinds of policies likely to emanate from the United States.

Interest Groups. In the mid-1960s, political scientist Grant McConnell raised the question of whether private interest groups of various kinds (big business *and* big labor) were assuming some of the functions of the U.S. government, and yet because of constitutional protection and political influence could not be held accountable for their actions.[7] In the mid-1970s Samuel P. Huntington raised a related point when he asked whether the success of interest groups in placing major claims on public resources was sapping the strength of American political institutions and rendering the country all but ungovernable.[8] McConnell's concern, as Nathan and Oliver point out in their analysis of American foreign policy making,[9] was about the effects of private power on democracy; Huntington was suggesting that American democracy—including the area of foreign affairs—was becoming unmanageable and anarchic.

Actually, both problems are present in the American interest group system, rendering the making of a rational and coherent U.S. foreign policy all but impossible. First, McConnell's point: A major worry in Washington these days is whether the large U.S. interest groups may sometimes be running their own foreign policies quite independently of the U.S. government and almost entirely without accountability to the U.S. public. Through their private business and large associations representing the interests of a variety of firms, for example, as well as individually, major U.S. corporations and multinationals can sometimes mobilize more lawyers, more money, more influence, and more clout than can the entire foreign-policy-making apparatus of the U.S. government. When big business senses a weakness at the National Security Council or a vacuum in one of the regional bureaus at the State Department, it can sometimes move in and virtually take over entire areas of foreign policy. In other cases a private association may be given or invited to run a whole area of foreign policy in cooperation with the federal government because the government itself lacks the requisite skills, ability, time, or expertise to do so itself. We are not talking just about the powerful role and influence of multinational corporations abroad but about the domestic assumption by some business groups of whole regions of foreign policy. The lobbying and influence peddling by U.S. firms on behalf of foreign governments is still another major problem in this area.

The problem is often as acute with big labor as with big business. The AFL-CIO, for example, has been running for some twenty-five years a program to develop trade unions in third world nations, especially in Latin America. The program is rather like those developed with the business sector, involving cooperation between the government and a private group. This program operates through U.S. embassies and AID missions abroad, employs public funds, and is supposed to be coordinated with a myriad of other official U.S. activities abroad. Yet there is almost no public oversight of these activities and practically no accountability. Questions have sometimes been raised about the exact purposes, methods, and results of this program. Yet in political Washington a careful examination of these activities is unlikely to be conducted since so many politicians are dependent on or fearful of the political clout of organized labor. Big labor's hand can be heavy on congressmen or scholars who cross it, and organized labor still exercises veto power over many appointments and reelection possibilities. Hence both big business and big labor can sometimes carry out their own almost autonomous foreign policies, quasi-independently of the U.S. government, but using public funds and resources, a situation not guaranteed to ensure coherence in U.S. foreign policy.

Second, Huntington's point: The power of these groups is immense. They command immense resources, their own and the public's. A number of these groups have practically taken over whole areas of foreign policy for themselves, making them into semiprivate preserves. This privatization of public policy is very dangerous for a rationalized and integrated foreign policy since it gives rise to a variety of private "fiefdoms," each pursuing its special interests, sometimes with only partial regard for the public or national interest. This is interest-group pluralism gone far beyond Madison's precepts; it is really a Calhounian system of separate "concurrent majorities" with little attachment to a common core and each with veto power over public policy. The success of these interest groups in incorporating themselves into the system, taking over certain areas of foreign policy for themselves, and extracting resources from the public weal

219

to pursue their own interests in fact diminishes the strength and accountability of the American system and makes the country—in this case its foreign affairs—chaotic and ungovernable.

Third, we must discuss the rise of new, single-cause, interest groups. These include church lobbies, human rights groups, and others that have been especially active on Central American issues. The church and human rights groups have been particularly effective on Capitol Hill, not only because they provide useful information to congressmen but also because they sometimes take advantage of their religious ties. No congressman can afford to refuse seeing representatives of the church. The trouble with the new church and human rights lobbies is that they often have a private political agenda that goes beyond the commitment to human rights, they are selective in mobilizing moral indignation against some types of regimes and not others, and their focus is entirely on one set of U.S. foreign policy considerations, human rights, to the exclusion of all other U.S. interests—political, economic, security—that may have at least equal legitimacy. These lobbies have skewed the foreign-policy discussion into a unidimensional format and have on numerous occasions blocked and frustrated policies that are clearly in the broader national interest.

Overall, our interest group system has changed from one of genuine pluralism, which most of us believe to be among the best features of American democracy. Some private groups have assumed a great deal of public power but with almost no accountability. The independent power of these groups is eroding the governability of the American system. Some of these groups have usurped whole areas of public policy for themselves, thereby accelerating the disturbing trends toward a corporatized polity in the United States, and some have acquired virtual veto power over public policy. As a high-ranking State Department official once put it to the author, he was far more worried about the anarchic conditions prevailing in the U.S. foreign policy debate over Central America than he was over anarchic conditions then prevailing in El Salvador itself. These trends are not reassuring in terms of the prospects for a better American foreign policy.

The Think Tanks. The Washington-based think tanks have, it has been argued, also been agencies, and reflections, of the growing disagreement over foreign policy.

In their excellent book *Our Own Worst Enemy: The Unmaking of American Foreign Policy,* I. M. Destler, Leslie Gelb, and Anthony Lake present the intriguing thesis that the decline in influence of the older, New York–based Council on Foreign Relations has been paralleled by the rise of the Washington think tanks. They further believe that the bipartisan consensus that the council was a primary agency in shaping in the 1950s has now been replaced by discord and by political, even partisan, competition among five rival agencies.

In Washington, the five most influential institutes are the American Enterprise Institute for Public Policy Research (AEI), the Brookings Institution, the Center for Strategic and International Studies (CSIS), the Heritage Foundation, and the Institute for Policy Studies (IPS). Agencies such as the Carnegie Endowment for International Peace and the Overseas Development Council generally play a lesser role, usually on narrower issues.

Neither the products of the Heritage Foundation (conservative) nor those of the IPS (radical) have historically been accorded much attention in middle-of-the-road Washington foreign-policy circles. When a liberal Democratic administration is in power, however, the IPS enjoys some added legitimacy, and when a conservative Republican administration is in power the Heritage Foundation has increased influence. Essentially, though, it is AEI, Brookings, and CSIS that command the broad center of the political spectrum and therefore have influence no matter what the politics of the administration in power.

The ideological lines between these three agencies, while they do exist on some issues, have blurred considerably in recent years— although in the public's view the differences remain stark. Brookings was long known as a liberal think tank mainly because its economists were Keynesians and therefore critical of Eisenhower's economic policies and supportive of Kennedy's. But Brookings now has a Republican president, its analyses have drifted toward the center, it raises funds from the same corporate and business sources as AEI and CSIS do, and its foreign-policy publications are not distinguished by any clear ideological position. AEI was long thought of as a pro-business institution, but it has also moved toward the center, and its publications are viewed as serious, scholarly, and, especially on foreign affairs, middle-of-the-road; CSIS also does mainly centrist studies and serves as the current home of both Henry Kissinger and Zbigniew Brzezinski.

There is far more interchange, cooperation, and agreement among the major think tanks than the earlier histories and orientations of these institutions would lead one to expect. Nevertheless in the public mind and for purposes of the media, the ideological differences between them tend to be exaggerated. What too often passes for "good television" now, for example, is when a representative of the left says something far out and then is answered by an ideologue of the right. In television's view, the need for controversy and confrontation has thereby been satisfied and "all points of view" have been represented. Much the same kind of confrontations are characteristic of congressional hearings and other public forums.

This kind of confrontational encounter ignores the considerable degree of consensus on a centrist and pragmatic foreign policy among the major moderate Washington think tanks. The public perception, however, often exaggerated by the media, is of widespread disagreement on virtually all issues, which reinforces the perception of fragmentation and polarization in Washington. And, of course, in the media age perception may be more important than reality.

Congress and Divided Government. There is no doubt that since Vietnam Congress has become more assertive in foreign policy. This new assertiveness goes beyond the traditional congressional oversight of foreign policy and Congress's treaty-ratifying responsibilities, and is much more aggressive. Numerous congressmen and their committees are actively engaged in the formulation, initiation, and *making* of foreign policy.[10]

One of the causes of this new assertiveness is the remarkable growth of congressional staffs over the past twenty years and the devolution of important fact-finding and policy-formulation functions to the staffs, most of whom are considerably younger and more ideological than the congressmen they serve. Another cause is the decline of the seniority system and ʼof party discipline, which has enabled many congressmen to go their own way—sometimes in defiance of the leadership. A third cause is television, which enables virtually any congressman to share equal time with the secretary of state and allows almost any bizarre and outlandish view to air in millions of living rooms.

The War Powers Act gives the Congress extraordinary powers to hamstring American foreign policy by requiring congressional approval of the commitment of U.S. ground forces after sixty days. The requirements of human rights certification every six months in countries like El Salvador has led to some limited improvements in the human rights situation in that country, but it has taken up enormous amounts of State Department and NSC staff time and created further divisiveness. In addition, politicians have sometimes delayed political appointments for so long as to cause designees to withdraw their names from nomination. And Congress has held up legislation by making its vote on a foreign-policy issue hostage to some purely private pursuit. The fact that since 1980 we have been operating with a system of divided government, with either the House or Senate or both controlled by one party and the White House by the other, has added significantly to Congress's independence and assertiveness. The presence of so many would-be presidential candidates in the Congress is another factor.

The current situation goes beyond the checks and balances that the founders intended. It represents instead an advanced state of paralysis. At one end of Pennsylvania Avenue American presidents tend to promise more than they can deliver; they sometimes refuse to recognize the limits that now exist on American power and capacity to maneuver internationally; they often present overblown statements of our prospects and goals; and they continue to pursue a strategy that would have the United States serve as both policeman and missionary to the world. At the other end of the avenue, the Congress postures chiefly for reelection purposes, seeks constantly to embarrass a president of the other party, ties up his legislation, and prevents a rational and coherent policy from being carried out.[11] Rarely is a workable and effective compromise arrived at out of all this.

Not only can every congressman now command equal time with a secretary of state but often functions as if he or she were secretary of state. Some congressmen have taken to negotiating directly with a group of guerrillas or a foreign government, presenting their positions on national television, and then "inviting" the U.S. government to go along. Overall the Congress has become far more critical of foreign policy initiatives emanating from the White House, assuming a greater role for itself while absolving itself of responsibility for the result of its actions. The big losers in all this have been the American people and the interests of a centrist, pragmatic, and moderate foreign policy.

Bureaucratic Politics and Fragmentation. It is the bane of our allies that U.S. administrations always speak with several voices on foreign policy. Such divisions would not be possible or permissible in the larger Western European countries with their parliamentary systems and strict party discipline, but in the United States rivalries ("bureaucratic politics") among and between the several foreign policy–making agencies—State Department, White House, Defense Department, NSC, CIA, UN Mission, Treasury Department, and so on—are endemic. The question is not whether the United States can speak with one voice on foreign affairs—it cannot—but rather how manageable or paralyzing the divisions become.

The Carter administration was widely criticized for having an incoherent, confused, and self-contradictory foreign policy. Secretary of State Cyrus Vance, NSC adviser Zbigniew Brzezinski, and UN Ambassador Andrew Young frequently spoke with different voices, from distinct perspectives, and for different constituencies. The relations between NSC staff and the professionals in the regional and functional bureaus of the State Department were so strained at times that they could barely speak civilly to each other, let alone carry out effective policy.

The Reagan administration was determined to change all that. It insisted on speaking with one voice on foreign policy, subordinating the NSC adviser, and ensuring that everyone in the foreign policy bureaucracies was "on line" with overall administration goals. Early in Mr. Reagan's first term a high-ranking foreign policy adviser within the government noted that this administration had taken pains to ensure greater ideological unity in foreign policy appointments than any previous administration. There *was* such ideological conformity in the administration in its first two years, but at the cost of severe criticism for its departures from a more centrist foreign policy. Much the same thing had been true with regard to the McGovern wing of the Democratic Party during the first two years of the Carter administration.

It was only later that fissures began to appear and the familiar bureaucratic rivalries resurfaced. The Departments of State and Defense were frequently at loggerheads over U.S. policy in Lebanon and Central America, among other places, a conflict that was sometimes reflected in the policy statements of Secretaries George Shultz and Caspar Weinberger. A fierce battle was waged over Latin American policy pitting (according to press accounts) Team A (the so-called ideologues) against Team B (called pragmatists), with each group having its allies and sympathizers among the president's White House staff and other cabinet members. The battle was eventually won, at least partially, by the pragmatists at the State Department. Meanwhile the personal rancor and dislike also intensified. By late 1984 some astute foreign policy analysts were saying that they had never before seen such fragmentation on foreign policy—not even under President Carter!

The extent of the fragmentation was considerably exaggerated by the press and the administration's critics, although there was sometimes disagreement over strategy, and both groups needed to compromise and agree on a single policy. On the one hand, the "ideologues" articulated a clear and unambiguous foreign-policy vision, but they were forced to give way on some issues. On the other hand the State Department professionals, who served as their chief foes, have in the past not always distinguished themselves for their expertise on Latin America or other areas to which they are assigned. Some of them share what may be termed the "Princeton syndrome"—

the belief that the broad understanding imparted by a general liberal arts education at an Ivy League college is sufficient to enable one to understand any world area. More specialized knowledge has often been viewed as unnecessary, even as an impediment by some officials. That attitude and the assumptions that all developing countries must inevitably follow the Western example, that the developmentalist processes learned in "History of Western Civ" will have universal applicability, have been at the root of our lack of understanding of third world areas.[12]

Actually, a considerable learning process has gone on within the administration. American foreign policy is now not only more sophisticated and nuanced than it was in the early months of the administration, but also more moderate and prudent. During the early months of any new administration those who dominate the headlines and the foreign policy discussions are often the politicians who accompanied the candidate during the campaign and accompanied him into office. Gradually, the foreign-policy professionals and those with more expertise on areas and functional issues begin to recapture policy. The Reagan administration has been undergoing this change over the past two years. Secretary Shultz and the State Department have reasserted their suzerainty over foreign policy, but the process has been particularly prolonged. Some policy makers do not speak to others beyond their formal obligations, and it appears that the infighting, the bureaucratic and personal rivalries, and the conflict, divisiveness, and fragmentation will continue—and may even get worse. A better balance is required between the president's political advisers, who often closely reflect his political mandate, and the career professionals who have specialized expertise and tend to push policy back toward the center.

The Media. The media, since Santo Domingo and Vietnam, the two major foreign policy crises of the 1960s, have played an increasingly important role in foreign policy—chiefly as critics. The media no longer present news only in a neutral fashion; instead, their positions are increasingly those of advocacy.

The causes of this new advocacy journalism are various. In part it stems from money and the immense profitability and "star quality" of network television; in part from the new style of aggressive, investigative reporting; in part from Vietnam and its legacy; in part from a new wave of more radical, Berkeley-generation reporters; in part from the widespread desire by young journalists to reap the same level of gold and glory that Woodward and Bernstein did from their disclosures of Watergate; in part from the desire to expose and attack all established institutions; and in part from the media's perception that the First Amendment guarantees it a position akin to a fourth branch of government.

Media coverage of foreign policy tends to be on the liberal and radical sides. We know from opinion surveys that the "elite media" (such as the *New York Times*, the *Washington Post*, network news, and the wire services) are overwhelmingly liberal, supporting Democratic presidential candidates over Republicans in recent elections by ratios of four or five to one. The elite media also tend to share the counter-culture view that the United States is among the major causes of the world's problems, that CIA-sponsored covert activities are inherently evil and should be made illegal, that there should be a mammoth resource allocation from North to South, that U.S. embassy officials are seldom to be trusted, and that guerrilla revolution likely represents the future of Latin America.[13] These views are often reflected in the news they print and broadcast.

Another problem is media inexperience in foreign affairs and the resulting ethnocentrism of the coverage. Many of the reporters sent to Central America by the major news organizations, for example, had never been in the area before, knew little or no Spanish, and had little understanding of Latin America. The coverage was thus exceedingly ethnocentric, often based on the simplistic categories of undergraduate history or political science courses, or on an idealized version of U.S. society and institutions (an apolitical military, middle class family farms and the like) which presumably Guatemala or El Salvador would try to imitate.

The problem, of course, is media (especially television) with immense power to influence opinion but not always with the knowledge, responsibility, or neutrality to do so fairly and adequately, or so oriented toward "entertainment" that their news coverage is fatally skewed or lacks depth. One is constantly amazed at the biases and prejudices that creep into the news reporting, at the one-sidedness of much of the news coverage, at some of the stories that should be covered but are not, and at the inability of the journalists and commentators to look at Central America on its own terms. The media's influence is enormous, but the reporting has not been commensurately balanced, evenhanded, or accurate. As a consequence the press, the general public, and policy making have all suffered.

Without presuming to judge the wisdom of the policy decisions made we can recognize without doubt that the coverage of the truck-bombing in Lebanon that killed 240 U.S. servicemen was a key factor, perhaps *the* key factor, in the withdrawal from that country of American troops. The coverage of the brutal rape and murder of the four nuns and religious lay women in El Salvador may have poisoned U.S. opinion about that country and helped lead to fundamental changes in U.S. policy. The coverage of Nicaragua was initially and rather romantically sympathetic to the Sandinista revolution, though by now some of that has changed.

A case can be made that in Central America some media coverage did help force the administration back to the mainstream of U.S. foreign policy, with its emphasis on democracy, human rights, socio-economic assistance, and good neighborliness along with the military buildup. Insofar as that is the case, there is something to be said in favor of the media's role in this regard. What remains objectionable, however—regardless of the policy outcome—are the political biases, the ethnocentrism, and the distortions of so much media coverage. In many areas the media have placed themselves above and beyond the electorate and political processes, presuming that they know better for the country than the electorate itself—a posture that is extremely dangerous in a democracy. Or they have placed themselves in a position of having "superior knowledge" to those inside and outside of government with real expertise on particular nations and countries. The media have far too often appropriated *for themselves*, arrogantly and presumptuously, a specially privileged position, in the process frustrating and hamstringing foreign policy, and thereby serving as an additional factor in our foreign policy paralysis. Sometimes it is difficult to tell if U.S. foreign policy is driven by the U.S. government or by the media.

Conclusions

Ultimately, U.S. foreign policy is a reflection of American society itself. We have become, since the 1960s, a much more divided and fragmented society, less sure of ourselves, less powerful in relative terms, more partisan and ideological. Building a domestic consensus around a foreign policy is less easy than it used to be; the foreign policy consensus that prevailed through the mid-1960s ("politics stops at the water's edge") has broken down, replaced by a myriad of special interests, partisan posturing, and highly vocal and often politically motivated spokesmen. During an era, after all, when all established verities and institutions are questioned or under attack, we should not be surprised that foreign policy is subjected to the same treatment.

Some would argue that the immobility that now frequently confronts us shows merely that the historic system of checks and balances is working properly. Actually, neither Madison nor anyone else in the pluralist tradition intended for pluralism to be carried to the

227

point of paralyzing the policy process or of seeing special interests hiving off pieces of foreign policy for themselves. Moreover the case can be made that Congress, public opinion, the media, the human rights lobbies, and other interests did force upon the Reagan administration a considerable degree of restraint and tempering of foreign policy. That is healthy to the degree it is true, but the criticism of the opposition has often been far more insidious than that: it has been aimed not just at moderating Reagan's foreign policy but sometimes at subverting it, undermining it, and perhaps if possible at *removing* the administration altogether. In this sense the system is not working; it tends toward polarization, impotency, ineffectiveness, and incapacitation. We are in deeper trouble than we think. Foreign policy–making has in many areas reached a stage of advanced sclerosis.

It requires a president of truly extraordinary political skills to overcome the system's now powerful tendencies toward immobility. This is not a partisan brief, but surely one must admire Mr. Reagan's skills in this regard. He has been masterly at dealing with a divided Congress; he is an effective communicator in getting his message to the public; he handles skeptical and hostile media with aplomb; he has skillfully played the interest groups against each other; and he has adroitly managed to keep separate his strong rhetoric (for domestic political purposes) from his actually quite moderate actions. Moreover, when the full prestige of the presidency is put on the line, the system does sometimes respond effectively—as in Grenada and more recently in Haiti, the Philippines, and the Mediterranean. While this may sound like praise for Mr. Reagan, its intent is to show that under a president with lesser skills the *system* would possibly be entirely immobilized. Moreover, it took President Reagan at least two years after his election in 1980 to grasp effectively these handles of foreign policy; and now only shortly into his second term after receiving an overwhelming electoral mandate, he is being treated as a lame duck while the political preparations for 1986, 1988, and even 1992 are already under way. The immobility and paralysis built into the system, furthermore, are such that Democratic presidents are now almost as likely to be tied down and hamstrung as Republicans.

What can be done about these disturbing tendencies? We can perhaps ask that the decibel rate in the debates be lowered somewhat and that the debates be conducted rationally and on the real issues; we can request less verbal overkill, we can try to rebuild the domestic consensus (as Senator Lugar sought to do in his Foreign Relations Committee hearings in early 1985); we can provide better training programs on foreign policy issues for journalists, congressional staff, clerics, and others now involved in the policy process; we can expose the private and partisan agendas of various groups and individuals; we can allow the president some greater discretion in foreign policy matters; and we can work for some greater prudence, restraint, and moderation both in foreign policy and in foreign-policy discussions. In fact, all these steps are already being taken. But since the fragmentation, polarization, and *immobilisme* that mark our foreign policy are to such a large degree a reflection of the divided, fragmented, and egocentric society we have become, it is unlikely that we will soon or easily see very much change for the better. We are beginning to break out of that cycle, but we still have a considerable way to go.

A Postscript:
Overcoming Paralysis: Reagan Administration Foreign Policy Accomplishments

The theme of a fragmented, incoherent, semi-paralyzed foreign policy-making apparatus is now becoming familiar in the literature. Certainly all of the elements analyzed here—and others besides—have helped contribute to the immobilism that we now face and which seems likely to become worse in the future.

But the more interesting issues may not be *immobilisme* and sclerosis—important though those are—but rather how we still manage, sometimes more than occasionally, to conduct a rational foreign policy at all, given the incoherence that we see all around us. In fact, our foreign policy accomplishments are many and profound, and it is important that these be acknowledged. For very often the accomplishments are drowned in the sea of fault-finding and nit-picking that goes on and that is itself a product of our divisiveness.

At the most general level one must credit the increased military preparedness, the stronger defense, the restored economy, the renewed confidence and faith in ourselves and our system that has occurred over the last several years. It is now the Soviet Union that is most often on the defensive and no longer quite so often the United States.

Looking at one specific area, Latin America, some major accomplishments have occurred. El Salvador is a model of stability and democracy as compared with six years ago. Grenada's not-so-comic-opera revolution has been reversed. The Caribbean Basin Initiative and the Kissinger Commission recommendations constitute a solid basis for a multipronged policy in the area. Democratization—in many cases with U.S. assistance—has gone forward to encompass sixteen of the twenty countries and over 90 percent of the population. We now have more mature and even "normal" relations with most of

South America than ever before in our history. Among the list of successes, only policy toward Nicaragua stands out as so far unsuccessful; and even there, while the United States has not rid the country of the Sandinistas, it has helped keep their revolution from succeeding or from being freely exported to neighboring countries.

The real news,[14] therefore, may not be that we are stalemated and often incoherent in our foreign policy but that policy goes forward at all and that there are some real accomplishments to show for it.

As indicated, this chapter was originally written in the spring of 1985 at the height of our recurring debate and accompanying paralysis over Central America policy. The Congress had just voted down the president's request for assistance to the resistance groups (usually referred to as the *contras*) struggling against the Sandinista regime in Nicaragua and had refused even to compromise. Then it watched in acute embarrassment as Daniel Ortega flew to Moscow to cement Nicaragua's ties with the Soviet Union—thus leaving the congressmen who had voted against the contra aid not only with egg on their faces but extremely vulnerable to strong attack the next time they faced the voters. Senator John Kerry and other members of Congress went to Central America to conduct their own versions of foreign policy. The church and human rights groups had begun a new campaign, in violation of U.S. law but rationalized as civil disobedience, to provide "sanctuary" to Central American refugees—carefully coaching them in what to say before sending them to well-meaning congregations throughout the United States. The nation's universities were becoming increasingly hostile to U.S. foreign policy, in many cases using violent protests and guerrilla tactics to silence one side in the debate and thereby denying the fundamental rights of free speech. It seemed at that time as though any kind of coherent foreign policy was being unraveled thread by thread almost daily.

But following the wrenching 1985 debate, policy seemed to settle down and a considerable degree of consensus was achieved. The administration and the Congress finally reached agreement later in 1985 on a program of humanitarian aid to the contras—though when President Reagan in 1986 proposed anew a program of military assistance the issue proved as divisive as it had been the previous year. Duarte proved to be an effective democratic leader in El Salvador, thus justifying the efforts of the administration to help organize the elections and assist that tragic country. Duarte also demonstrated that the guerrillas really did lack the popular support some advocates had attributed to them. The human rights performance of both the Salvadoran armed forces and the Nicaraguan contras improved. Nicaragua's revolution looked less and less attractive to unbiased

230

observers. Meanwhile the media and the Congress had gone on to other issues: South Africa, the U.S. deficit, tax reform, Bhopal, Ethiopia, the Philippines.

Indeed, by the end of 1985, one could almost have said that the administration had "won" its case on Central America (and there are some within the White House who privately made such claims). Particularly in Washington (if not yet in the universities and among some church groups) agreement had been reached that:[15]

• Nicaragua is really a Marxist-Leninist regime and has very little intention of going in a more democratic direction.
• Nicaragua has been aiding the guerrillas in El Salvador and nefariously intervening in the internal affairs of its neighbors, though the precise extent of this aid is still open to debate.
• There is broad-based disillusionment in Nicaragua with the revolution; the revolution has not been successful particularly in the economic and political spheres.
• The contras really do have considerable popular support: they consist not just of the followers of the old dictatorship.
• The United States should take strong action to keep MIGs and other sophisticated offensive weaponry out of Nicaragua and to prevent it from militarily threatening its neighbors.
• Some kind of pressure should be kept on Nicaragua to help maintain even a limited degree of freedom and pluralism, to prevent Nicaragua from intervening in its neighbors' internal affairs, and to force Nicaragua to negotiate with the United States.

With regard to El Salvador there is similar consensus that:

• Duarte has done an excellent job.
• The Salvadoran military is improving.
• The guerrillas are not necessarily the wave of the future.
• Military and other assistance to the Duarte government should be continued, enabling it to negotiate with the guerrillas for greater democracy from a position of strength. Indeed there are even some in the Democratic opposition who have come to the same conclusion regarding Nicaragua: if we give military aid to Duarte in order for him to have a strong base for the building of democracy, we should also give aid to the contras to help force a democratic resolution in Nicaragua.

In short, the administration came to believe that it has been, over time, proven correct in all its major assessments of and policies toward Central America, that its policies there were all on the right track, and that the Central American problem has been essentially "solved." Significantly, and with greater or lesser degrees of reluctance, a good part of the Congress and of informed opinion in Washington has come to share that view—although many in the opposition cannot yet bring themselves to say this publicly and though there is still disagreement over some aspects of the policy.

My own sense is that the problems in Central America and in Latin America more generally have not been so readily "solved" and that there may be even greater problems (such as the explosive potential of the debt issue and other continued economic problems in the region) coming down the pike. But there is no doubt that the Central America issue has been significantly turned around in recent years. One could even say that all the pulling and tugging between the various interests, between the Congress and White House, and then the compromises and growing consensus in fact proves the American system still does work.

One needs therefore to keep an open mind about the themes presented in this paper and to reserve a final judgment. On the one hand, there can be no doubt that the Reagan administration, and particularly the president himself, has effected a real revolution in the Untied States in the way we think and act, about foreign affairs as well as other matters.[16] Some of us have been reluctant to admit that fact (and some still will not). But there is now more confidence in the air, more hope for the country, more vigor, more consensus, more agreement that in foreign policy we are doing some good things and may even be sometimes on the right track. Our actions in Haiti, the Philippines, and the Mediterranean, as well as Central America, seem to indicate that. At the same time many of the divisive, negative, polarizing, and paralyzing tendencies are still with us. They are deeply rooted, and they could again be reasserted—especially if we had a less-determined president or an even more obstreperous Congress. Hence we shall simply have to wait and see if the Reagan revolution in its better aspects can be sustained or whether we will revert again to the immobilism described earlier, potentially paralyzing our ability to conduct the long-term bipartisan foreign policy that many of us see as a crying American need—coherent, rational, and middle of the road.

That is why the unraveling that has occurred as a result of the revelations about the secretive U.S. policy in Iran and its domestic reverberations is so worrisome. The one force that has heretofore tended to hold the foreign policy-making system together—the president and his immense popularity—is now being undermined. The debate will continue as to whether the fallout from the Iran venture stems from the wisdom of the controversial policies of the president and his advisers or from the press and opposition politicians eager to take advantage of every slip. Whatever we decide on this issue, the facts are that the president's authority has been considerably undermined. As a result, fragmentation and incoherence are likely to spread. Since the opposition will not allow the issue to be forgotten, the immobilism and paralysis threatening foreign policy are likely to be a long-term problem lasting beyond the 1988 election.

Notes

1. Graham Allison, *Essence of Decision: Explaining the Cuban Missile Crisis* (Boston: Little, Brown and Co., 1971).

2. John A. Reilly, ed., *American Public Opinion and Foreign Policy* (Chicago: Chicago Council on Foreign Relations, 1975).

3. William M. Leogrande, *Central America and the Polls* (Washington, D.C.: Washington Office on Latin America, 1984).

4. See the series of articles on the attitudes of these several elites by Stanley Rothman and Robert Lichter, published in *Public Opinion,* 1981–1984. See also their book *The Media Elite: America's New Powerbrokers* (Bethesda, Md.: Adler and Adler, 1986).

5. David Mayhew, *Congress: The Electoral Connection* (New Haven, Conn.: Yale University Press, 1974).

6. Robert Packenham, *Liberal America and the Third World* (Princeton, N.J.: Princeton University Press, 1973); and Howard J. Wiarda, "At the Root of the Problem: Conceptual Failures in U.S.-Central American Relations," in Robert S. Leiken, ed., *Central America: Anatomy of Conflict* (New York: Pergamon Press, 1984), pp. 259–78.

7. Grant McConnell, *Private Power and American Democracy* (New York: Vintage Press, 1966).

8. Samuel P. Huntington, "The Governability of Democracies: USA" in Michael Crozier, Samuel P. Huntington, and Joji Watanuki, *The Governability of Democracies* (Trilateral Commission, 1975), also published as "The Democratic Distemper" in Nathan Glazer and Irving Kristol, eds., *The American Commonwealth* (New York: Basic Books, 1976).

9. James A. Nathan and James K. Oliver, *Foreign Policy Making and the American Political System* (Boston: Little, Brown and Co., 1983).

10. Thomas M. Frank and Edward Weisband, *Foreign Policy by Congress* (New York: Oxford University Press, 1979).

11. I. M. Destler, Leslie H. Gelb, and Anthony Lake, *Our Own Worst Enemy: The Unmaking of American Foreign Policy* (New York: Simon and Schuster, 1984).

12. Howard J. Wiarda, *Ethnocentrism in Foreign Policy: Can We Understand the Third World?* (Washington, D.C.: American Enterprise Institute, 1985).

13. Stanley Rothman and S. Robert Lichter, "Media and Business Elites," *Public Opinion* (November 1981), pp. 42–46, 59–60; also Howard J. Wiarda,

PART FOUR

Positive Approaches

12
The Future of Latin America: Any Cause for Optimism?

It is difficult these days for any objective and realistic student of Latin America to be optimistic about its future. The facts and figures add up to a picture that offers scant cause for encouragement.

The Present Crisis

Economic Aspects. Economically the region is a disaster area. Latin America has been particularly hard hit by the world depression that began in 1979 and still continues in many countries. That crisis came on top of the earlier oil shock of 1973 and the generally unstable and depressed prices for Latin America's primary exports during much of the 1970s. The world depression of the past six years has led to stagnant or contracting economies throughout Latin America, that lack adequate cushions or safety nets, social or otherwise, on which to fall back on.[1] Several economies of the area have experienced negative growth rates for over half a decade now; in most of the others there has been zero or very little development. Meanwhile, inflation is well over 1000 percent per year in several countries, and unemployment and underemployment combined may be as high as 40–50 percent throughout the area. Even the oil exporters (Venezuela, Mexico, Ecuador), which initially benefited from the oil crisis, are now facing very difficult times.[2]

The debt crisis adds to the problems. Latin America's debt is so large that there is no hope whatsoever that it will ever be paid. Banks have by this time quietly written off the possibility that they will ever collect much of the principal; they can be persuaded to stay in the foreign loans game only on the grounds that by doing so they will

Paper presented at the American Enterprise Institute's Public Policy Week Forum, "The Alternative Futures of Latin America," Washington, D.C., December 5, 1984, published in *AEI Foreign Policy and Defense Review,* vol. 5, no. 3 (Winter 1985).

continue to collect a trickle of interest. In this sense a major plank of the South's agenda in the North-South dialogue—the massive transfer of resources from North to South—has already been carried out, de facto and without anyone's admission that it has occurred. By stretching out the repayment period, reducing interest charges, forgoing some fees and commissions, rescheduling the debt over a multiyear period, and agreeing to some form of "cap" on interest rates (elements in the recent Mexican and Argentine agreements) the fig leaf may be kept in place. One should have no illusions, however, that these new arrangements will solve the problem. They preserve the twin fictions that the big debtor countries have avoided or can avoid default and that the banks will continue to collect. Fiction and romance serve certain essential functions but they should not be confused with reality, which is that the debt cannot be paid, no matter how severe the consequences for the banks, the Latin American countries, and, as always, the poor taxpayer.[3]

There is almost no new investment in the region. Given the instability and potential for chaos throughout Central America and the Caribbean particularly, a business or corporation would have to be almost irrational to invest in the region today—unless it could be done with ironclad U.S. government guarantees. Unfortunately, we in the United States do not sufficiently discriminate between countries; the violence and instability we have seen recently in Nicaragua and El Salvador have frightened away investment from the region as a whole. American and multinational business will be extremely reluctant to go into an area that seems as potentially unstable as Latin America.

Many of the large companies already there are, in fact, getting out of the region. Recent statistics indicate that not a single large American corporation has more than 10 percent of its holdings in Latin America. This is a major change from the days when W.R. Grace & Co., United Fruit Co., Kennecott Company, International Petroleum Corporation, and others had major investments in the area. Many companies are selling their Latin American holdings and abandoning the region in favor of the more lucrative investment fields of the Pacific Basin, Western Europe, Canada, and the United States itself. These are rational steps from the companies' point of view, but over the long term they will be devastating for the future of Latin America.

Until very recently, the U.S. government has not seemed willing to take up the slack. Since the late 1960s and the unofficial end of the Alliance for Progress, there has been little public assistance for Latin America. U.S. monetary assistance and personnel were severely cut. This was in keeping with the attitude of "benign neglect" that characterized U.S. policy toward Latin America for a decade, stemming from the assessment after Che Guevara's failure in Bolivia that all of Latin America was not about to go the way of Castro's Cuba after all. Only after the revolutionary threat developed again, this time in Central America in the late 1970s and early 1980s, did U.S. public assistance again begin to increase, as it had immediately after Castro's revolution twenty years earlier. The new aid took the form of the Caribbean Basin Initiative (CBI) and the "Marshall Plan for Central America" growing out of the report of the National Bipartisan (Kissinger) Commission on Central America. But the CBI, Latin Americans complain, has thus far produced precious little money or benefits, and some of the Kissinger Commission recommendations continue to languish in the political and bureaucratic labyrinths of the Congress.

Moreover, Latin American capital is also fleeing the region. Even at the height of the massive bailout of Mexico in 1982 more capital actually left that country than came in. Such losses are occurring all over Latin America: not only are U.S. companies abandoning the field, but local capital is also getting out as fast as it can in favor of the safer havens of Geneva, Miami, Houston, and Los Angeles. Even in such rich and nationalistic countries as Brazil and Venezuela, which never before had capital flight problems because the business elites believed in their countries' futures, money is now leaving in unprecendented amounts. If there is neither foreign nor local investment, nor much public assistance to fill the void, where will the capital necessary for growth come from?

It will not, apparently, come from either Eastern or Western Europe. The Soviet Union is a growing presence in Latin America, but its share of trade is very small; although it seems willing to continue massively propping up the Cuban economy, it appears unwilling to bail out the troubled economies of other Socialist regimes such as the one in Nicaragua. Nor will Western Europe fill the vacuum. In recent years many Latin Americans have clung to the hope that they do not really need the United States any more, that they could reduce their dependence on the U.S. because the Socialist and Social Democratic parties and governments of Western Europe would surely come to their rescue. Instead, Western European financial help has been meager, and it is certainly inadequate to make up for lost U.S. aid and investment. And no substitute for U.S. and local Latin American money has come forward.

Social Aspects. The spiraling economic crisis in Latin America has worsened the difficult social situation. There are few new jobs, unemployment is high, inflation is devastating the lower and middle classes, and poverty and malnutrition are increasing. Even in such third world successes as Brazil, Venezuela, and Mexico, the gaps between rich and poor are widening rather than narrowing. The conditions of life of Latin America's poor are becoming worse at a time when heightened expectations make them increasingly unwilling to accept that fate. Small wonder that under these conditions radical and revolutionary appeals can find widespread receptivity. Unfortunately, the belt-tightening measures demanded by the major lending agencies may well make the already grim social conditions worse, piling further pressures on the political systems of the region while doing little to solve the economic crisis.

Political Aspects. The political systems of Latin America have similarly been undermined. In other writings,[4] I have described a model of the Latin American political systems that had shown them to be, while not always democratic by our lights, at least somewhat flexible and accommodative. That model had been posited on the understanding that new social and political groups could be brought into the system if (1) they tempered their demands and (2) were willing to coexist with the old groups. Such an accommodative political process was possible, however, only as long as the economy continued to expand, as it did in the 1950s and 1960s, providing new benefits that could be doled out to the newer, rising groups at the same time the older groups' share continued to be augmented.

The economic crisis of the past six years thus not only has been devastating for the economies of the region, but also has undermined, or threatened to undermine, the existing political order. There are simply no new pieces of the economic pie to hand out. The competition for the existing shares, therefore, has become increasingly intense and in some countries violent. The governments of the region can no longer cope with the pressures that modernity and rising expectations, in a time of downward-turning economies, have thrust upon them. It is not just any particular regime of the moment that is threatened but a whole, more-or-less functional and accommodative *system* of politics.

Fragmentation and polarization are setting in everywhere, and in some countries there is increased potential for revolution and civil war. Moderate military regimes are threatened by extremism, the democratic governments of the region are increasingly imperiled, and the celebrated period of "returns" or "transitions" to democracy may be halted and even reversed. Already there has been a coup in Panama; Bolivia and Peru are threatened; Honduras and Ecuador are shaky; Brazil's fate is still uncertain; Argentina's democratic government is facing increased problems; even Venezuela, a bastion of democracy since 1958, is being shaken by talk of a future coup. The current situation augurs ill not just for democracy but for *any* possibilities of stable or moderate rule.

Soviet and Cuban Presence. Finally the Soviet Union, through Cuba as well as on its own, has become a significant influence in Latin America politically, militarily, economically, and diplomatically. And Latin America, for the reasons already discussed, is now particularly vulnerable, prey to internally based but externally directed revolutionary movements. The roots of revolution in Latin America, virtually all serious analysts of the region agree, lie in indigenous, social, economic, and political conditions. But these may be exacerbated and exploited by a more activist Soviet Union and its revolutionary proxies, particularly Cuba. That was the situation—of the Soviet Union taking advantage of local conditions, exacerbating the difficulties, playing on home-grown anti-Americanism, providing the ideology, funds, and organization that local revolutionaries lacked—in Cuba, and it became the pattern in Nicaragua, Grenada, Suriname, and now El Salvador. To the severe indigenous difficulties that Latin America faces has been added a strong and mischievous Soviet presence. The Soviets are intent on increasing their influence in the region, contributing further to the fires of instability that already exist, and embarrassing the United States in its own backyard.[5]

All of these dismal scenarios, of course, carry immense implications for U.S. policy in Latin America. They suggest that things are likely to get far worse in the region than they are now. Without capital and investment from *any* source, the Latin American economies are destined to founder. Social and political disintegration may well set in.

If crisis, polarization, and breakdown, rather than development, are the prospects for the region, what kind of bases are there for U.S. policy? We have limited economic assistance levers to manipulate, the democracy initiative seems doomed to fail if the Latin American economic pie continues to shrink, and the austerity measures that we and the international banks have insisted upon will certainly increase the social tension and the possibilities for revolutionary backlash. In this context of a spiraling and still down-turning economy, of increased social tension, of governments and political systems incapable of coping with or resolving their crises, the fear is that the United States would be left with only a reactive policy whose major (and virtually sole) component would be military intervention. That is an outcome that almost no one inside or outside the U.S. government would like to see.

Hope amid Despair?

The prospects for the future of Latin America need not be entirely pessimistic, however. Indeed, taking into account some factors other than the bleak ones discussed earlier, one could even come away with a hopeful view.

Limits of Crisis. First, the crisis in Latin America has likely been overstated. Putting the issues in crisis terms is a way to get foreign aid money from a reluctant Congress, to mobilize popular support, and to coordinate the foreign affairs bureaucracies. Nor are the Latin Americans above exaggerating their own plight for the sake of getting the U.S. assistance conduits flowing again. Latin America seems perpetually to be in "crisis"; one suspects that there may be some hidden private or political agendas at work here.

There is, to be sure, a crisis in Latin America, but it may not be quite as severe as pictured. In fact, life in Latin America goes on even in such crisis countries as Nicaragua and El Salvador, regardless of the grand political and ideological controversies that swirl about. Even in the major areas of conflict in Central America foreign visitors are often surprised to find people going to work, growing their crops, doing their daily tasks, and eking out a form of subsistence despite the disruption all around them. Most people cope and survive in one form or another, without joining the revolutionaries. I do not wish here to understate Latin America's problems, only to indicate that there are strong interests in some quarters in magnifying the problems and therefore that one should not overstate the case either.

Differences Among Countries. One must also distinguish between countries. Colombia and probably Mexico will likely succeed in muddling along through the foreseeable future with time-honored institutions, applying a little money here and a large amount of patronage there to get them through this and the next crisis. Bolivia will probably have a coup, but it may come from any one of three or four directions, and in the process Bolivian politics will not likely change very much. Argentina remains fragmented and will probably face another cycle of political division; but what about that is new? The Brazilians will artfully apply some grease, and a political accommodation is likely. In Honduras, Guatemala, Panama, Ecuador, and elsewhere the military and civilian elites will continue to coexist in a shifting, often uneasy relationship that may make purists uncomfortable but that reflects the power realities in these countries. The purpose of these comments is not to offer some superficial analysis of each Latin American country but only to indicate that there may be more than one or two paths to development. Indeed one of the leading texts in the field concludes there may be at least *nine* different routes to development for the Latin American countries.[6] In one form or another, most countries will continue to muddle along.

Glimmers of Economic Health. Economically, the prospects are not altogether dismal. If the U.S. economic recovery continues, the Latin American nations which are so heavily dependent on the "locomotive" of the U.S. economy will eventually begin to feel the beneficial effects. It usually takes two to three years for the full effects of a change in the U.S. economy to be felt in Latin America; since the U.S. recovery got under way in late 1983 it should not be long before Latin America too begins to reap some benefits. The evidence for 1984 and 1985 was mixed, but many countries in 1986 showed improvement.

In some quarters, furthermore, Latin America, particularly South America, is still seen as a promising market for investment, and there is still capital in considerable amounts flowing into that region. These same countries of South America, and Mexico, have substantial real assets that are considerably greater than their present debts. The CBI and the recently enacted Kissinger Commission recommendations will provide some funds and pump-priming—and some of these may stay in the country for which they were intended and a certain percentage may even "trickle down." An economic growth rate of 3–5 percent over the next several years in quite a few countries would not be wholly unexpected. If that should occur, some countries might even manage to pay a portion of their debt.

If one were to engage in instant risk analysis, one would probably say, echoing William Glade's careful assessment,[7] that the economic future looks hard in Chile, Mexico, and Peru, moderately hopeful though still uncertain in Argentina and Brazil, only a bit more assured in Colombia and Venezuela. The Central American countries (Costa Rica and Panama excepted) are so poor by comparison, in terms of both per capita income and natural resources and markets, that only a massive Marshall Plan–like bailout is likely to help them; we will have to wait and see how the Kissinger Commission aid package is implemented in the region and if it can be sustained. The English-speaking Caribbean countries are somewhat more promising and more peaceful than those of Central America, but that alone may take them out of the public mind and hence out of the assistance flow.

If the economic situation can be improved somewhat, perhaps the social situation can similarly be ameliorated. On the one hand, we should not expect social egalitarianism, social justice, and new social programs to flower suddenly throughout Latin America. On the other hand, these societies have not been entirely immune to social change in the past, when the economic situation was better. On the contrary, a good deal of social modernization has occurred in Latin America in the past thirty to fifty years. Elitist structures have increasingly given way to middle-class ones, trade unions have been organized, the peasants have been mobilized, and so on. Under pressure, the governing elites and middle sectors in Latin America have shown a considerable capacity to bend and accommodate. They have generally allowed (except in Nicaragua under Somoza or Guatemala and El Salvador in the 1970s) just enough benefits to be channeled to the lower classes to head off revolution from below while also maintaining themselves in power. The changes have been gradual and incremental rather than sweeping, and they are likely to remain so. That is not an unvarnished and magnificent picture and, again, it will be unsatisfactory to purists, but realistically that may be as much as we can hope for.

Political Prospects. The political outlook is, similarly, not entirely grim. The key to political stability is economic recovery and sufficient resources to allow governing elements to play an accommodative political game rather than a repressive one. In the situation of an expanding economic pie, there are always new pieces to hand out to the clamoring new groups, without this implying someone else must be deprived. Historically the Latin American countries have been quite adept at improvising and deriving new formulas, usually short of U.S.-style democracy and pluralism, that involve ad hoc and frequently mixed systems of civilian and military rule, or elements combining democracy and authoritarianism. These solutions often defy neat categorization, but they have often been at least partially functional in Latin America. With a modest break in the economic situation, there is no reason such solutions cannot be successful in the future—although the pressures and difficulties are now, assuredly, more intense. But the transition to democracy in so many countries is also a hopeful process.

The Latin American political system not only has proved quite flexible with regard to internal or domestic pressures, but has often been able to accommodate external pressures as well. Chiefly, these involve pressures from the United States and require adjustment to the American panacea of the moment, whether it is agrarian reform, community development, or basic human needs. Experienced observers of Latin America develop a sometimes grudging admiration for Latin America's ability to absorb and accommodate some aspects of whatever the current U.S. policy dictates, usually so as to qualify for further aid, while really not changing much. In this way Latin America may continue to adjust to today's changed international situation—including management of the debt crisis.

The Strategic Situation. Strategically, the situation looks similarly hopeful—or at least possibly so. The U.S. military and strategic commitment and presence in Central America and the Caribbean are currently very strong. They have been major factors in forcing a paranoid Nicaragua, convinced that it is next to experience a Grenada-like U.S. intervention, into a defensive strategy. It helped convince Bouterse in Suriname to expel the major part of the Cuban forces there. It has given Fidel Castro pause about the possibility of fomenting revolution elsewhere in Central America and the Caribbean. And it has forced the Salvadoran guerrillas into a defensive posture—they are short on new recruits, more and more confined to certain specific strongholds, unable to launch their expected offensive, and forced now, in meeting with Duarte on his terms, to look for a negotiated settlement rather than a military victory. It is one thing to wage a guerrilla war against a corrupt and ineffective Salvadoran army; it is quite another to face almost certain martyrdom by taking on the U.S. army. The guerrillas are clearly feeling the pressure.[8]

Finally, there is evidence the Soviet Union is reassessing its strategies in Latin America. With a minimum of effort or commitment on their part the Soviets have had a number of Latin American plums—beginning with Cuba—fall into their lap. Success with Cuba had encouraged them to expand their presence and commitments diplomatically, militarily, economically, and politically. But now, in the wake of the U.S. intervention in Grenada and the massive U.S. military-strategic-diplomatic-economic buildup in the Caribbean and Central America, the Soviets are having second thoughts: there have been strong questions about the reliability of such Caribbean clients as Grenada, the Soviets have proven unwilling to give much economic aid to Nicaragua, and they have told the Sandinistas they cannot expect the Soviet Union to come to their defense if they are attacked. The United States enjoys overwhelming local advantage over the Soviet Union in the Caribbean and has recently shown a willingness to employ and demonstrate its strength.

From the Soviet point of view, therefore, it is worthwhile to allow, maybe even to stimulate, these plums to fall into its lap; but it is not worth risking a major confrontation with the United States and certainly not in its own backyard. Latin America is simply not worth that much to the Soviet Union, and faced with the U.S. buildup the Soviets will likely concentrate on other areas. That is in accord with the revered Leninist principle that when you probe and hit mush you keep going; when you probe and hit steel you go elsewhere. In the Caribbean the Soviets have recently hit steel, and as a prudent and realistic power they are currently reassessing their involvements there. The result is likely to be not a full retreat but probably a turning back from some of its recent endeavors. That too is a major hopeful sign.

Out of the Morass?

In looking back over the preceding pages we find about 60 percent of the analysis pessimistic regarding Latin America's future and perhaps 40 percent more hopeful. In this day, that seems about the right balance. There are abundant reasons to be despairing about Latin America and its future, but there are sufficient glimmers of light to retain some measure of optimism.

Overall, rather than either a sparkling new takeoff or a precipitous descent into the abyss, it seems most likely that Latin America will continue to muddle along under diverse formulas. That has been Latin America's past and it will likely be its future. Those who know the area well also know Latin America has an enormous capacity to bend, absorb, and accommodate while retaining its traditional institutions. Latin America's institutions have often proved remarkably adaptable, bending to change but rarely being overwhelmed by it. The region has shown an amazing capacity to absorb changes and pressures both internal and external, to devise new and ad hoc formulas for resolving its problems. One would not be entirely surprised, therefore, if Latin America not only survived the present crisis in which it finds itself but also began a new process of recovery and then moved on to a new developmental plateau.[9]

Notes

1. For comparison see John Weicher, ed., *Maintaining the Safety Net: Income Redistribution Programs in the Reagan Administration* (Washington, D.C.: American Enterprise Institute, 1984).

2. Based on World Bank statistics and those provided in the annual Inter-American Development Bank publication entitled *Economic and Social Progress in Latin America*.

3. Some of the conclusions in this and the following paragraphs are based

on interviews with U.S. corporate representatives and banking officials; see also the special issue of the *Harvard International Review* (January–February 1984), devoted to "Development and the World Economy" and featuring articles by Hollis Chenery, Richard N. Cooper, Gunnar Myrdal, and Henry C. Wallich.

4. Howard J. Wiarda, ed., *Politics and Social Change in Latin America: The Distant Tradition* (Amherst, Mass.: University of Massachusetts Press, revised second edition, 1982); and Wiarda, *Corporation and National Development in Latin America* (Boulder, Colo.: Westview Press, 1981).

5. Howard J. Wiarda, "Soviet Policy in the Caribbean and Central America: Opportunities and Constraints," Paper presented at a conference on Soviet foreign policy, the Kennan Institute for Advanced Russian Studies, Woodrow Wilson International Center for Scholars and the United States Information Agency, Washington, D.C., March 2, 1984; forthcoming in a volume entitled *The Communist Challenge in the Caribbean and Central America* (Washington, D.C.: American Enterprise Institute, 1987).

6. See the discussion in Harvey F. Kline and Howard J. Wiarda, eds., *Latin American Politics and Development* (Boulder, Colo.: Westview Press, 1985), pp. 114–15).

7. See William P. Glade, Jr., "Latin America: Debt, Destruction, and Development," in Michael Novak and Michael P. Jackson, eds., *Latin America: Dependency or Interdependence?* (Washington, D.C.: American Enterprise Institute, 1986).

8. See the paper by the author entitled "Aftermath of Grenada: The Impact of the U.S. Action on Revolutionary Prospects in Central America," Prepared for the conference "Soviet/Cuban Strategy in the Third World after Grenada," Kennan Institute for Advanced Russian Studies, Woodrow Wilson Center, Smithsonian Institution and the Naval Postgraduate School, Monterey, Calif., August 15–18, 1984; published in Jiri Valenta and Herbert Ellison, eds., *Grenada and Soviet/Cuban Policy: Internal Crisis and U.S./OECS Intervention* (Boulder, Colo.: Westview Press, 1986), pp. 105–122. See also Clifford Krauss, "Leftists Lose Optimism About Soon Prevailing in Central America," *Wall Street Journal* (October 15, 1984).

9. On the advantages of incrementalist "muddling through" public policy see the classic statement by David Braybrook and Charles E. Lindblom, *A Strategy of Decision* (New York: The Free Press, 1963), especially p. 71.

13
U.S. Policy toward
South America:
A Maturing Relationship?

The United States has been so preoccupied with Central America and the Caribbean in recent years that it has paid relatively little attention to South America. That is certainly not a new situation. At least since the Spanish-American War of 1898, by which time the United States had become both a major industrial and a major military power, its Latin American preoccupations have been chiefly with those nations of the circum-Caribbean that lie close to our southern borders, within our sphere of influence, around our "soft underbelly"—as strategic thinkers then and now put it.

Inattention to South America

The reasons for this preoccupation with the Caribbean and Central America and the comparative inattention to South America are several. The first is sheer distance and logistics—South America is simply farther away, and we are less directly and immediately affected by events there than by the upheavals in the Caribbean. The second reason is that, because the the bigger nations of South America are, in general, more viable, more institutionalized, and more stable than those of Central America and the Caribbean, we have had to worry about them less. Historically it has been the smaller, less-institutionalized nations of Central America and the Caribbean whose chronic instability has preoccupied the United States—especially if their instability makes them susceptible to adventurism and manipulation by outside powers (Spain, France, Britain, Germany, and of course most recently the Soviet Union).

Published in *Current History* (February 1985), pp. 49–52 ff.

Third, the South American nations have, ironically, received less attention from the United States because of the very success of their development efforts. By almost any index of modernization, the South American nations (with the exceptions of Bolivia and, marginally, Ecuador and Paraguay) are considerably better off than the Spanish-speaking countries of Central America and the Caribbean. Their GNP is considerably higher, per capita income is higher, their industry is more developed, and their internal markets and possibilities are larger.

Countries such as Argentina, Brazil, Chile, Uruguay, Venezuela, Colombia, and Peru (as well as Mexico) are by no means hopelessly backward. Rather, they have developed considerably over the past forty years, and several of them have emerged from the ranks of the Less Developed Countries (LDCs) into the ranks of the Newly Industrialized Countries (NICs). Precisely because they are third world success stories, several of these countries no longer qualify for U.S. assistance. That is another and major reason for U.S. official neglect of the area: because our aid missions, number of personnel, and assistance programs are greatly reduced, so is the attention we pay to these countries.

Actually, our bilateral relations with most of the countries of South America are quite good. There are of course significant issues and differences with each of the countries of the area. Nationalism is also rising in South America and, with it, the desire for foreign policies more independent from the U.S. foreign policy. And one could further say that U.S. relations with Latin America as a whole are often strained, difficult, and unhappy. But that has almost always been the case regardless of the administration in office in Washington, and it derives chiefly from asymmetries in size, influence, wealth, and power. Despite the persistent frictions, however, bilateral relations are more or less normal, even satisfactory in most cases. Perhaps that indicates a certain maturation of the U.S.–Latin American relationship and the promise of sounder bilateral relations with the major South American countries on a basis like those with European countries.

One could even speculate that there may be a cause-and-effect relationship between the relative inattention devoted to South America and the maturing of our bilateral relations. South America is not, currently, a crisis area as Central America is; the United States is not especially concerned with the potential for continent-wide revolution in the region; and the Soviet Union seems unlikely soon to establish a ring of satellites there. In this noncrisis atmosphere, our bilateral relations have been able to grow and mature, and some semblance of normality in our relations may be in the process of being formed. That would represent a major step in putting U.S.–Latin American relations on a more solid footing.

Major Issues

But there are of course still significant issues affecting U.S.–South American relations. Although there are signs of growing maturity in the relationship, that is not to say that no controversies remain.

The Ongoing Debt Crisis. Foremost among these is the debt issue—and, related, the continuing economic crisis in Latin America. During 1984 there was significant progress on this front. Mexico reached a historic agreement with its lenders that provided for lower interest rates and a longer-term schedule of payments. That in turn increased the pressures on the other big debtor nations—Argentina, Brazil, Peru, and Venezuela—to come to similar terms.

Although there was encouraging progress in this regard, one must keep in mind the differences between these countries that made the Mexican agreement much easier to reach. Mexico, unlike the others, has virtually limitless petroleum reserves and therefore a continuous source of foreign exchange earnings that these other countries (Venezuela excepted) do not have. More recently, Mexico has been hurt by falling petroleum prices, but it is still the case that it is better to be oil-rich than oil-poor.

Second, in reaching an agreement, Mexico is not as constrained by democratic give and take as these other countries are. Mexico is an authoritarian system that can reach authoritative decisions comparatively easily; in the new democracies of South America, public opinion, election and reelection considerations, and democratic debate discourage agreements that seem to represent a cave-in to foreign interests, the banks, and the United States.

Third, Mexico shares a 2,000-mile border with the United States. When the crunch comes, the United States will not allow Mexico to become destabilized. Mexico knows that as well as the United States.

No one knows how the debt issue will finally be resolved. There is considerable sentiment in the South American countries not to pay their debts, to treat the debt as part of the obligation of the northern nations to the southern ones for past exploitation, to force the United States and the private banks to absorb the losses. Many bankers also have privately determined virtually to give up on their South American loans. They have concluded that they will never collect any of the principal and only a token amount of interest; their main concern now is to avoid having to write off these loans as uncollectable. A major side effect of the banks' conclusions, of course, is that there will be no more loans to the South American debtor nations except under duress or with generous U.S. government guarantees. But in 1984 and 1985 there was at least less talk of outright default or repudiation by the debtor nations and less talk of system-wide disaster or collapse by the bankers. The debt appeared "manageable." For the time being at least the fig leaf has been kept in place.[1]

Troubled Domestic Economies. The more general economic crisis in South America also remains acute. The economies of the area have been generally stagnant or have even contracted for approximately five or six years. Growth rates in almost all sectors are down, unemployment and underemployment combined may reach half the work force in several nations of the area, and inflation is rampant. New investment is very hard to get for most countries, and capital flight has reached dangerous levels. Quite a number of U.S. and multinational firms, in addition, are liquidating their holdings in South America and pulling out, afraid of the potential for region-wide political instability and attracted by more lucrative profits in Western Europe, the Pacific Basin, or the United States itself.

The economic crisis in South America has its roots in the two major oil shocks of 1973 and 1979, the fluctuating world market prices for the region's primary products, the world economic downturn that set in in 1979 and deepened thereafter, and bad planning, corruption, and mismanagement on the part of the South American nations themselves. The depression of the early 1980s not only has had a devastating effect on the economies of the area but also has undermined their political systems, made it increasingly difficult to maintain open and accommodative politics, and slowed down the transition to democracy in some countries and threatened to reverse it in others (Bolivia, Panama, Peru). With the world economy now apparently on the road to recovery, especially in the United States, the South American economies have also begun to show signs of recovery. But the process has been very slow and painful.

Nationalism. The economic downturn came at a time when the intellectual and political elites of South America were in the process of becoming increasingly independent and nationalistic. There had been a lot of talk, some of it romantic, about breaking their ties of dependency with the United States, diversifying their foreign relations, opening greater trade with China and the Soviet Union, and reducing

251

U.S. influence in the area. These views were widespread throughout Latin America in the 1970s.

Obviously a political agenda was involved in this move by Latin America toward lesser dependence on the United States, as well as an economic one. By the 1970s those who had grown up in Latin America in the 1960s were in positions of influence in the government, the media, the universities, the church, and other institutions. Many among the younger generation were anti-American, thought in Marxist terms, and favored a radical restructuring both of their internal societies and of their external relations—including the widespread desire to redefine their relationship with the United States. These sentiments were shared by many in the ministries, the autonomous agencies, the bureaucracies, and elsewhere in the South American countries. Revolution, restructuring, and radical change seemed everywhere in the air.

The economic downturn of 1979 and later reversed this process— or at least put it on hold. For one thing, the European nations to whom Latin America had looked to diversify its relations and to break or renegotiate its ties to the United States did not come through. The European countries provided disappointingly little aid, certainly not enough to substitute for that of the United States. European markets also dried up as the demand for Latin America's products fell dramatically with the world depression. Nor did Europe provide the investment, the trade, and the capital markets that Latin America desperately required. Certainly the Soviet Union, China, and Eastern Europe could not fill the void.

That left South America with nowhere to turn—except back to the United States. Indeed one of the unanticipated consequences of the world depression of the past six years was to remind the South American nations just how dependent they were on the United States. That message became clear even to those on the left. Hence there has developed in virtually all the South American countries a new pragmatism in dealing with the United States. Recognizing that they absolutely need U.S. capital, technology, and markets and that they have nowhere else to turn, the political leadership of South America has, for the most part, come to grips with this fact realistically. There is still a desire to diversify their external relations and trade, to loosen the ties to the United States, and to increase their relationships with other nations. But prudence and practicality also demand that commercial, political, and economic ties with the United States remain close. The old saw still holds: Latin America frequently has a hard time living with the United States, but cannot live without the United States either.

The Drug Trade. Another issue of concern in U.S.–South American relations has been the drug traffic. The U.S. government has determined that since it may not be able to change consumer habits in the United States, it will try to cut off the flow of drugs at the source. The strategy will likely fail and strain our relations with several of the South American countries.

The facts are simple: the drug traffic is very big business. In Colombia the export of drugs is now bigger business than the export of coffee. Those who know Colombian history will realize how big a change that is. In Paraguay, Bolivia, Brazil, Peru, Venezuela, and Argentina drugs are also a major export if not (in some of those named) *the* major export.

Solving the dilemmas caused by those facts is more difficult. First, cutting off the flow of drugs from one country does little to stem the overall tide; it only changes the source. The drug traffic in Colombia, for example, boomed when Mexican sources began to dry up, so the total volume available remained the same and even increased. Second, drugs have become a major source of earnings for many people in South America. The United States and the governments of these countries can hardly persuade farmers who are making 250 dollars a month growing marijuana or coca to go back to earning only 25 dollars raising traditional crops. Taking strong action will not be politically palatable for most governments of the area because the stakes are so high and so much money is involved.

Third, the local governments and the local police and armed forces are often themselves involved in the trafficking of drugs, and they are not inclined to enforce restrictions that would cut off their own cash or tax flow. Although such behavior is illegal, it is an easy way of supplementing their meager salaries. Fourth, the Latin Americans, and especially the democratic governments, cannot condone the widespread spraying of agent orange or paraquat, which may harm their own populations. Many of them fear also the world will not buy their coffee and other crops if it fears these crops have been contaminated by spraying.

Nor is the U.S. government wholeheartedly behind the drug eradication drive. The Drug Enforcement Agency (DEA) supports the drive because that is its responsibility, and the White House has been strongly involved in the campaign, but some U.S. ambassadors and foreign service political officers have been lukewarm. Their job, after all, is to maintain cordial relations with the countries to which they have been assigned; they do not want to antagonize those governments with a vigorous antidrug campaign. U.S. embassies in the South American capitals have sometimes been uncooperative when

DEA officials push their eradication programs strenuously. Because of such bureaucratic politics within the U.S. family of operations abroad, little is done to stamp out drugs at their source. The DEA knows that without the full support of the embassy or of the host government, it alone cannot resolve a hopeless situation.

Democracy and Human Rights. In Bolivia, Peru, Brazil, Uruguay, Ecuador, and Argentina, we have witnessed in recent years a remarkable transition from authoritarianism to democracy. The United States has strongly supported these developments as well as efforts to secure greater respect for human rights in these countries.

Several clouds loom on the horizon, however. The first is that the transition in several of the South American countries may be only temporary and not irreversible. In Peru rumors of a pending coup or coup attempt abound. In Bolivia, several recent coup attempts have been put down, and in that beleaguered country one cannot take democracy or stability for granted. The Brazilian generals are not unanimously convinced that the *abertura* has been a success or that it might not be reversed. Ecuador has, to understate the case, a certain history of *coups d'etat*. In Argentina people say only half in jest that the first year of Alfonsín was the year of euphoria, the second was the year of disillusionment, and the third will have to be the year of the coup.

If this is indeed democracy's moment in South America, as some scholars have claimed, there is reason to fear that in some countries the moment may already have come and gone. Certainly the transitions to democracy in the region will be difficult to maintain if the economic slump continues. The world depression, which had particularly devastating effects in Latin America, threatens not only to damage the economies of the area but also to undermine the region's political systems.

A second cause for concern, Chile, has shown almost no movement toward democracy or greater respect for human rights. For a time the democratic opposition in Chile seemed to be growing, and elements in the armed forces were thought to be inclined to get rid of Pinochet. But Pinochet's position seems stronger than ever, and the democratic opposition is fragmented and discouraged. Chile remains a pariah state, an outcast among the community of Western democratic nations, a characterization that weighs heavily in Chile but seems not so far to have shaken Pinochet's grip.

A third concern is that the mere presence of democratic governments in Latin America does not guarantee warmer relations with the United States. We of course prefer democratic to authoritarian regimes, but that will not automatically result in stronger pro-American attitudes. In some Washington circles in recent years there was romantic talk that if only we could put democratic governments into power in Latin America, our difficulties with the countries of the region would disappear. But the U.S. differences with Brazil, for example, are fundamental, substantial, and over real issues and interests, both economic and political; they will not disappear, whether a military or a democratic government is in power.

The same is true in Argentina. Former Secretary of State Alexander Haig found at the height of the Falklands/Malvinas War that the Argentine generals could be prickly people to deal with; we have recently discovered in the debt negotiations and over other issues that democratic president Alfonsín can be at least as difficult. Let us face the fact that democracy is no magic doorway to better relations between the United States and Latin America. Our relations with a proud nation like Argentina will always be touchy, whether it is under democratic or military rule. Realism demands that we recognize this fact and not engage in wishful thinking about the presumed harmony of democratic nations.

The fourth point is that we have formulated no policy should democracy in South America be reversed. The Reagan administration has become strongly supportive of democracy in Latin America not just because it believes in democracy but also because it knows a prodemocracy stance helps get the Congress, the media, and public opinion on its side; it encourages our European allies to support our policies; and it legitimizes American foreign policy initiatives. The administration also believes that in the long run democracies in Latin America are better able to preserve stability, to carry out reforms, to achieve justice, and to keep out mischievous foreign powers—which are the bedrock of U.S. foreign policy in the area.

Although all these things may be fine and true in the long run, in the short run we may be facing the strong possibility of a new wave of military coups—especially if the economic downturn continues. The administration has no real plan to deal with such an eventuality and has not fully thought through the consequences of its prodemocracy position. Will the United States suspend diplomatic relations and cut off assistance to such military regimes if they seize power? In the early 1960s, President Kennedy tried this strategy which succeeded neither in restoring democracy in any of the countries affected nor in endearing us to the successor regimes. We have interests in these countries besides democracy; if we couch policy purely in terms of supporting democracy, we will have more difficulty later defending strong ties to nondemocratic regimes that we may in our own interest want to support. The democracy agenda, therefore, is both an opportunity for U.S. policy and a potential trap, particularly if we are faced with another wave of military regimes for which we have not adequately planned.

Administration Policy

In dealing with the South American countries U.S. policy has been considerably more flexible, prudent, and moderate than might have been expected from some of the early statements of the administration. Moreover, despite the rhetoric and the election campaign posturing to the contrary, there has been considerable continuity in foreign policy from the Carter to the Reagan administrations, particularly in South America. Each new administration sounds ideological and even strident at the beginning; but eventually, in each administration pragmatists, centrists, and professionals come again to dominate policy, particularly on a day-to-day basis and in noncrisis areas.

The crisis for U.S. policy in the region has been in Central America and the Caribbean, not in South America. While Central America and the Caribbean have been dealt with at the highest levels of the U.S. government, in the White House, and by the president's key political advisers, relations with the South American countries have been handled mainly at lower levels in the foreign-policy bureaucracies, for the most part by career professionals. South Americans (and many students of Latin America in the United States) sometimes lament the lack of attention at high levels that their part of the world has received. We suggest here, however, that may be a blessing in disguise, for it has enabled U.S.–South American relations to be conducted on a more professional, regular, mature, and normal basis than before. Of course, gaffes, misunderstandings, and real differences continue to exist; but at rather quiet and mundane levels we may have finally begun to place our everyday relations with the major South American nations on a mature bilateral basis similar to our relations with other civilized countries.

Most aspects of U.S.–South American relations are likely to continue on this pragmatic, more mature course in President Reagan's second term. The United States has shown itself to be quite flexible and realistic in its dealings with the South American nations. It has also been demonstrated that the United States can get along with a variety of regimes, including one with Communists in the cabinet (Bolivia). The U.S. government has supported democratic openings (in Brazil) and Social Democratic regimes (in Argentina). It has shown less friendliness to military regimes than seemed likely in the early months of the administration (Chile), and overall it has shown a greater sense of moderation and willingness to maintain normal relations with regimes of diverse stripes.

Yet the possibilities exist for a scrambling of this new and stabler picture. Great uncertainty lies ahead in such countries as Argentina, Bolivia, Brazil, Chile, Ecuador, Paraguay, Peru, and Uruguay (to say nothing of those troublesome outposts on the South American continent not dealt with here, Guyana and Suriname). A new wave of coups and human rights violations would surely set off another round of recriminations and conflict over policy. The economic situation remains precarious, and economic crises in Latin America have long been closely associated with political upheaval. Poverty, underdevelopment, inferiority, deprivation, bitterness, immense social gaps, and strong anti-Americanism remain.

The great hope of every American president and his advisers is that when and if trouble comes, it will happen in the next administration. So far, our comparative neglect of and lower-level dealings with South America have produced not altogether unhappy results, but beneath the surface calm the situations in these various countries remain precarious. Our future relations with them are similarly uncertain; but if the mature relationship analyzed here, often talked about in the past but seldom implemented, continues and is strengthened, U.S.–South American relations may at last be put on a sounder basis.

Notes

1. For a full discussion see Howard J. Wiarda *Latin America at the Crossroads: Debt, Development and the Future* (Boulder, Colo.: Westview Press, 1987).

14

President Reagan's Second Term: Prospects for Central America

Ronald Reagan's overwhelming electoral victory in November 1984 was more than just a personal victory for the president. It was also a mandate for his program and for a continuation of that agenda during the second term. At the same time, the results of the congressional, gubernatorial, and state and local elections indicate that it was not an unqualified mandate and that the American public still prefers gradualism, incrementalism, and the historic system of checks and balances. I interpret the 1984 electoral results as implying that the president should not just maintain the status quo but go forward with his programs while at the same time not going off unrestrained in new directions, as some of his supporters urge.

The election turned not so much on foreign affairs issues but on domestic considerations: the economic recovery, declining inflation and unemployment, renewed self-confidence and national pride, strong presidential leadership—America on the move again. Nevertheless these aspirations are easily translatable into preferences and recommendations for foreign policy. In Central America pursuing these same goals means standing firm, defending our interests, refusing to be pushed around, maintaining a posture of strength and continuity in a context that Americans know to be difficult and complex, and living up to our ideals. But it also means getting involved in no more Vietnam-like imbroglios. The American public wants no "second Cuba" in the Caribbean; at the same time it clearly does not want to get involved in a ground war on the Central American mainland using American troops. That is the public sentiment—and the delicate balancing act—that Ronald Reagan carried with him into the second term.

Disasters Avoided

In foreign affairs one often has to be content with the news of disasters that did not happen rather than expecting many positive

Published in *The American Spectator*, vol. 18 (February 1985), pp. 24–27.

accomplishments. Let us review the missteps the Reagan administration did not take before moving on to the more positive accomplishments of its first four years, remembering that avoiding mistakes can be viewed as every bit as big an accomplishment as any bold new initiatives.

First, we did not "go to the source" as former Secretary of State Alexander Haig once urged. By this he meant, presumably, taking strong actions against the source of our difficulties in Central America (to say nothing of the Horn of Africa, the Yemens, Southern Africa, and elsewhere): the Cubans. Cuba is a thorn in the American side, a kind of panic button (rather like Berlin in decades past) that the Soviets and the Cubans themselves can push from time to time and get a predictable American response.

But military action against Cuba would have involved such a wrenching, bloody battle as to tear America apart again; it would have diverted attention from other important agendas such as the president's economic recovery plans and the defense buildup; and it quite conceivably might have destroyed the Reagan presidency and his possibilities for a second term. In the end a more restrained policy prevailed. An invasion or quarantine of Cuba, never seriously considered (except perhaps as a bluff to frighten the Cubans), was put on the back burner where it remains.

Second, we have not sent ground combat troops into Central America. Rather our response has been gradual, measured, and controlled. We sent military trainers to El Salvador, strengthened the Caribbean fleet, built up a large military presence in Honduras, sent a strong message in the Grenada intervention, and put immense pressure—military, political, economic, and diplomatic—on the Sandinista regime in Nicaragua. But we have not, so far, used U.S. ground forces. Invading Nicaragua would be a bloody mess. The Sandinistas would fight strenuously before eventually fading across their borders. We would then have to bomb their sanctuaries in Honduras and Costa Rica, and at that stage we would really have a "second Vietnam" on our hands, which we do not have at present—something both the public and the Pentagon want strongly to avoid.

Such a strategy would play right into the hands of the president's foes and, again, carry the potential to destroy the Reagan presidency. Nor is the Defense Department eager to jump into an invasion of a mainland country that would not have the support of the American people, which would not have entirely clear objectives, which would divide the government itself, and which would again involve our forces in a protracted, interminable quagmire that might eventually discredit the military institution itself. On this issue also the cooler heads prevailed, foreseeing the negative consequences that out-weighed the advantages.

Nor did the president abolish the State Department's human rights office, as once seemed in the offing. He did not abandon the reformist and humanitarian urges that have long been at the heart of American foreign policy. And he did not forsake the country's commitment to expanding democracy abroad—as shown by the Reagan administration's efforts in Haiti and the Philippines and by its creation of the National Endowment for Democracy. We have to be cognizant of these missteps that, despite fears in some quarters, did *not* happen as well as appreciative of the positive steps that did.

Continuity and Change

Under Ronald Reagan, there has been at least as much continuity in foreign policy as change. Exact calculations depend on the measure used. The president returned to the historic bedrock of U.S. policy toward Central America without abandoning what is useful in the newer approaches. That is, he restored U.S. leadership in the Caribbean and Central America, he reasserted the primacy of U.S. strategic purposes in the region, and he renewed the emphasis on having safe, stable, friendly nations to the south. At the same time he emphasized democratic development, democracy, and the protection of human rights as effective means to help accomplish these goals. In that sense President Reagan sought to combine both strength and noble purpose as the twin pillars of his policy, thereby returning to the bases of past successes in American foreign policy. In this he stood in marked contrast to Jimmy Carter who, at least during the first two years of his presidency, emphasized one side of the equation at the expense of the other.

A long-term educational process has been under way in the Reagan presidency which has helped produce a more effective, pragmatic, and centrist policy. In the 1980 campaign, in the transition team papers, and in the early weeks of the new administration, there was a lot of talk about abandoning human rights concerns, putting aside the agrarian reform initiatives in El Salvador, and focusing exclusively on the military and strategic aspects of the Central American crisis. Only gradually did the administration realize that to retain public support, ensure congressional votes, and gain the help of our allies it would have to follow a more comprehensive policy. It needed to combine its military-strategic interests with a broader program of socioeconomic assistance, support of human rights, and aid to democracy. Such a broad-based and consensus-building program would help defuse domestic and international opposition to the administration's policy, secure the higher road, and enable the president to carry out the plans he and his advisers had formulated. Of such considerations were born the Caribbean Basin Initiative, the Kissinger Commission, and the far more sophisticated, nuanced, and multipronged strategy for Latin America.

In part, this more sophisticated policy grew out of the protracted—and continuing—tension between the White House on the one hand and the foreign affairs bureaucracies, principally the State Department, on the other. Every new administration seems to go through this process, and Mr. Reagan's is no exception. During the first months or years of a new administration, the policy debate and the headlines tend to be dominated by the president's political advisers, those who helped articulate his positions during the campaign, accompanied him into office, and have new and often controversial ideas. Eventually, these ideas are tempered in the bureaucratic arena by long-time professionals, who generally have greater functional or area-specific expertise than the president's political advisers, and who eventually reassert their influence over policy making.

Such an evolution, although obviously starting from a different end of the political spectrum, happened under Mr. Carter and it happened under Mr. Reagan. There is an almost constant interplay between the more ideological and political of the president's advisers and the foreign policy professionals at the State Department and elsewhere. This battle has raged, on and off again, throughout Mr. Reagan's first term, and it continues in his second term. It is reflected in part in the debate over whether the United States can live with the Sandinista regime in Nicaragua or whether it should eliminate that regime. It is reflected also in the debate over human rights policy, over the precise parameters and thrusts of the president's democracy initiative, and over a variety of other policies. It is also reflected in rivalries over personnel appointments to high foreign-policy-making positions.

The debate has sometimes been unseemly, and it is the stuff of which *Washington Post* and *New York Times* headlines (always eager to find cracks in administration policy) are gleefully made. But it has also been salutary for policy, helping produce the more sophisticated and multifaceted policy we have now and enabling us to ensure that the expertise found in the professional bureaucracies is combined with the overwhelming popular mandate that Mr. Reagan has now twice received.

Positive Accomplishments

Let us turn from missteps that did not happen in the first term to more positive accomplishments that did. The list is rather impressive,

261

although that fact cannot ever be admitted by the Democratic opposition.

Let us begin with Grenada. Grenada demonstrated, to the Cubans, the Nicaraguans, the Surinamese, the Salvadoran guerrillas, and above all the Soviets that the United States was serious about defending its interests. Our allies (including those in Latin America), despite some public fulminations to the contrary, were generally pleased to see the United States act decisively. The Latin Americans are usually publicly opposed to intervention, and Grenada is a small and not so significant island. But in governing circles in the region there is always a glad sigh of relief when the "colossus of the North" takes decisive action to defend its interests *and* those of Latin America, and demonstrates that it is not just a paper tiger.

The documents captured in Grenada attest that that island's revolution was much more serious than we had previously thought. The documents reveal, among other things, that it was a Marxist-Leninist revolution and not just a merry bunch of Robin Hoods, that the Cubans were everywhere and the Grenadans did almost nothing without consulting their Cuban mentors, and that the Soviets were trying to use the Grenadans to stimulate revolution in Suriname and Belize. Grenada was to be a proxy for the Cubans just as the Cubans themselves were a proxy for the Soviets. The documents reveal a bloody, disorganized, unpopular revolution that had lost the support of the Grenadan people and violated their democratic civic culture. The American invaders were thus looked upon as saviors and heroes. The U.S. action not only succeeded in rescuing the endangered American medical students and returning Grenada to democracy, but also offered a powerful lesson to the Nicaraguans, Cubans, and Soviets—a theme discussed in more detail below.

Second, there is the democracy agenda. When President Reagan first broached this subject in his speech before the British Parliament, it was greeted with skepticism on various fronts. The Democratic opposition was appalled because the president was stealing its agenda, and many of them could not believe in any case that this president was genuinely serious about democracy. Many scholars were likewise skeptical because they believed the democracy agenda, if pursued too enthusiastically, would result in another patronizing, missionary-style campaign, in the mold of Woodrow Wilson or Jimmy Carter, to export North American institutions to Latin America, where they would not work or work as anticipated and, worse, would probably help undermine the feeble institutions existing in those countries. The early statements of some of the true believers in the program lent credence to these fears.

As written in the legislation, however, the democracy program seems on a sounder footing. Carl Gershman, the president of the Democracy Endowment, is calm, level-headed, and politically savvy, not an ideologue. Many of the early congressional fears have abated. Rather than a large-scale missionary campaign to bring the benefits of democracy to "less fortunate" or "less developed" peoples (the terms used indicate the patronizing and condescending attitudes contained in the early proposals), the democracy program is appropriately modest. It provides limited funds for research on where democracy works and how. It serves as a conduit for the building of democratic trade unionism in Latin America and for assisting private commerce and entrepreneurship. It provides for a greatly expanded and long-needed student exchange program. It recognizes limits on what the United States can do in this arena while also suggesting that a nudge and push in favor of democratic groups in Latin America can in appropriate circumstances make a decisive difference. It recognizes elections and human rights as crucial to democracy. It is a serious program that merits the support of serious people.

Third, the debt issue. We should have no false optimism about this fundamental matter. Latin America's debt will never be fully repaid—though it is important to keep alive the illusion that it will be. The big debtor nations—Argentina, Brazil, Mexico—are incapable of fully repaying their debts without ruining their domestic societies and polities. This they cannot and will not do.

Nevertheless the pretense that the debt will be repaid must be maintained. If the debtor nations formally default, they will not be able to get another foreign loan for a long, long time. Nor can the banks entirely write off these loans without raising havoc in international financial circles. Several of the banks would face a bleak future indeed if they were forced to write off these staggering amounts as bad loans. In addition, they would be unable to collect on the interest that is still trickling in, as distinct from the principal that will never be repaid.

This is one of the most elaborate "smoke and mirrors" operations that the fertile minds of economists and politicians have ever concocted. The Reagan administration has handled the whole debt issue quite adroitly, sounding tough here, caving in there, stretching out the loan period, renegotiating the interest charges, and so on. The whole strategy hangs by a thread, but as an exercise in crisis management with multiple dimensions, political as well as economic, it is a fascinating show to watch.

Fourth, the enactment of the Caribbean Basin Initiative and of the recommendations of the National Bipartisan (Kissinger) Commission on Central America constitute further major accomplishments of the administration. Here again illusion and reality must be separated. We should have no illusions that by our efforts we can do much to create democracy in Central America where it does not now exist, that we can reform the Central American militaries to make them honest and professional by our lights, or that we can create in the region happy, socially just, middle-class societies that look just like ours. These initiatives and programs are devices a clever administration uses both for their own value and for the support they build for its policies. By pursuing these policies the administration secures greater assistance funds from Congress, defuses the criticism of other Western allies, and satisfies world public opinion.

But the aid funds *are* important to get money flowing again in the devastated economies of the Caribbean and Central America. Not all the money will find its way to Miami or Geneva. Some reforms will be enacted, and a few may be implemented. Even if the part that finds its way into private pockets reaches 30 percent (something that can never be said publicly for fear of repercussions from the public, the Congress, and the General Accounting Office) 70 percent may still do some, though modest, good. In the current circumstances that is about all we can realistically expect. It requires a clever foreign policy to maintain the required fictions while recognizing realistically what the United States can and cannot do in this part of the world.

Fifth, major accomplishments can be cited with regard to specific countries. Perhaps the most important is preventing the collapse and guerrilla takeover of El Salvador. During the first three years of the administration the political-strategic situation in that unfortunate country was far worse than any official spokesman ever admitted publicly. The Salvadoran government and the armed forces were several times on the verge of disintegration; it appeared that a guerrilla triumph was imminent.

Today the situation has turned around: the armed forces are stronger than before, El Salvador now has an elected democratic and therefore legitimate government in power, and the guerrillas are on the defensive. The guerrilla movement may atrophy, perhaps the best outcome in this kind of war. The weakness of the guerrillas and the strength and legitimacy of the government were in fact what enabled Duarte to take his dramatic initiative to begin discussions with the guerrillas in October 1984. Having placed so many of our hopes in democracy, however, one shudders to think of the ramifications should Duarte be overthrown or assassinated.

In Nicaragua the policy has produced more ambiguous results. One cannot, finally, be sure whether the immense pressure put on the

Sandinista regime will make it more moderate or only solidify its hold and push it further into the Soviet camp. On balance, I believe the U.S. pressure has helped retain whatever vestiges of pluralism still exist in Nicaragua. Moreover, the U.S. pressure is also responsible for getting a paranoid Nicaragua, convinced the American invasion could come at any minute, to the bargaining table and for keeping open the possibilities for negotiations. In addition, it has helped keep open the possibility for future moderation of the regime.

Ultimately, U.S. policy in the Caribbean and Central America must be judged by its influence on Cuba and the Soviet Union. There is now abundant evidence that the Soviets are having second thoughts about their circum-Caribbean adventurism. The Cubans have begun to conclude that Central America may not be as ripe for revolution as it appeared in 1979 when the Sandinistas came to power; and in this part of the world the Soviets pay attention to Cuba's expertise. The Soviets have also told the Nicaraguans they should not expect Soviet help if they are attacked by the United States. The U.S. invasion of Grenada and the buildup of our military forces in Central America and the Caribbean have demonstrated to the Soviet Union that it risks confrontation with the United States if its mischief-making goes too far. All the evidence indicates that the Soviets do not want a showdown now with the United States, and certainly not in the Caribbean region where the United States has overwhelming local advantage and where the Soviet Union has only limited interests and political leverage. Hence we may see a turning away from the Caribbean by the Soviet Union and an attempt to exploit other regions where they have the advantage and the U.S. commitment is not so strong.

What to Expect

The prospects for U.S. policy in Central America in President Reagan's second term are probably: more of the same. The administration believes it has finally, after many false starts, achieved a viable U.S. policy for the region and that its policy has begun to pay off. The democracy agenda enables the administration to stand for traditional American ideals while also pursuing a large part of its original policy. By standing steadfastly for democracy the administration has won the loyalty and allegiance of much of the professional bureaucracy, taken the argument away from congressional critics, satisfied our allies, and won considerable legitimacy for its policies. There are traps in pursuing the democracy agenda too enthusiastically across-the-board, but so far the advantages outweigh the disadvantages. In any case it

265

seems unlikely the democracy agenda would be permitted to go into the unrealistic flights of fancy that some of its adherents envisage. Pursuing democracy too strenuously in Saudi Arabia, for example, could have devastating effects on U.S. oil supplies; pursuing democracy in Mexico could destabilize our southern neighbor.

The administration's policy has started to show success. In the Caribbean Basin Initiative and the Kissinger Commission recommendations we finally have the tools to deal with the area's problems. We have a democratic government in El Salvador that is both pursuing reform and successfully carrying forward the war effort. Our policies in Nicaragua have forced the Sandinistas into discussions with the United States, have helped unmask the true nature of that disingenuous regime, and have produced in Managua a bunker mentality that may lead to future changes in the nature of that government. The Cubans and Soviets are also on the defensive and reassessing their prospects, which at the moment seem quite bleak. The Europeans are now, on balance, supportive of the strong but tempered policy President Reagan has pursued.

None of the alarmist or radical predictions about U.S. policy in Central America seem likely, at this writing. There will be some shuffling of personnel in the foreign-affairs bureaucracies but not the wholesale changeover in the cabinet and the White House that once was expected. Nor are the main lines of policy likely to change much: Mr. Reagan will not feel "unleashed" during his second term to do irreparable harm to the world, as some radical critics have suggested; nor will he return to being the "true" (presumably more conservative) Reagan that some of his supporters are suggesting. He has been masterly at keeping his declared views, which are aimed at a domestic political audience and are often quite strident, separate from his real policies, which have been much more prudent and traditional. The fusing of the declared and the real did not happen in the first term and is unlikely in the second.

The main lines of current established policy will likely continue. It is unlikely that we will see many dramatic new departures. This is especially so given that the administration now has a firmer handle on policy and that, once established, an existing consensus on policy in Washington is difficult to change.

With regard to Nicaragua, the policy will probably remain largely the same: maintain (and perhaps increase) the pressure on the Sandinista regime while keeping open the negotiating process through Contadora and other forums. In part, this two-track policy stems from the administration's ambivalence over whether to get rid of the Sandinista government or to seek to modify it through increasing pressures. In the absence of any final decision, the policy will likely continue to follow both paths.

In the meantime, the administration would clearly not be unhappy if the regime collapsed, through a combination of external contra pressure and internal mismanagement, without the direct commitment of U.S. forces. The Pentagon is skeptical about the use of such forces; it draws a distinction between the two major interventions of the 1960s: the Dominican Republic ("successful") and Vietnam ("unsuccessful"). Grenada, a small island, was patterned after the Dominican intervention: we went in quickly, we accomplished our objectives, and we got out quickly. But Defense Department planners believe Nicaragua, a mainland country, would be more like Vietnam or perhaps Lebanon: a bloody imbroglio with ambiguous purposes, thus inviting constant political sniping and criticism and bringing blame on the military for whatever results were produced. Hence an invasion there seems unlikely.

The presence of Soviet MIGs in Nicaragua would obviously change our policy. The administration has said clearly that it would not allow MIGs in Nicaragua, and it has unambiguously conveyed that message to Nicaragua, Cuba, and the Soviet Union. Should we discover that the Soviet Union has secretly supplied Nicaragua with such weaponry strong action from the United States could be expected, probably in the form of an ultimatum. An equally tough question remains with regard to the progressive buildup of ever more sophisticated arms in Nicaragua itself.

In El Salvador the administration also believes that it is on the right track and that U.S. ground forces will not be necessary. The Salvadoran armed forces are more cohesive and better trained than they were, the guerrillas are weaker than they were, and Salvadoran civil society has proven to be more durable than expected. An elected government is in power, and we will continue to support it. Should that government be overthrown, however, the situation could become hazardous: civil society could unravel, the rationale for the administration's policy of aiding democracy would be undermined, Congress would be reluctant to vote for more funds, and the war would go badly. Barring these developments, the administration expects El Salvador to stabilize as the guerrillas become more confined to remote areas of the country, thereby eliminating the need to introduce U.S. ground forces.

In the meantime the administration needs to move forward with the Caribbean Basin Initiative and the Kissinger Commission recommendations. These plans have been put forward with great fanfare, but if there is little follow-through the Caribbean countries will be in the worst of predicaments, their hopes and expectations raised high once again and then dashed. Those are the forces—raised hopes and dashed expectations—of which revolutions are made.

But if there are some possibilities of achieving our goals in Central America, we should move toward a more mature and long-range relationship with these countries. That is what we have been doing with the larger countries of South America, and it is what we should do in Central America as well. For too long U.S. policy there has been crisis-oriented and almost exclusively reactive. If we can begin to resolve some of the region's pressing and immediate problems, and thus reduce our proconsular role over the long term, then we will find it opportune and prudent to establish sounder, stabler, and more normal relations—similar to those we have long had with Europe and are beginning to have with South America.

The greatest current danger is complacency. El Salvador is out of the headlines for the moment, and therefore we may turn our attention to other issues. But benign neglect of Central America will no longer do: it may have been an appropriate strategy for an earlier and sleepier time, but it allows smaller problems to fester until they become major trouble spots. Benign neglect practiced by earlier American administrations is precisely why we have such deep problems in Central America today. We should carry through our aid commitments, keep working on the debt, maintain our strategic and political presence, implement student exchanges, support the Duarte government, and walk a fine line in Nicaragua between applying pressure and keeping negotiations going. As in the past, the U.S. president may have to involve himself personally in the process to keep the legislation in Congress moving and the foreign affairs bureaucracies on course. Otherwise, a prudent and sensible Latin America policy that has taken years to fashion may again be sidetracked by indifference and lethargy.

15

Political Development in Central America: Options and Possibilities

In the academic literature the term "political development" conveys a variety of meanings. It is used ambiguously, unclearly, and in different ways by different authors—sometimes by the same author. To some, it means institutionalization, to others differentiation and specialization of functions, to others simply democratization. Political scientist Lucian Pye once counted at least twelve distinct uses of the term political development.[1]

In the foreign policy community, however, political development is most often used synonymously with democratization. At the popular level, in the media, and among informed citizens, that is the meaning most closely associated with the term. Thus, when we speak of assisting the "political development" of Central America, we generally mean assisting democratization in that area. Although the equation of political development with democratization is problematic, conceptually as well as practically, that is the meaning we will employ in this chapter. In the concluding section we return to the matter of the ambiguities in the term and the implications of this for policy.

Absence of Political Development in Central America's History

Democracy has always been a rather fragile flower in Central America. It remains so today, though there are signs of its possible blossoming.

During the three centuries of Spanish colonial rule, roughly from the 1520s to the 1820s, there was little of what we would call democracy in Central America. Rather, the political system was au-

Statement prepared for the National Bipartisan Commission on Central America, Washington, D.C., November 1983; published in *AEI Foreign Policy and Defense Review,* vol. 5, no. 1 (1984), pp. 6–13.

thoritarian, from the top down; the economy was feudal, exploitative, and mercantilist; the society was elitist and hierarchical, consisting of only two classes; the church reinforced the authoritarianism of the state; and learning and intellectual life were similarly dominated by revealed truth, rote memorization of authoritative principles, and deductive reasoning. Nor did Spain ever provide much training in self-governance or seek to incorporate the large indigenous populations into the political life of its colonies.[2]

Considerable variation existed, however, up and down the isthmus. Mexico and Guatemala had the most gold and silver for the Spaniards to exploit and the most Indians to enslave. Hence they felt the strongest impact of the Spanish colonial system. Panama and Costa Rica, having small indigenous populations and little gold or silver and being far from the main centers of Spanish rule, felt the Spanish colonial impact the least. El Salvador, Honduras, and Nicaragua occupy intermediate positions on this scale.

These different colonial experiences were profound in terms of the future political development of these countries and can almost be stated as a historical law: where the Spanish colonial system in all its manifest forms was the strongest—politically, socially, economically, religiously, and legally—as in Mexico and Guatemala, the possibilities for later democratic development were the weakest. Where the Spanish colonial system was the weakest, as in Costa Rica and Panama, the possibilities for later democratic growth were the strongest. The intermediary countries would be, during their independence histories, condemned to great instability and frequent oscillations between nascently democratic and traditionally autocratic rule.

After independence from Spain, a legitimacy vacuum existed in Central America. The authority of the Spanish crown had been withdrawn, but what was to replace it? Some argued for monarchy. Some looked to another protector, such as England, France, or the United States. Some favored representative democracy and adopted, essentially, a Spanish-language translation of the U.S. Constitution, almost as if that alone would be sufficient to guarantee democracy. For a time, from 1824 to 1838, a confederation of Central American states existed, but it broke up in confusion and disarray.[3]

It is important to note that although the Central American states had achieved political independence, no accompanying social or economic revolution took place. The landholding system, the class structure, the system of castes, the pattern of elite rule were all largely unaffected by independence. Into the vacuum left by Spain's withdrawal came men on horseback and the newly created national armies.

The first thirty years of independent life were hence chaotic and disruptive. Several of the countries reverted to a more primitive subsistence. Order, stability, and progress were virtually nonexistent. Central America had the worst of all possible worlds: it had repudiated its colonial political institutions but had not yet begun to develop viable democratic ones to replace them.

From the 1850s to the 1880s some stability was brought out of the disorder that had gone before. The earliest wave of men on horseback had died off. The landholding elites began to reconsolidate their power. Immigration grew and the population expanded. British investment began to flow in. Using W.W. Rostow's aeronautical metaphor, the preconditions for takeoff were set.[4] But there was still precious little democratization.

The period 1890–1930 was the heyday of oligarchic rule in Central America. The older landed oligarchy was supplemented by a commercial import-export class. Considerable economic growth occurred. The middle class grew. Gentlemanly rules were established enabling the military and civilian elites (usually a combination of the two) to rotate or alternate in office. Greater stability was ensured through the modernization and centralization of the army, with U.S. Marine reinforcement in several countries.

It is again important to stress that while considerable economic growth and major social changes were occurring in Central America during this period, they came exclusively under elite or oligarchic auspices. Except in Costa Rica, which built upon its earlier democratic roots, there was still little movement toward democracy. When Central America became convulsed in the political and economic upheavals precipitated by the depression of the 1930s, it had not yet developed an infrastructure—parties, regular elections, pluralism, representative institutions—on which to build genuine democracy.[5]

The Search for New Accommodations, 1930s–1960s

The 1930s were extremely disruptive in Central America, economically, politically, and sociologically. Not only did the bottom drop out of the market for Central America's products, but there was also a wave of revolutions in 1930–1931 and major challenges by the emerging middle classes of the region demanding a share of power. Central America began to search for a new set of economic and political models and a way to accommodate as well as control the rising social forces.

Democracy was one of the contenders, but it succeeded fully only in Costa Rica following the 1948 revolution. Democracy was also tried

in Guatemala from 1944 to 1954; but it remained weakly institutionalized, veered off in some radical directions, and was overthrown
in a coup supported by the United States. In El Salvador, Honduras,
Guatemala, and Nicaragua, long-term dictators appeared in the
1930s, committed to order and discipline but also seeking to modernize their economies and societies. They often ruled with strong-arm
methods, but they also represented the aspiring *mestizo* middle
classes, not necessarily the old-time oligarchies; and they enjoyed
considerable popularity—at least for a time—because of the economic
development and social modernization they initiated.

By this point two main political traditions were operating in
Central America—and a nascent third one. First, the older and historically dominant authoritarian tradition was still present. Difficult
though it is for Americans to understand, that tradition had considerable support in Central America largely because of its often unhappy
experiences with liberal-democratic forms and the widespread convic-
tion on the part of the Central Americans that democracy did not
always work very well in the fragmented, violent, disintegrative context of that region.

The liberal-democratic tradition was also present. But except in
Costa Rica it was not well institutionalized in the form of political
parties and workable representative institutions. The democratic preference emerged from time to time (in Guatemala in 1944, in El Salvador in 1972, in Honduras in 1963), but it lacked the legitimacy and
stability democracy has in the advanced Western democracies and
may not even have enjoyed majority support in the several countries.
A third strain, socialism, in a variety of forms, was also present in
Central America from the 1930s.

The problem for Central America was to devise a political formula
to satisfy or perhaps ameliorate these diverse tendencies and world
views, none of which could command the support either of an absolute majority or of the main power contenders in society.

Only in Costa Rica was the formula a democratic one, involving
regular elections and a rotation in power by the two dominant groups
following that country's brief but decisive revolution in 1948.
Elsewhere, efforts were made to combine, and perhaps even to reconcile, the traditional and the liberal orientations, and maybe even to
hint at a move toward the socialist one.

In Nicaragua, for example, following the death of the senior
Somoza, various attempts were made by his elder son, Luís, to relax
the harsh controls of the old authoritarianism, to allow greater pluralism and freedom, and even to share power with some outside the
Somoza family. In Honduras the military and the civilian parties

rotated in office or ruled jointly in an arrangement where the military retained control of security matters and was the ultimate political arbiter, while the civilian elites managed the economy, held key cabinet positions, and dominated most agencies of the bureaucracy. In Guatemala, whose politics after 1954 had been more divisive, polarized, and violent than that of its neighbors, there were similar efforts—not all of them unviable or inappropriate—to combine civilian and military rule, or to alternate between them, in various shaky and uneasy blends.

In El Salvador the system also worked moderately well from 1948 to 1972. There, a group of younger, progressive majors and colonels came to power; they were reform-oriented, nationalistic, and semi-populist. The military remained the final authority but, recognizing its own limitations, put the finance, planning, and economic ministries, as well as various development agencies—such as housing, agriculture, and water resources—in the hands of capable civilian technicians. It allowed the major trade union organizations to grow and to have a measure of political participation. The officers who governed enjoyed considerable popularity and pursued many populist strategies. The army created its own political party, modeled after the Mexican PRI, which was more or less pluralistic and not entirely undemocratic. It held elections regularly in which the official candidates generally won; however, through a system of corporate representation within the party, most major groups were represented and had some voice in national affairs.

None of these systems (except Costa Rica's) were entirely democratic by our lights. But they were not entirely undemocratic either. They represented some interesting combinations and fusions of the liberal and the authoritarian traditions, both strongly present in Central America. Moreover, they tended to represent quite realistic and pragmatic modernizing responses of the Central American countries, given the profound social changes occurring in all of them since the 1930s and also given the reality of their own cultures and societies. By the criteria we normally use to assess democracy, none of these regimes fully measured up; but the trend was certainly *toward* greater democracy, pluralism, and representation—on their terms if not yet on ours.

Cloture and Sclerosis of the System

The systems we have described functioned not entirely intolerably for most people in most of the Central American countries during most of the 1960s and early 1970s. Then, instead of the political opening that had gone before, a period of political cloture and sclerosis set in that snuffed out the possibilities for greater democratization and pluralism. It is the domestic legacy of these reversals in Central America that now presents American policy with so many difficulties throughout the region.

What happened? Why did increasingly open societies give way to increasingly closed ones? The causes are general, relating to the region as a whole, and specific, having to do with the characteristics of each of the countries affected.

The general causes include the following:

- *New mass challenges.* The Central American systems had been generally able to accommodate the rising middle-class demands of the 1950s and 1960s. When the demands grew from the lower classes as they did in the late 1960s–early 1970s, however, the systems were less able to cope. Increasing economic difficulties in the 1970s compounded the problem and made it more and more difficult for democratic public policy to be carried out.
- *Outside intervention.* If the challenges had been purely internal, they might have been manageable. But by the late 1960s all these nations, and especially Guatemala where the conflict was most intense, had externally inspired guerrilla movements. These movements and the responses to them by those in power produced severe fragmentation and polarization.
- *Bureaucratic authoritarianism.* In Central America as in the larger South American countries (Argentina, Brazil, Chile), accelerating social change that threatened to get out of hand provoked a form of military interventionism that was long term, unlike the short-term tenure of most military juntas. In addition the new system was military-bureaucratic, unlike the historic pattern of one-man *caudillo* rule, and it strongly repressed trade union and political movements that challenged the dominant position of the military.
- *Greed and power.* The military career had become a route not only to power but also to wealth and social status. Those who challenged that system had to be kept out of power at all costs.
- *Benign neglect by the United States.* A key turning point in three of the countries (Guatemala, El Salvador, and Nicaragua) came in the early 1970s. Preoccupied by Vietnam, Watergate, war in the Middle East, and other concerns, the United States did not adequately use its influence to prevent the political cloture that occurred then.

In Nicaragua, the earlier political opening was closed off by Somoza's second son, Anastasio, Jr.[6] Part of his undoing came from the blatant greed and corruption that he showed in reaping immense private profit from the relief efforts after the 1972 earthquake; part stemmed from his refusal to share any of the wealth of his realm with other Nicaraguan elite families as his father and brother had done; part derived from the severe and gruesome suppression of his growing opposition; part also stemmed from the corruption that went beyond the more or less tolerable levels of the past. Had Anastasio Somoza Jr. been less greedy, less corrupt, less repressive, and more politically adept, we would probably not face the serious problems in Nicaragua that we do today.

In Guatemala the more-or-less centrist civilian and military regimes that governed in the 1960s similarly gave way in the 1970s to a succession of extremely repressive regimes. The administrations of General Eugenio Kjell Laugerud García and General Fernando Romeo Lucas García were among the most repressive in the recent history of the hemisphere, or in Guatemala's own often bloody past. All possibilities for accommodation, assimilation, and further democratization were thus lost.

In El Salvador the same pattern prevailed. A military regime that had been quite progressive in the early 1960s had become more and more corrupt and repressive by the 1970s. The victory by civilian Christian Democratic candidate José Napoleón Duarte in the 1972 election—and the annulment of that election by the armed forces—ushered in a period of severely repressive rule, until a new coup in 1979 further polarized the society. It is in this context, with its striking parallels to the developments in Nicaragua and Guatemala, that the crisis with which we are now grappling in El Salvador began.

It is no accident that it is in precisely these three countries—El Salvador, Guatemala, and Nicaragua—where the internal crisis, and the crises for U.S. policy, are the strongest. Allowing for distinct national variations, all three went through a roughly parallel process where a trend toward more open, pluralistic, and democratic societies gave way to increased cloture, sclerosis, and polarization, precipitating not only an internal crisis in these societies but also major problems for U.S. foreign policy.

What Is to Come?

The debate over whether it is possible for the United States to assist democratic development in Central America—and how, where, and by what means—has been long and arduous. It is related to the historic debate between idealism and realism in American foreign policy—and whether it is possible to combine or reconcile the two.

275

Arguments in Support of a Policy of Democratization. The arguments in favor of a vigorous U.S. commitment to support and encourage democracy in Central America are strong and forceful.[7] They include:

- *A moral argument.* A fundamental American belief is that democratic principles have a universal applicability, that democracy is the best form of government, and that we as a nation have a moral obligation and responsibility to help expand democracy's possibilities in other nations.
- *An economic argument.* Support for programs or democratic political development assist and reinforce our programs of foreign economic assistance. Stable political institutions are conducive to stable economic growth.
- *A national security argument.* Strengthening democracy abroad enables the United States to compete more favorably with its ideological adversaries. Democratic development takes away the argument of revolutionary groups that they alone stand for change. Therefore democracy abroad helps preserve stability and reinforces legitimate U.S. security concerns.
- *Making the world a safer place.* Democratic nations tend to be more peaceful, less bellicose, and less desirous of pursuing expansionist policies toward their neighbors that may lead to war.
- *Furthering the evolution of Latin America.* It has been suggested that this may be democracy's historic time in Latin America, that with the decline or disappearance of authoritarian regimes and the emergence of democracies or democratic trends in Argentina, Bolivia, Brazil, Ecuador, El Salvador, Guatemala, Haiti, Honduras, Panama, Peru, and Uruguay, it may be a propitious time to expand democratic institutions in some of these countries and to pursue new possibilities for democracy in the other countries of the isthmus.

All of these purposes, it is argued, would be served simultaneously by strengthening democracy abroad. And within the United States, labor, business, Democrats, Republicans, Congress, the president, liberals, and conservatives all favor an approach by the United States to support the development of democratic values and institutions around the world.[8] The plan has both compelling logic and widespread domestic political support.

Arguments against a Policy of Democratization. The arguments against a concerted U.S. campaign to support democracy in Latin America are also strong.[9] They include the following:

• *U.S. capabilities.* It has been suggested that neither the general public nor the Congress is ready to support another major foreign assistance program, especially one that may cost U.S. jobs; that we no longer have the financial resources to carry out the program successfully; and that we may no longer have the will or the commitment for such a major prodemocracy campaign. The costs, both financial and psychic, of bringing democracy to Central America would be enormous, and we may not have the capabilities.

• *Destabilization.* The literature on development strongly suggests that such programs of economic assistance and social modernization as would be involved in the democracy campaign, instead of promoting stability and political development, may actually undermine both, by weakening traditional and transitional institutions before new ones have a chance to take root.

• *Latin American wishes.* Latin America is now more independent, nationalistic, and assertive; it may not want to listen to our advice or follow our example, including our advice about democracy. In addition, while many Central Americans support democracy and representative government in the abstract, they are less convinced that democracy works well or is viable in their own context.

• *Interventionism and proconsularism.* The democracy campaign could involve the United States even more deeply in the internal affairs of the Central American nations, not always in appropriate ways. Therefore it may be both damaging to them and self-defeating for us.

• *Latin American realities.* Although we wish that Central America could be democratic, the realities of the societies and politics of the area make that unlikely, at least in several countries over the short term. Is a campaign of exporting democracy to Central America therefore doomed to failure? And would such failure imply severe costs for U.S. policy?

What Is Likely? Central America, as we have seen, is undergoing immense changes—economic, social, political, ideological, and in terms of the increased impact of the outside world on its internal affairs.[10] Yet, despite all these changes, these nations also have remarkable continuity of historic ideas and institutions. The changes in Central America, as well as in our own values, rule out the possibility of the U.S. standing obdurately against all alterations in the status quo; yet the heavy weight of the past and the persistence of many traditional institutions mean that the U.S. cannot push too fast either, for fear of destabilizing the area further.

Central America is going through not only a crisis of change but also a period of major questioning and experimentation. While Central Americans have little sympathy for a Soviet-style economic or political model, they also consider the formal machinery of the U.S. political system not entirely appropriate in their circumstances either. They want democracy, but they want it adjusted to their own realities and not as some pale imitation of the United States.

Many Central American thinkers and political leaders are searching for a new political formula, derived in part from outside their own borders but combined with revered national and local institutions. While this experimentation with new models goes on—involving some special role for the military, some particularly Latin American modes of representation, forms of more populist-style democracy, and types of social and economic as well as political democracy—we may expect considerable uncertainty and some instability. Central Americans also plead for understanding by the United States as they search for new political and developmental formulas.

In the meantime, the Central American political process is likely to reflect the same uncertainties of the transition from traditionalism to modernity that it has exhibited in the past. That transition is likely to involve overlaps and fusions of civilian and military elements, various blends of extended family-style and city-state politics[11] with the newer realities of mass-based political parties as well as combinations of traditional patronage politics and the newer requirements of serving the public interest. Mixed solutions are likely, not entirely democratic by our criteria and not always living up to democracy's high standards. We may lament these occasional departures from the democratic path, but we must also be prepared to deal with them prudently and realistically.

Recommendations

We believe the United States should follow a policy of democratic developmentalism in Central America. But realism dictates that this policy may have to be more restrained and less heavy-handed than under some U.S. foreign assistance programs in the past.[12] We must avoid the overblown rhetoric and the exaggerated (and therefore unrealistic) expectations raised by some past policies and concentrate on realistic and practical goals. We will not succeed in transplanting our institutions intact into Central America, but we can appropriately provide some aid and incentives in the right directions to assist the Central Americans in their own institutional and democratic development.

We should avoid laying down a Procrustean bed of criteria for democracy in Central America so pure that no government in the world could live up to it. While it is unlikely that the United States can successfully export its own democratic institutions to Central America, we should explicitly reject the notion that the United States therefore do nothing at all to assist democracy throughout the region. While democracy is not an "export commodity," as a recent report put it,[13] it can be nurtured, encouraged, and strengthened. But our assistance to democratic regimes and institutions must be tempered and realistic, building on Central America's own viable democratic traditions and institutions. We cannot prematurely sweep away Central America's existing institutions without inviting the instability and fragmentation that would enable the enemies of democracy to triumph, but we should certainly lend support to the democratic openings that do exist.

The United States cannot entirely reverse centuries of Central American history, wipe the blackboard clean, and begin anew. But there are regimes and movements in Central America—those that flagrantly violate human rights, that suppress the democratic forces, that violate both our own and Central America's sensibilities—that both our moral sense and practical political realities cannot allow us to support. Such regimes not only are repulsive to us but also lay the groundwork in which Castro-like and pro-Soviet groups can grow and gain support.

The United States cannot impose its own solutions on nations unwilling to abide by them, with cultures and histories different from our own. But we can and should assist the Central American nations in finding their own developmental formulas. We can and should help their trade unions; we should support a broader exchange program between the United States and Latin America; we should encourage the private sector and various private groups; we can provide technical assistance and advice in various substantive policy areas; we can encourage the Central American armed forces to act more responsibly; we can work for justice and human rights; and we can encourage democratic outcomes.

By these and other strategies we can assist democratic forces throughout the area, while avoiding flamboyant campaigns and interventionist stances not in keeping either with Central American wishes or with our own realistic possibilities. We can thus assist the development of more open, pluralistic, and democratic societies in Central America in accord with their desire to find their own way and with our interests and democratic preferences. It is a noble course, and a prudent and realistic one, which combines a hardheaded commitment to defending our national interests in the region with the powerful moral thrust the United States has always represented.

Notes

1. Lucian Pye, *Aspects of Political Development* (Boston: Little, Brown, and Co., 1966), chapter 2.

2. The best treatment is Murdo J. Macleod, *Spanish Central America: A Socioeconomic History* (Berkeley, Calif.: University of California Press, 1973).

3. Thomas L. Karnes, *The Failure of Union: Central America 1824–1975* (Chapel Hill, N.C.: University of North Carolina Press, 1976); and Ralph Lee Woodward, *Central America: A Nation Divided* (New York: Oxford University Press, 1976).

4. W. W. Rostow, *The Stages of Economic Growth: A Non-Communist Manifesto* (Cambridge: Cambridge University Press, 1960).

5. For a comparative overview as well as treatment of the individual countries see Howard J. Wiarda and Harvey F. Kline, *Latin American Politics and Development*, 2nd ed., rev. (Boulder, Colo.: Westview Press, 1985).

6. For comparative case histories see Thomas P. Anderson, *Politics in Central America* (New York: Praeger, 1982).

7. William A. Douglas, *Developing Democracy* (Washington, D.C.: Heldref Publications, 1972); and Michael Samuels and William A. Douglas, "Promoting Democracy," *The Washington Quarterly* (Summer 1981).

8. The materials in this section are summarized from *The Commitment to Democracy: A Bipartisan Approach (An Interim Report of the Democracy Program)* (Washington, D.C.: The Democracy Program, 1983).

9. For an expanded discussion of these ideas, see chapter 5 in this volume.

10. These changes have been treated in more detail in another paper by the author, "Changing Realities and U.S. Policy in the Caribbean Basin: An Overview," in James R. Greene and Brent Scowcroft, eds., *Western Interests and U.S. Policy Options in the Caribbean Basin* (Boston: Oelgeschlager, Gunn and Hain for the Atlantic Council, 1984), pp. 55–98.

11. Roland H. Ebel, "The Development and Decline of the Central American City-State," in Howard J. Wiarda, ed., *Rift and Revolution: The Central American Imbroglio* (Washington, D.C.: American Enterprise Institute for Public Policy Research, 1984).

12. For elaboration of these themes see Howard J. Wiarda, "United States Policy in Central America: Toward a New Relationship," Statement prepared for the National Bipartisan Commission on Central America, United States Department of State, Washington, D.C., September 28–29, 1983; published in *Appendix to the Report of the National Bipartisan Commission on Central America* (Washington, D.C.: Government Printing Office, 1984), pp. 207–251.

13. *The Americas at a Crossroads: Report of the Inter-American Dialogue* (Washington, D.C.: Woodrow Wilson International Center for Scholars, April 1983), p. 30.

Index

A NOTE ON THE BOOK

*This book was edited by Dana Lane
and Janet Schilling of the Publications Staff
of the American Enterprise Institute.
The index was prepared by Patricia R. Foreman.
The text was set in Palatino, a typeface designed by Hermann Zapf.
Coghill Book Typesetting Company, of Richmond, Virginia,
set the type, and Edwards Brothers Incorporated,
of Ann Arbor, Michigan, printed and bound the book,
using permanent acid-free paper.*